D1030142

The Canada Merchants
1713-1763

J. F. BOSHER

CLARENDON PRESS · OXFORD
1987

Oxford University Press, Walton Street, Oxford OX2 6DP
Oxford New York Toronto
Delhi Bombay Calcutta Madras Karachi
Petaling Jaya Singapore Hong Kong Tokyo
Nairobi Dar es Salaam Cape Town
Melbourne Auckland
and associated companies in
Beirut Berlin Ibadan Nicosia

Oxford is a trade mark of Oxford University Press

Published in the United States
by Oxford University Press, New York

British Library Cataloguing in Publication Data
Bosher, J.F.
The Canada merchants 1713–1763.
1. Merchants—France—History—18th century
I. Title
380.1′0944 HF3555
ISBN 0-19-821134-1

Library of Congress Cataloging in Publication Data
Bosher, J. F.
The Canada merchants, 1713–1763.
Bibliography: p.
Includes index.
1. Merchants—Canada—History—18th century.
2. Canada—Commerce—France—History—18th century.
3. France—Commerce—Canada—History—18th century.
4. Huguenots—Canada—History—18th century. 5. Canada —History—To 1763 (New France) I. Title.
HF3225.B67 1987 382′.0944′071 86-12586
ISBN 0-19-821134-1

Typeset by Joshua Associates Limited, Oxford
Printed and bound in Great Britain by
Biddles Ltd, Guildford and King's Lynn

TO KATHRYN CECIL

Preface

THIS is a social study of merchants, not an economic study of their trade. It touches on the lives of scarcely a hundred families, few enough to be treated by name rather than boiled down into nameless statistics. Yet they are seen at a certain distance because the surviving records are mostly impersonal business papers revealing impersonal business lives. The meagre information that can be gathered from them does not, in my opinion, lend itself to statistical treatment, but some of it I have compressed in twelve tables.

Writing the story of these merchants has been an exercise in making sense of countless tiny facts gathered slowly over fifteen years from scattered sources bearing mainly on other subjects. Inspector Maigret and Sherlock Holmes were faced with similar problems with which they became similarly obsessed. For them, a moment came in every case when they knew they had got it right, and the moment came in this case, *toutes proportions gardées*, when I realized that the Canada merchants lived in family and church groups rather than in social classes of the kind we are taught to believe in nowadays. Some men in history may fit into economically determined classes, but family tradition and the human mind or spirit intervened between the Canada merchants and their material circumstances, turning one man this way and another that. As a result, most of them belonged to social groups that were Roman Catholic, Protestant, or Jewish. These were the affiliations that mattered most in their business and family lives.

I am sincerely grateful to the many archivists in France, England, and Canada who went out of their way to assist an importunate researcher: Françoise Giteau and her tireless staff at La Rochelle; Étienne Taillemite at the Archives nationales; the willing archivist with the Baby Collection at the University of Montréal; Claude Hohl at Auxerre who drove me out to visit an irascible village notary; the British Museum staff at Ashridge who brought as many boxes as I needed day after day; those at Bordeaux who saved me endless time and trouble by allowing me to find my own documents in the store-rooms; the naval officer at Rochefort willing to open as early as my train arrived; all those with provincial courtesy, such as the part-time archivist at St Antonin-en-Rouergue who left his school class in order to unlock the archives in the town hall for an unidentified foreigner; the lady who took home likely-looking documents and pushed them under my door with the morning's mail. . . .

For funds or research time, I owe grateful acknowlegements to the Killam Foundation, the Social Sciences and Humanities Research Council of Canada, the Nuffield Foundation, the Franco-Canadian Cultural Exchange Programme, York University, and the Guggenheim Foundation (whose fellowship, offered in 1972, I unfortunately could not accept).

Many friends have helped me along the way, more than I can name, and I tender my gratitude here. For various services, I thank Hubert Mondor in Paris, Simone Bonthonneau in La Rochelle, Denis Vatinel *pasteur* at Poitiers, Gareth Bennett at Oxford, R. M. Middleton in Québec and Ottawa, Jean-Pierre Poussou, Paul Butel, P.-L. Coyne, Dominique Geffré, Dr Claude Massé and Jane McLeod in Bordeaux, Nicholas Rodgers, Joseph Ernst, Ramsay Cook, Paul Lovejoy in Toronto, and those colleagues who have listened to my papers over the years. Most of all, the book has had the benefit of my wife's devotion and concern.

Contents

List of Tables

List of Maps

List of Plates

List of Genealogical Charts

List of Abbreviations

A. D. Ch. Mar	Archives départementales de la Charente Maritime (La Rochelle)
ADG	Archives départementales de la Gironde (Bordeaux)
AN	Archives nationales (Paris)
ANQ	Archives nationales de Québec (St Foy, Québec)
BN	Bibliothèque nationale (Paris)
Bibl.	bibliothèque
Bx.	Bordeaux
DCB	*Dictionary of Canadian Biography*
inv.	inventory of property and papers etc.
LR	La Rochelle
MC	Minutier central des Notaires de Paris
PAC	Public Archives of Canada (Ottawa)
PHSL	*Proceedings of the Huguenot Society of London*
PRO	Public Record Office (London)
Que.	Québec
RHAF	*La Revue de l'Histoire de l'Amérique française*
RHES	*Le Revue d'Histoire économique et sociale*
RHMC	*La Revue d'histoire moderne et contemporaine*
SSP	*sous seing privé*, a contract signed privately and not notarized, though sometimes left with a notary later.
tx.	*tonneaux*, a measure of ship's capacity, variable and complicated, but cited here as in the documents and serving as a rough order of magnitude, a ton.

EXPLANATORY NOTE

What looks like an abbreviation following the name of an archive is usually an archival reference number.

A proper name followed by a town in parentheses and a date, for example, Bernard (Bx.), 26 Feb. 1748, refers to a notarial minute of a notary by that name at that town filed under that date. When the name is a saint, for example, Saint Jean-du-Perrot (LR), 14 Oct. 1753, the reference is to an entry of that date in the registers of that parish church.

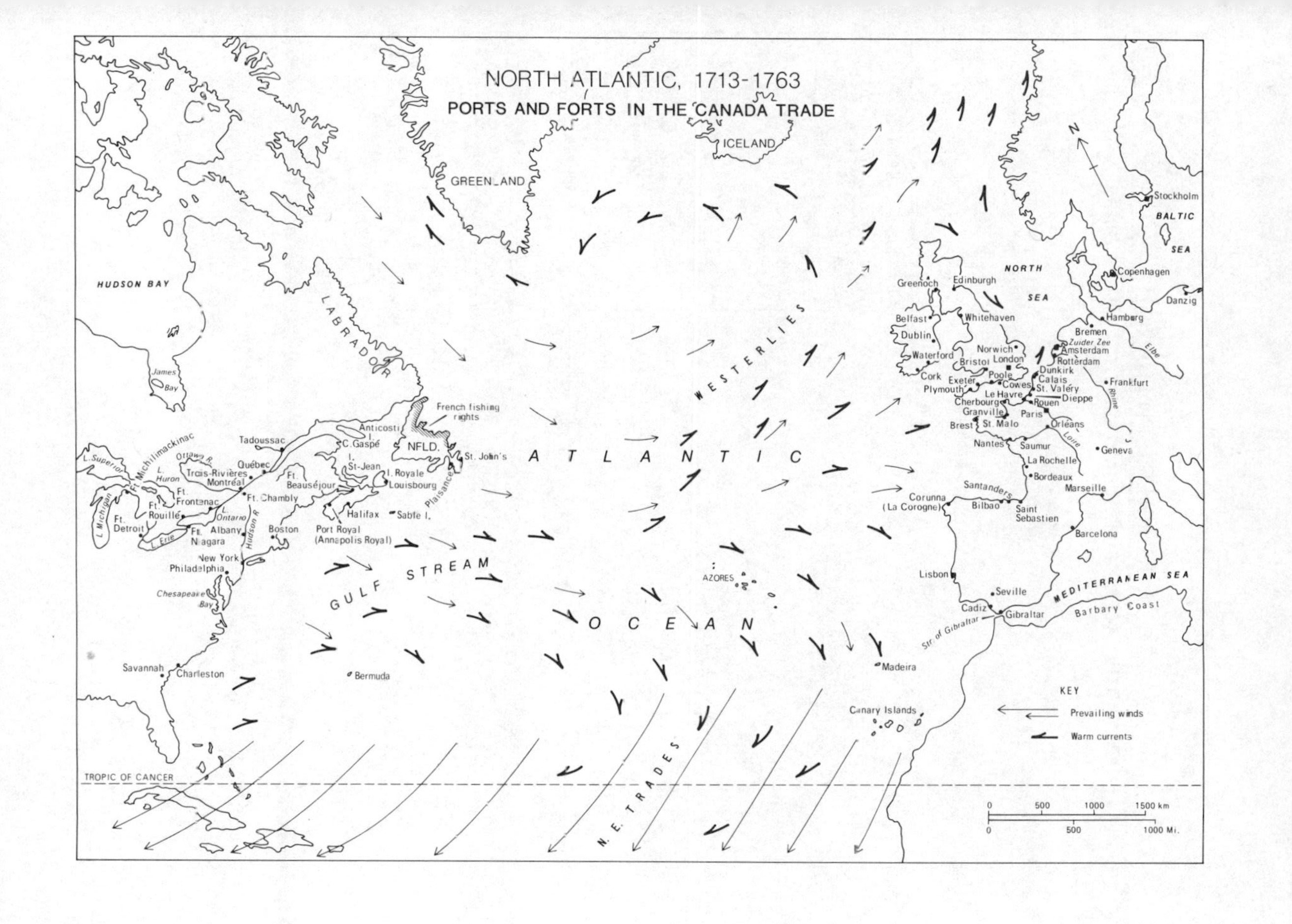
NORTH ATLANTIC, 1713-1763
PORTS AND FORTS IN THE CANADA TRADE
GREENLAND
ICELAND
HUDSON BAY
James Bay
LABRADOR
French fishing rights
NFLD.
St. John's
Plaisance
Anticosti I.
C. Gaspé
I. St-Jean
I. Royale
Louisbourg
Sable I.
Halifax
Port Royal (Annapolis Royal)
Ft. Beauséjour
Tadoussac
Québec
Trois-Rivières
Montréal
Ft. Chambly
Ottawa R.
L. Superior
Michilimackinac
L. Huron
L. Michigan
Ft. Frontenac
Ft. Rouillé
Ft. Detroit
L. Ontario
Erie
Ft. Niagara
Albany
Hudson R.
Boston
New York
Philadelphia
Chesapeake Bay
Savannah
Charleston
Bermuda
TROPIC OF CANCER
GULF STREAM
ATLANTIC
OCEAN
WESTERLIES
N.E. TRADES
AZORES
Madeira
Canary Islands
Greenoch
Edinburgh
NORTH SEA
Belfast
Whitehaven
Dublin
Waterford
Cork
Norwich
Bristol
London
Exeter
Plymouth
Poole
Cowes
Dunkirk
Calais
St. Valery
Le Havre
Dieppe
Rouen
Cherbourg
Granville
Paris
Brest
St. Malo
Orléans
Loire
Nantes
Saumur
La Rochelle
Bordeaux
Corunna (La Corogne)
Santander
Bilbao
Saint Sebastien
Lisbon
Seville
Cadiz
Gibraltar
Str. of Gibraltar
Barcelona
Marseille
Geneva
Frankfurt
Rhine
Zuider Zee
Amsterdam
Rotterdam
Bremen
Hamburg
Elbe
Copenhagen
Stockholm
BALTIC SEA
Danzig
N
MEDITERRANEAN SEA
Barbary Coast
KEY
Prevailing winds
Warm currents
0 500 1000 1500 km
0 500 1000 Mi.

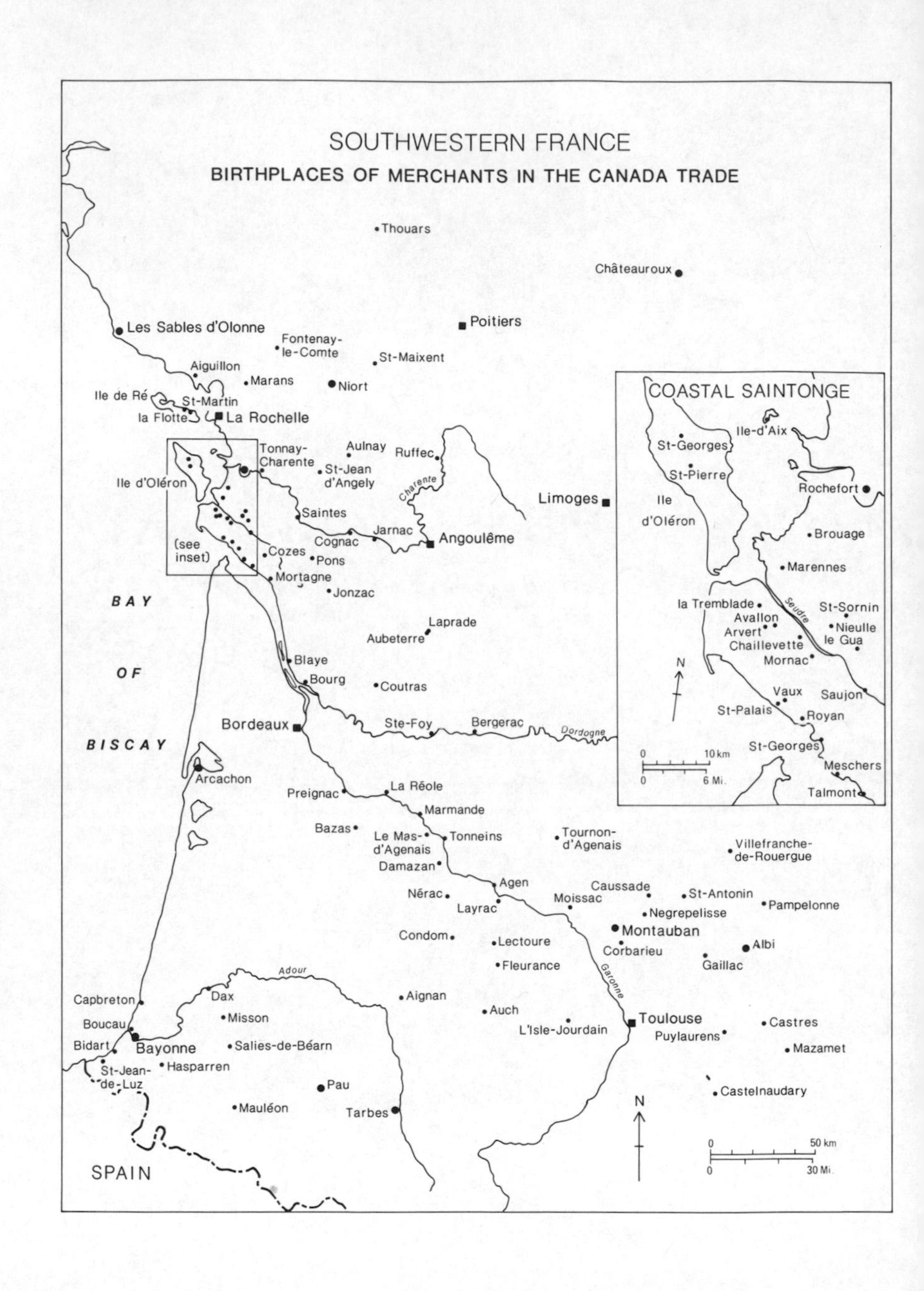
SOUTHWESTERN FRANCE
BIRTHPLACES OF MERCHANTS IN THE CANADA TRADE
Thouars
Châteauroux
Les Sables d'Olonne
Poitiers
Fontenay-le-Comte
St-Maixent
Aiguillon
Marans
Niort
Ile de Ré
St-Martin
la Flotte
La Rochelle
Aulnay
Tonnay-Charente
Ruffec
St-Jean d'Angely
Ile d'Oléron
Charente
Limoges
Saintes
Jarnac
Cognac
Angoulême
(see inset)
Cozes
Pons
Mortagne
Jonzac
BAY OF BISCAY
Laprade
Aubeterre
Blaye
Bourg
Coutras
Bordeaux
Ste-Foy
Bergerac
Dordogne
Arcachon
Preignac
La Réole
Marmande
Bazas
Le Mas-d'Agenais
Tonneins
Tournon-d'Agenais
Villefranche-de-Rouergue
Damazan
Agen
Caussade
Nérac
Layrac
Moissac
St-Antonin
Pampelonne
Negrepelisse
Condom
Montauban
Lectoure
Corbarieu
Albi
Gaillac
Fleurance
Garonne
Adour
Aignan
Capbreton
Dax
Auch
Toulouse
Castres
Boucau
Misson
L'Isle-Jourdain
Puylaurens
Bidart
Bayonne
Salies-de-Béarn
Mazamet
St-Jean-de-Luz
Hasparren
Pau
Castelnaudary
Mauléon
Tarbes
N
0 50 km
0 30 Mi.
SPAIN
COASTAL SAINTONGE
Ile-d'Aix
St-Georges
St-Pierre
Rochefort
Ile d'Oléron
Brouage
Marennes
la Tremblade
Seudre
St-Sornin
Avallon
Arvert
Nieulle
Chaillevette
le Gua
Mornac
N
Vaux
Saujon
St-Palais
Royan
St-Georges
0 10 km
0 6 Mi.
Meschers
Talmont

I

Introduction

I

Canada in the French Empire

i. *A Colony, Not a Nation*

VISITORS to Canada in the eighteenth century were impressed by the public order that had been established in the wilderness by authorities of Church and State. The town of Québec seemed like a tiny capital in one of the French provinces, hierarchical in every way, with merchants and mariners in the lower town near the St Lawrence River, above them in the upper town, the Admiralty and *Prévoté* law courts, several religious orders and the seminary, and houses of the wealthy and well-born, the whole crowned by the governor's Fort St Louis and the *palais* of the Intendant and the bishop. Montréal, too, was well ordered, surrounded like Québec by walls with gates, ruled by a military governor, laid out in Maréchal Vauban's grid or *bastide* shape on an island *seigneurie* held by the Sulpicians, with a fort, a parade square (*place des armes*), and a market square. The autumn fur fair no longer brought the Indian bands because the *voyageurs* now went west to meet them in the up-country, the *pays d'en haut*, and there, too, forts and soldiers maintained order and justice in the Bourbon fashion. The colony stretched southward from Montréal up the Richelieu River valley to Lake Champlain for nearly a hundred miles, and north-eastward down the St Lawrence River for more than three hundred miles. Beyond the Gaspé Peninsula near the river's mouth, on the south bank, the small settlements on Île St Jean (Prince Edward Island), Île Royale (Cape Breton Island), and various bays in the Gulf of St Lawrence were under similar military and ecclesiastical government. Everywhere the militia and militia captains were regulated and supervised. Little or nothing was left to local or 'Canadian' initiative. The wig-wearing classes–seigneurs, officers, magistrates, and merchants–wore their wigs as in France and felt quite at home, at least in the social scene.

The story of this colony is usually written as an early chapter in the history of Canada. Seen in the framework of Canadian national history, those tiny French colonies in the valleys of the St Lawrence and the Richelieu, and on the coasts of the present maritime provinces, appear to be much more than merely the first European settlements in Canada. New France appears to be cut off from old France as though it were already a separate sovereign country. The Atlantic Ocean turns into a great gulf of separation posing major problems, such as the celebrated 'problem of communication'.[1] Differences between France and Canada come into sharp focus, such as the jealous rivalries of established Canadian merchants and the *marchands forains* who used to come and go with the ships, the nostalgic memories of Canada, its harsh winter and bracing life remembered by Madame Bégon, Joseph Cadet, and other Canadians in France.[2] Whatever seems distinctively Canadian floats to the top of the Canadian historian's mind; whatever seems distinctively French or European sinks like the dregs to the bottom.

The geography of North America was uppermost in the minds of Harold Innis (1894-1952) and Donald Creighton (1902-79), two of Canada's most original and influential historians. In Innis's famous books on the cod fisheries and the fur trade, New France appears as the principal source of two commodities that Europeans wanted badly enough to send out men and ships for, to fight each other and the native tribes for, and to establish colonies for. All other French motives seemed minor to Innis, even the centralized paternal authority which he thought 'characteristic of a colony dependent on the fur trade'.[3] The five chapters on the French regime in *The Fur Trade in Canada* (1927) treat the history of New France geographically as a series of widening circles beginning at the Atlantic coast (chapter 2) and going on to the Ottawa region (chapter 3), the Great Lakes (chapter 4), the West (chapter 5), and the Hudson's Bay (chapter 6), regions where Innis travelled on foot and by canoe to know them for himself. Geography marked Donald Creighton's work even more firmly in *The Empire of the Saint Lawrence* (1937) which presents the history of New France as shaped by 'the unity of the Saint Lawrence', a result of Canadian geography more than of any other factor.

These influential writers have persuaded two generations that Frenchmen came to Canada above all for fur, fish, and timber, staple

[1] See H. A. Innis, *Empire and Communication* (Oxford, 1950); and *The Bias of Communication* (Toronto, 1951).

[2] 'Correspondance de Madame Bégon (1748-53)', *Rapport de l'Archiviste de la Province de Québec* (1934-5), pp. 1-278;L. F. G. Baby, 'Une lettre de Cadet, le munitionnaire de la Nouvelle-France', *Canadian Antiquarian and Numismatic Journal* (Montréal), 3rd series, vol. i (1898), pp. 173-87; P. Desfontaines, *L'Homme et l'hiver au Canada* (Paris, 1957).

[3] H. A. Innis, *The Fur Trade in Canada* (1930); rev. ed., Toronto, 1956), p. 115.

products which imposed a commercial way of life on Canadian society. Trade and traders have seemed fundamental to other distinguished historians. Guy Frégault (1918-77), did not scruple to write of merchants as part of a 'bourgeoisie' which he believed to be a major element in the society of New France. 'It is not easy', he wrote, 'to show the precise limits separating the middle class from the *grande bourgeoisie* and these from the aristocracy. To tell the truth, the latter two groups were really one.'[4] This was a conclusion based on a great deal of research, to which Cameron Nish later added much evidence of what he described as a class of 'bourgeois gentilshommes'.[5] Other historians have recently expressed this idea in descriptions of the mixed ruling class that grew rich, during the last twenty years of the French regime, in the shipping, supply, and retail trades as well as the fur trade.

These descriptions have provoked a contradictory view that the ruling class of New France was not composed of bourgeois moved by economic motives, but by noblemen with military and social motives. 'The dominant group, pre-Conquest,' wrote W. J. Eccles, 'was made up of the officer corps in the colonial regulars and the holders of senior judicial and administrative posts, many of whom engaged in commerce in order to maintain themselves in the dominant social position. Commerce, for most of them, was merely a means to a social rather than an economic end. It was this group that was eliminated by the Conquest and replaced by the British placemen and merchants with their *bourgeois* values. . . .'[6] A similar view, though with more detail and nuance, is expressed by Fernand Ouellet who believes that there was no Canadian bourgeoisie to fall in 1760-5: there was only a 'collusion of administrators, military leaders, seigneurs, business opportunists, such as Cadet, and of the metropolitan entrepreneurs . . .'.[7] Ouellet believes the dominant group in this mixed ruling class to have been the nobility.

Thus, Eccles and Ouellet take a view of Canadian society different from that of Innis, Creighton, and Frégault. These older historians were, of course, well aware of what Innis described as 'the pronounced

[4] Guy Frégault, *La Société canadienne sous le régime français* Brochure de la société historique du Canada, no. 3 (Ottawa, 1954), p. 14.

[5] Cameron Nish, *Les Bourgeois-gentilshommes de la Nouvelle-France, 1729–1748* (Montreal, 1968).

[6] W. J. Eccles, *France in America* (Vancouver, 1973), p. 214 note.

[7] F. Ouellet, *Economic and Social History of Québec, 1760–1850* (1966; trans., Ottawa, 1980), pp. xiii, 46 ff.

militaristic development of New France'.[8] Creighton called it 'a commercial and military state' and Frégault 'a military type of establishment', even though they believed trade to have been fundamental.[9] The difference was that when Eccles, for example, described Canada as 'essentially military in its framework', he went on to declare, after more thought and research, that 'for over half a century the fur trade was used by France as an instrument of its foreign policy'.[10] In his view Canadian society was founded on war rather than on trade. And Ouellet continued to see the nobility and the officers of the militia as more influential than the merchants who, he wrote, 'represented only a minority'.[11]

Geographic, economic, and military factors continue to impress the readers and writers of early Canadian history. Books devoted to them have a wider appeal nowadays than the books about French institutions transplanted to the New World. Since Innis and Creighton, it has become conventional to dispose of French institutions in a few summary passages that acknowledge their importance but imply that they are not very interesting. 'Fundamentally,' Innis wrote, 'the civilization of North America is the civilization of Europe, and the interest of this volume [*The Fur Trade*...] is primarily in the effects of a vast new land area on European civilization.'[12] 'Fundamentally,' Creighton echoed, 'the civilization of each society in North America is the civilization of Europe.'[13] Then they went on with studies that had nothing to do with European civilization. Their books are still justly famous and capable of weathering many a belated review: my point is that the example set by Innis and Creighton has been more influential than their desultory remarks quoted above.[14] Hence, it seems natural in our generation that the most successful book on the seigneurial system in Canada is a study of its geography by R. C. Harris; seigneurial society and institutions take second place.[15] Hence, too,

[8] Innis, *The Fur Trade*, p. 391.

[9] D. Creighton, *The Empire of the Saint Lawrence* (Toronto, 1937), p. 16; Frégault, *La Société canadienne*, pp. 11, 13.

[10] Eccles, *France in America*, p. 210; Eccles, 'The Fur Trade and Eighteenth-Century Imperialism'. *William and Mary Quarterly*, 3rd series, vol. xl (1983), p. 362.

[11] Ouellet, *Economic and Social History*, p. 99; Ouellet, 'Officiers de milice et structure sociale au Québec (1660-1815)', *Histoire sociale*, vol. xii (1979), p. 49.

[12] Innis, *The Fur Trade*, p. 383.

[13] Creighton, *The Empire*, p. 2.

[14] Such as W. J. Eccles's harsh and not wholly convincing 'A Belated Review of Harold Adams Innis, *The Fur Trade in Canada*', *Canadian Historical Review*, vol. lx (1979), pp. 419-41.

[15] Harris, *The Seigneurial System in Early Canada* (Madison, 1968); W. B. Munro, *The*

studies of trade have flourished, whereas the history of the Church has attracted fewer writers and readers than its enormous role in New France warrants.[16]

Innis, Creighton, Frégault, Eccles, and Ouellet have tended to set aside the most controversial features of Canadian society in the French regime, features which used to appear in earlier histories. In the past, there were basically two different histories, one written in Québec for Québécois, and the other written in the English-speaking world for its readers. A good example of the Québec histories, one of the latest and best, is by Canon Lionel Groulx (1878-1967), an eloquent and learned priest who believed that France gave Canada a 'type of family and parish strongly impregnated with Christian spirit', a 'social composition duly hierarchical', a 'living Catholicism that sprang from the best sources', and a 'sociological milieu of rare moral hygiene'.[17]

Other patriotic historians of Québec, too, have stressed the formative power of the Roman Catholic Church and its ally, the Bourbon monarchy. Marcel Trudel (1917-) once described the disintegration of the Jesuit Order after the Conquest as 'a great misfortune', their college having been 'a fundamental and essential force for our Canadian civilization'.[18] Even the detached and sophisticated Guy Frégault, more inclined to take a materialist view of New France, concluded with Benjamin Franklin that the British Conquest has 'shattered [the Canadians] as a people' (*brisé en tant que peuple*); it was a *crise de structure* for them, not merely a *crise de conjoncture*, because

Seigniorial System in Canada: a Study in French Colonial Policy (NY, 1907); Marcel Trudel, *Le Régime seigneurial*, Brochure de la Société historique du Canada, no. 6 (Ottawa, 1956).

[16] Daniel Francis and Toby Morantz, *Partners in Furs: A History of the Fur Trade in Eastern James Bay 1600–1870* (Kingston, 1983); A. J. Ray and D. Freeman, *'Give us Good Measure': An Economic Analysis of Relations Between the Indians and the Hudson's Bay Company before 1763* (Toronto, 1978); A. J. Ray, *Indians in the Fur Trade* (south-west of Hudson's Bay) (Toronto, 1974); Jacques Mathieu, *Le Commerce entre le Nouvelle-France et les Antilles au XVIIIe siècle* (Montréal, 1981); Maurice Filion, *La Pensée et l'action coloniale de Maurepas vis-à-vis du Canada, 1723–49* (Ottawa, 1972); D. S. Macmillan, ed., *Canadian Business History* (Toronto, 1972), part 1; E. E. Rich, *The Fur Trade and the Northwest to 1857* (Toronto, 1967); E. E. Rich, *The Hudson's Bay Company* 3 vols. Compared with these riches, and the growing literature on the history of the native tribes, the few short books by C. Jaenen, A. J. B. Johnston, J. S. Moir, and H. H. Walsh, useful though they are, show how little scholarly work is devoted to the history of the clergy and Church life.

[17] L. Groulx, *Histoire du Canada français depuis la découverte*, 4th ed. (Montréal, 1960), vol. 1, p. 366; see the important brief study by Serge Gagnon, *Québec and its Historians, 1840 to 1920* (Montréal, 1982), 161 pp.

[18] M. Trudel, *L'Église canadienne sous le régime militaire, 1759–64* (Montréal and Québec, 1956 and 1957), vol. 2, p. 177.

Canadian society had lost its leadership and suffered a permanent blow.[19] The leaders had gone because they were 'unable to survive outside the political and economic framework of New France and the French empire'.[20] The influence of the monarchy and the Church was not lost on Frégault.

Those were historians writing for Québécois much as their predecessors had done. For the English-speaking public the history of New France had been written by the American, Francis Parkman (1823-93), who in *The Old Régime in Canada* (1874) described the people of New France as lacking in self-reliance because their condition was that 'of a child held always under the rule of a father', and pointed out that the seminary schools of Québec taught humility and obedience but neither truth nor independence.[21] Years of research and careful thought lay behind Parkman's work, but pronouncements such as these only embarrass Canadian historians today who, in their efforts to be fair-minded, dismiss them as merely the fatuous prejudices of Victorian imperialists.[22] A two-volume history by G. M. Wrong (1860-1948), *The Rise and Fall of New France* (1928), has been discarded for the same reasons, though it was based on much learning and was once considered a standard work. Wrong thought, with Bourlemaque, that 'the religious policy was wrong; the country should have been thrown open to all comers, to Protestants and to foreigners, and the king should have helped their settlement'.[23]

Whatever their faults, these older books, French and English, had the merit of raising certain subjects that are quietly dropped in our time. The religious, political, and social differences between New France and New England, between old France and old England, were substantial and fundamental, but they are neglected in historical research and shrinking in the general histories. Sound old histories, like those by A. R. M. Lower and Edgar McGinnis, discuss them briefly as differences between 'the English race' and 'the French race', terms that are mysterious and unpalatable to this generation of students.[24] An embarrassed silence is growing up around these

[19] Frégault, *La Guerre de la conquête, 1754–60* (Montréal, 1975), pp. 456-8; F. Ouellet disagrees with this (*Economic and Social History*, p. 46).

[20] Frégault, *La Société canadienne*, p. 15.

[21] F. Parkman, *The Old Régime in Canada* (Toronto, 1899), pp. 163, 198, etc.

[22] W. J. Eccles, 'The History of New France according to Francis Parkman', *William and Mary Quarterly*, 3rd series, vol. xviii (1961).

[23] G. M. Wrong, *The Rise and Fall of New France* (Toronto, 1928), vol. 2, pp. 628-30, 880.

[24] A. R. M. Lower, *Colony to Nation*, 4th ed. (Toronto, 1964), e.g. pp. 66-71; Edgar McGinnis, *Canada: A Political and Social History*, 4th ed. (Toronto, 1982), pp. 149-54.

differences. As they fade in the collective memory, they come to seem unreal, superficial, or irrelevant. Students are ignorant of them, colleagues sceptical. This may be well and good in the realm of Canadian politics, but in the history of New France it is doubtful whether a knowledge of demographic trends, price series, and the fur trade, interesting though they are, can make up for an ignorance of the prevailing religious, political, and social systems. And these call for study of the France whence they came, as well as the New France where they went.

Here and there, the best Canadian historians have always acknowledged the French origins of New France. 'By contrast (with the Thirteen Colonies)', Eccles wrote, 'New France was merely an underpopulated province, a provincial backwater, separated from the rest of the kingdom by the Atlantic. Given the political structure, and the dependent nature of Canadian society at the upper level, ambitious men of ability were obliged to make their careers in the imperial forces or the administration in competition with men much better advantaged in France.'[25] But then, like the rest, and for the same reasons, Eccles went on treating New France as a separate subject, its society as a self-contained entity. Consequently, the economic, geographical, and military features of Canadian history have stood out boldly. They are what stand out as Canadian to the historian who sees history from the banks of the St Lawrence or of the Great Lakes, and they stand out against what he takes to be a European background of social, political, and religious features.

The history of New France seen from a Canadian national standpoint is not unlike the history of Brittany or Gascony apart from the rest of France. That is, it has a character and charm of its own but lacks both depth and breadth, like any provincial history. The reader of it is continually reminded of fundamental events that have been left out merely because they came from abroad, that is, outside the province. Of what use to remind the historian that the people of Québec also came from abroad bringing with them their religion and their social and political institutions? The compelling mythology of America prompts him to distinguish between 'us' and 'them', between Canadians and Frenchmen, between the history of Canada and the history of France. Consequently, he has little to say about the Counter-Reformation, the Roman Catholic Church, the absolute monarchy, or the European commercial empires which gave birth to

[25] Eccles, *France in America*, p. 133.

Canada and which explain the colony's meaning and character. He knows that economic development was the work of French officials but apparently thinks their story foreign to Canadian history.[26] He is interested in the thirteen royal Intendants and eleven governors posted to Québec, and the Superior Council there, but indifferent to the main body of Intendants, governors, and sovereign courts in France. French merchants may interest him a little more, because the colony was so dependent on transatlantic trade, but he can be counted on to ignore their social history, especially the vital difference between the merchants at the seaports and the royal financiers who dominated the Paris monopolies, the Company of New France and the Indies Company.[27] The social and religious differences among merchants will never even come to his attention unless he leaves the banks of the St Lawrence and settles himself on the banks of the Seine, the Garonne, the Thames, the Zuider Zee, or the Elbe.

In Canada, the religious differences among merchants are scarcely even perceptible. The few Huguenots who came to Canada seem almost as insignificant as the Jews, but taken together with those in the Canada trade at La Rochelle, Bordeaux, Montauban, Rouen, and Paris, they appear as part of a different and successful element in the French business classes. If we broaden our view still further, we find that New Converts in France and New France belonged to that Protestant society of merchants in Holland, Germany, England, and New England which dominated the North Atlantic. Amsterdam, London, Hamburg, and Geneva, these were the great international centres of trade and banking in that age. Their merchant bankers were a weighty political force in the 'republican' governments of the Protestant trading nations. Merchants ranked high in Holland, in Hamburg, in the England that had recently become the greatest seapower and was soon to become the first modern industrial power, and ranked even higher in the English colonies of North America.[28] As Louis XIV and Colbert knew, the Huguenots in France were an intrusion of that cosmopolitan republic of merchants which was a serious threat to the Roman Catholic Church and its ally, the Bourbon monarchy.

It is a commonplace in European history that three Protestant or anti-Catholic countries rose to the ranks of the great powers in the

[26] F. Mason Wade, *The French Canadians, 1760–1945* (NY, 1955), p. 32.

[27] See for instance, W. J. Eccles, 'A Belated Review of Harold Adams Innis, *The Fur Trade in Canada*', *Review*, vol. lx (1979), p. 436; and see below, p. 88.

[28] See below, p. 152.

eighteenth century: Great Britain, lately ruled by the Dutch House of Orange, firmly attached to Calvinist Scotland from 1707 and to Lutheran Hanover from 1714; Brandenburg-Prussia, Lutheran with a Calvinist ruling house and a special reputation for religious tolerance; and Russia, Orthodox Christian and at odds with Rome since AD 1054. If their foreign policies did not express religious purposes and if they were not always allies, their expansions and their victories nevertheless put a stop to the Counter-Reformation so vigorously championed by the greatest powers of the seventeenth century, Habsburg Austria and Spain, and Bourbon France.

In the throes of defeat and decline, these powers began to lose their crusading ardour, as had Catholic Poland earlier, and near the end of the age of New France they drove out the Jesuits, those commando troops of the Counter-Reformation, from Portugal in 1759, from France in 1762-4, from Spain in 1767, from Austria and the Papacy in 1772.[29] The French Crown turned its back on New France, colonial mission of the Counter-Reformation, at the same time that it turned its back on the Society of Jesus. As part of the same change in religious policy, the Crown began to relax censorship of the press and religious persecution. The French ruling classes grew more curious about the 'republican' civilization of the Protestant countries, and a new liberal-minded public sprang up that was to bring down the authoritarian Church and monarchy in 1789. Thirty years before the French Revolution, a British military victory in Canada broke the authority of Church and State there, as it had broken it in Acadia and Newfoundland in 1710. By these stages, New France and at last old France itself, were brought into the Protestant trading society of the North Atlantic.

These events appear to lead us a long way from the history of the Canada merchants, but the appearance is deceptive. The international conflict was also a political and social conflict; the conflicting religious groups were also social groups. Bourbon official society was quite different from Atlantic trading society, and the Canada merchants belonged to the one or the other, according to whether they were Catholic or Huguenot.[30] A typical Catholic merchant was related to priests, officials, officers, or financiers, perhaps all four, and his ambition was to found a noble family by buying a royal office and arranging noble marriages for his children.[31] A Huguenot merchant

[29] Dale Van Kley, *The Jansenists and the Expulsion of the Jesuits from France, 1757–1765* (New Haven, 1975).

[30] See below, p. 43.

[31] See below, pp. 56-67.

could not hope to rise in Bourbon official society unless he truly gave up his Protestant faith and social relations. Some families did so and rose accordingly–Beaujon, Depont de Grange, Mouchard, and Maurin (in Canada), to name a few–but most could hope for no more than the life of the prosperous banker unless they fled to a Protestant country.

There the avenues of social progress were different and, as many Huguenot careers showed, even a foreign merchant might become a town councillor in Amsterdam or Hamburg, a member of Parliament or a Lord Mayor in London, a member of a colonial council in Boston, Philadelphia, or New York. In the eighteenth century, Huguenot merchants in the Canada trade were seldom rich enough, or desperate or bold enough, to flee abroad and so to risk losing what wealth their families had accumulated. A few who stayed in Canada after 1763 shared the advantages that had made possible the careers of their fellow-Huguenots posted to Canada as officers in the British army.[32] For those who returned to France, a relaxing of persecution during the middle of the eighteenth century, in some of the major seaports especially, encouraged them to hope for a better future.

ii. *The Canada Trade*

The Canada trade was small because the population of the colony was small, and the furs and fish that were the principal exports did not take up much cargo space. No more than eleven or twelve thousand French people ever came out to Canada; the population in 1713 was eighteen or nineteen thousand, and in 1760 some sixty-five or seventy thousand. About a quarter of these lived in the three towns, Québec (about 8,000), Montréal (5,000), and Trois Rivières (1,500). Louisbourg, on the coast of Cape Breton Island, had some 2,000 inhabitants by the middle of the century. Three-quarters of the Canadian population lived on rural *seigneuries*, some 250 of them, along the banks of the St Lawrence River and up the major river valleys leading into it. There were tiny settlements on Île St Jean (Prince Edward Island) and at other places in the estuary of the St Lawrence. To this French-Canadian population must be added, in describing commercial markets, the native tribes served by western forts that were also trading posts: Fort Frontenac (Kingston), Fort Rouillé (Toronto), Fort Detroit, Fort Michilimackinac at the joining of Lake Michigan and Lake Huron, and smaller posts. Other forts traded with Indians to the

[32] See below, pp. 165-7.

south on the Richelieu River leading to Lake Champlain and the Hudson River beyond, and to the north and north-west on James Bay and beyond. Few though the tribesmen were, they took more merchandise than they required for themselves and traded it with more distant tribes.[33]

Soldiers, sailors, and militiamen played a large part in the commercial life of Canada and all of New France. The primary 'industry' of these colonies, as W. J. Eccles has shown in some detail, was war.[34] Every able-bodied man was a militiaman, and the regular garrison included Colonial Regular Troops (*Troupes franches de la marine*) numbering some 2,600 with 112 officers in the Seven Years War. To these were added a varying number of French regiments numbering several thousand troops. The Franco-Canadian army assembled at Québec in summer 1759 numbered between 12,000 and 15,000 men.[35] Just before its capture in 1758, Louisbourg had a garrison of about 8,000 men.

With a population and a civilization such as this, Canada tended to import more than it exported, and its balance of payments with France was nearly always unfavourable. The result for French shipping merchants was that return cargoes could often not be found at all. A few ships carried furs, timber, ginseng for China in some years, dried peas or wheat in other years; most went on to the West Indies for cargoes of sugar or indigo, or stopped at Gaspé for fish, or took back as ballast those stones that were used (or so every Canadian visitor is assured) to pave the streets of La Rochelle. For all this Atlantic trade, Québec was the Canadian port, for ships did not yet sail up to Montréal. Though the St Lawrence was frozen from December to April, in the shipping season Quebec was a busy port with ships coming and going from the West Indies and Louisbourg, the all-weather port on Cape Breton Island, as well as from France.[36] Shipyards near Québec built at least seventy seagoing craft, probably

[33] Jacques Henripin, *La Population canadienne au début du XVIIIe siècle* (Paris, 1954); Hubert Charbonneau, *Vie et mort de nos ancêtres: Étude démographique* (Montréal, 1975); Louis Edmond Hamelin, 'La Population totale du Canada depuis 1600', *Cahiers de géographique de Québec*, vol. ix (1965), pp. 1-11; J. N. Biraben, 'Le Peuplement du Canada français', *Annales de démographie historique* (1966), pp. 104-39; Guy Frégault, *Le XVIIIe siècle canadien* (Montréal, 1968), ch. 1; Bruce G. Trigger, *Handbook of North American Indians*, vol. 15, 'Northeast' (Washington, 1978), 924 pp. in 4° (see 'population' in the index).

[34] W. J. Eccles, 'The Social, Economic and Political Significance of the Military Establishment in New France', *Canadian Historical Review* (1975), pp. 1-21.

[35] George F. G. Stanley, *New France: the Last Phase* (Toronto, 1968), pp. 153, 223.

[36] Gilles Proulx, *Between France and New France: Life Aboard the Tall Sailing Ships* (Toronto, 1984), 173 pp.

more, in the half-century before 1763, and repaired and careened many more.[37] As the records of the Québec admiralty court have disappeared, information about Canadian maritime life during the French regime is fragmentary, but the large number of mariners registered in crew rolls at French ports as 'born at Québec' or 'settled at Québec' shows a vigorous seafaring population.

Canada was anchored firmly in the French empire by the course of its trade, as well as by imperial administration and by the personal ties of immigrants. Whatever the volume of the smuggling trade with New England and New York–and at some periods it was substantial–most of the trade at Québec and Louisbourg was with ports in France and the French West Indies.[38] No reliable lists of shipping or of imports and exports were drawn up in the age of New France, and historians have so far compiled only partial lists.[39] From 1713 to 1743, when war began, there were seldom more than a dozen ships a year from France, and these were seldom of more than 150 tons burden. Traffic between Québec and the West Indies was even smaller until 1724, when it began to increase, so that twenty or thirty vessels a year plied the West India trade from about 1730.[40] From 1743, about twenty or thirty French ships reached Québec each year, many of them between two and three hundred tons, and in the 1750s there were sometimes as many as three score ships in a year. My list of ships dispatched to Canada in 1758 now names more than seventy, though perhaps half were lost to the enemy or the sea, or re-routed to the West Indies. Many ships in these war years, sometimes a third or even a half of them, brought cargoes or troops on government account, and the prosperity that government spending brought to the colony had

[37] Réal Brisson, *La Charpenterie navale à Québec sous le régime français* (Québec, 1983), 318 pp.

[38] Mathieu, *Le Commerce entre la Nouvelle-France et les Antilles*; Clarence P. Gould, 'Trade Between the Windward Islands and the Continental Colonies of the French Empire, 1683-1763', *Mississippi Valley Historical Review*, vol. xxv (1938-9), pp. 473-90.

[39] The statistical lists in the scholarly article by James Pritchard, 'The Pattern of French Colonial Shipping to Canada before 1760', *Revue française d'histoire d'outre-mer*, vol. lxiii (1976), pp. 189-210, show the problem, for they are much lower than my figures, and mine are still too incomplete to publish. The only reliable lists now are partial ones, such as those in Dale Miquelon, *Dugard of Rouen*, appendix; James Pritchard, 'The Voyage of the *Fier*: An Analysis of a Shipping and Trading Venture to New France, 1724-28', *Histoire sociale*, vol. 6 (1973), pp. 75-97; J. F. Bosher, 'Une Famille de Fleurance dans le commerce du Canada à Bordeaux (1683-1753): les Jung', *Annales du Midi*, vol. 95 (1983), pp. 180-4.

[40] Estimates of shipping from France are based on my unpublished lists, those of West Indian shipping on lists in Mathieu, *Le Commerce entre la Nouvelle-France et les Antilles.*

stimulated a further growth of trade. The name, tonnage, and destination of a ship tells us precious little about its cargo. Cargoes are even less well known than ships. Such evidence as I have gathered points nevertheless to a pattern of imperial trade such as we might expect to find in an age when the French government made a policy of having seagoing trade serve imperial purposes.[41]

Almost all the Canada trade was carried on in French-owned vessels. Many of them were built abroad, especially in Holland early in the century and at Boston later on, or acquired as wartime prizes or purchased at Louisbourg or elsewhere. In 1733 Robert Dugard sent one of his captains to buy a ship in England.[42] Several in my shipping lists were built at Québec.[43] The crews, especially in wartime, included foreign sailors, but with few exceptions, the owners, officers, and shipping merchants were French or French-Canadian in this period.

Not until near the end of the French empire in North America did the Crown issue passports to foreign vessels. When they did it was in the agony of the Seven Years War, to make up for shortages in French shipping to Canada and to disguise French ships as neutral ones. In 1758 Jean-Henry Goossens of Bilbao sent *Le St Thomas* (140 tx., Captain Antoine Albarez), *La Ville de Bilbao* (150 tx., Captain Pierre Platenzia), and *Le Jesus-Maria-Joseph* (150 tx., Captain Jean de Zubaras) to Canada loaded with flour provided by his Bordeaux agent, Vignes.[44] In 1758 also, Desclaux sent a Spanish vessel, *La Pastoriza de la Coragne* (Captain Augustin Dios Rosalis), to Québec with a false passport for the Terceres Islands to mislead any British captors. In 1759, *Lamalétie, Latuilière et Cie.*, late of Québec, sent off *Le St Augustin* of Bilbao.[45] There was also talk of Scandinavian vessels. However, foreign vessels such as these sailed under French government contracts merely as short-term emergency measures of the type the government of Louis XIV had sometimes resorted to in seventeenth-century wars.[46]

[41] Of the many works on French imperial trade policy, the most useful for the period include Jean Tarrade, *Le Commerce colonial de la France à la fin de l'ancien régime* (Paris, 1972), 2 vols., and Filion, *La Pensée et l'action coloniale de Maurepas.*

[42] AN, 62 AQ 39, *Livre de délibération*, entries for 28 Jan. and 10 Mar. 1733. Arrangements in London were made by Jean Le Quesne; the company named the ship *La Ville de Québec.*

[43] Brisson, *La Charpenterie navale*, appendix B.

[44] AN, Colonies B 108, fols. 91, 118, 146.

[45] Arch. Ville de Bx., fonds Beaumartin, letter of Jean de Navarre, *Lt. Gén. de l'Amirauté de Guienne*, 1758; AN Colonies B 110, fol. 31; AN Z^{1D} 132 (1 June 1764).

[46] Issuing a passport in 1692, for instance, for *Le St Jacob* of Copenhagen (200 tx.,

Most ships were sent by merchants seeking a profit. The conditions affecting the Canada trade were as complex as any in that age, and the reasons for the bankruptcy of one merchant and the success of another are far from clear. For one thing, they were all at the mercy of markets where prices rose and fell not only in response to the usual factors of supply and demand, but also as a consequence of the isolation resulting from slow and scarce news. The passage from Louisbourg to France seldom took less than three weeks, from Québec seldom less than four, and voyages from France to New France usually took twice as long because of the prevailing westerly winds and currents of the Atlantic which move in a clockwise direction. Only between January and June did eighteenth-century vessels find the following winds they needed to reach Newfoundland or Canada by John Cabot's direct route rather than the very long circular 'Spanish' route using the trade winds to the Caribbean.

French transatlantic trade was hindered by a scarcity of printed news. Reports of markets and prices circulated mainly in those short, informal business letters that merchants were continually writing and receiving. These show much uncertainty and speculation. For instance, in May 1757 Antoine Giraudeau of La Rochelle sent his vessel *La Petite Suzanne* (80 tx., Captain Mathurin Fouché) to his friend, Pierre Meynardie at Québec, and in one of his covering letters he wrote:

> Judging by sales of furs by Monsieur Dumas of Montauban, there will be big losses on these return cargoes, as you will see by the prices I shall quote you at which he sold. Fortunately, I was silly enough (*assez étourdi*) to sell my marten skins long before my other peltries. I say fortunately, for I never would have got 8 livres apiece at the entrepôt as I did. . . . As for oils, as they were worth 165 livres per 30 *veltes* before the arrival of the Canadian vessels, I was sufficiently badly advised to refuse 150 livres for the lot, and today I shall sell them barrel by barrel for only 137 livres 18 sols. There has been a dreadful waste on the dried cod, having had on delivery, as I did, only 3,841 livres instead of 4,550 livres which your invoice stated. I sold it much too soon . . . the smallness of my ship prompts me to beg you to sell it if you find a suitable price . . . etc. etc.

Appended to the letter, a typical one in this trade, is a list of the prices at which Dumas had sold his bearskins, wolf, marten, fox, otter, and

Captain Christophle Eckoft, or Captain Jacques Vivier) which sailed from Bordeaux for Québec on 22 June. (ADG, 6 B 75*, fol. 90, 6 B 296 (23 Apr. 1692); ANQ, Chamballon (Que.), 3 Oct. 1692.)

other skins in Montauban.[47] Again, in spring 1756 Pierre Fesquet of Bordeaux, attracted by reports of high prices at Québec, sent off his ship, *Le Bon Amy* (60 tx., Captain Nicolas Pizane), with a cargo of brandy, wine, beef, pork, flour, and ironware. In his accompanying letter he asked his Québec agent, who was his clerk's brother, Joseph-Abraham Dérit, to load the ship with dried cod or timber for Martinique, 'and add twenty or thirty natives (*sauvages*) or even more if they can be suitably lodged without their numbers causing illness. These natives should not cost more than 150 to 200 livres or at most 300 livres'. If no cargo can be found, he added, then sell the ship. 'She is worth 7,000 livres.'[48]

The speculative element was somewhat reduced by the almost universal practice of dealing in a wide variety of merchandise in the hope of gaining on some what might be lost on others. In general, it is rare to find someone in the transatlantic Canada trade specializing in one commodity. Even Étienne Augier, a brandy merchant at Tonnay-Charente, down the river Charente from Cognac and Jarnac, dealt in butter, codfish, and whatever else was ordered or sent by his son at Louisbourg.[49] Mixed cargoes were partly the result of the practice whereby shipping merchants at the ports assembled cargoes of whatever seemed likely to sell, or whatever was asked for, so that bills of lading rarely carry the names of the local fur, fish, or other specialized dealers. By definition, indeed, a *négociant* was a dealer in mixed or variable cargoes, and so distinguished from a specialized cloth merchant or any other.

A ship's cargo was normally made up of a dozen, a score, or more lots of mixed goods, each assembled by a *négociant* for his own agent or customer in Canada, and loaded on the ship by arrangement with the manager (i.e. the *armateur* who might or might not be the owner). Even what looks like a specialized fish carrier, *La Providence* (80 tx.) of Granville, sailed by her owner-captain, Thomas Destouches, to Gaspé for a cargo of cod in 1755, turns out to have delivered a mixed cargo at Gaspé–pork, beef, butter, salt, wine, and brandy–in exchange for the fish with which she was captured on 29 October during the return voyage.[50] As bills of lading show, New France imported not

[47] PRO, HCA 32: 234, *La Petite Suzanne*, Giraudeau (LR) to Meynardie (Que.), 11 May 1757.

[48] PRO, HCA 32: 169, *Le Bon Amy*, Fesquet (Bx.) to Derit (Que.), 18 Mar. 1756.

[49] PRO, HCA 323: 224 pt. 2, *Le St Martin* of Dunkirk, bills of lading, seized 9 Jan. 1757; J. F. Bosher, 'French Protestant Families in Canadian Trade', *Histoire sociale* (Ottawa), vol. vii (1974), p. 193.

[50] PRO, HCA 32: 235.

only hardware, textiles, wine, and brandy, but enormous quantities of flour, beef, fruit, butter, and other foodstuffs. Eastbound cargoes seem to have been somewhat more specialized, but the names on the bills of lading are usually those of general *négociants* rather than fur or fish dealers, at least in the later period.

The element of speculation in the trade was much greater in the case of merchants without resident agents. They usually relied upon ships' captains to sell goods and buy return cargoes, or to engage agents at Québec. When Jean Saint Marc of St Malo fitted out *Le Rubis* (280 tx.) for a voyage to Canada and the West Indies in spring 1757, the many merchants of St Malo who sent shirts, cloth, butter, wine, candles, paper, etc. named no agents at Québec and entrusted everything to the captain, Allain-Charles-Marie Magon de Coetizac.[51] A West Indian cargo of sugar, coffee, and rum would have been in Captain Louis Guilman's charge on another St Malo vessel, *La Mutine* (80 tx.), dispatched that year by the firm of *Despechers, Guillemant et Bodiniers* on a voyage to St Dominique, then to Québec and finally home with a cargo of Gaspé codfish.[52]

Such merchant captains were usual on ships sailing directly from St Malo, for in the middle of the eighteenth century the trade between Québec and St Malo was irregular and there were few of those trading partnerships that merchants in Canada had with people at La Rochelle, Bordeaux, Bayonne, and Rouen. To avoid the uncertainties of such expeditions, on which the ship's captain was in the position of a pedlar, merchants at the small ports of St Valéry-sur-Somme, Cherbourg, Dieppe, or even Rouen, usually sent their vessels to Canada by way of La Rochelle or Bordeaux where a cargo could be had from a regular Canada merchant with an agent at Québec. In 1755, for example, this practice was followed for at least nine vessels from St Valéry, three each from Honfleur and Dieppe, two each from Cherbourg and Calais, and one each from Le Havre, Boulogne, Carteret, and St Malo.[53]

As a result, the principal French ports in the trade were surrounded by satellite ports which gave them resources that Québec, Louisbourg, and other colonial ports did not have. But in addition to the relatively

[51] PRO, HCA 32: 238 pt. 1; various other vessels were sent from St Malo under government contract, negotiated through the Magon family with its many connections in Paris.

[52] PRO, HCA 32: 220, *La Mutine* of St Malo seized 17 Apr. 1757.

[53] ADG, 6 B 101*; Perrens (Bx.), 23 May 1755; A. D. Ch. Mar., 4 J 2269, p. 22; AN, Z[1D] 132; PRO, HCA 32 *passim*.

distant and often large ports mentioned above, there were many more tiny satellite ports, often fishing ports near at hand, from which La Rochelle, Bordeaux, Rouen, and Bayonne drew ships, crews, and even some merchants and merchandise. Bordeaux was notoriously dependent for ships and sailors on Royan, Blaye, and Talmont; La Rochelle on Marennes, Brouage, St Martin-de-Ré, and the island of Oléron. Both ports had ships and sailors from the little ports of the Arvert Peninsula between the Gironde and the river Seudre: Chaillevette, Mornac, La Tremblade, and others. What men from these satellite ports sought at the centres of the colonial trades was the financial backing in the form of bottomry loans, marine insurance, and the cargoes and markets that only merchants with agents overseas might offer.[54]

The special qualification of the Canada merchants at La Rochelle and Bordeaux was that they either had formal agents or partners, often relatives, in Canada, or else they used the services of friends' or relatives' agents at Québec. In any case, personal connections or introductions were necessary. *Courtez et Foussat* of Bordeaux sent *La Nouvelle Constante* (240 tx., Captain Joseph Audoire) to *Delannes et Gauthier* of Québec in 1757 'on the assurance that Messieurs Risteau, father and son, have given us', and they enclosed a brief letter of introduction from Risteau and son.[55] When Admyrault of La Rochelle sent *La Surprise* (110 tx., Captain Jacques Radiguet) to Louisbourg in 1757, he addressed it to the Delort brothers there who had begun the relationship a few months before with a letter and references dated 3 December 1756. 'I am most flattered', Admyrault wrote in reply, 'to have the honour of your acquaintance. I very much hope there will be occasion to convince you of the favourable idea I have of your firm. Please be assured that if I undertake any speculation at your colony, I shall address myself to none but yourselves. . . .'[56]

Admyrault was one of those Canada merchants with no relatives in New France; nor had he ever visited the colony. He was therefore in the habit of signing formal partnerships with merchants of Québec for

[54] The bottomry loan, 'prêt à la grosse aventure', was the most usual form of loan to managers or ships' captains who needed cash for the customary two-months' advance of wages to seamen at the beginning of a voyage. There was an element of insurance in it, as the interest or premium was high but the lender lost the principal if the ship was lost. Interest was 20%, 25%, or as high as 40% or more in wartime.

[55] PRO, HCA 32: 225 pt. 1, *La Nouvelle Constante* seized 21 July 1757 and taken to Falmouth, *Courtez & Foussat* (Bx.) to *Delannes & Gauthier* (Que.), 18 June 1757.

[56] PRO, HCA 32: 242, *La Surprise*, dogger of La Rochelle, Admyrault (LR) to Delort (Louisbourg), 26 May 1757.

the brief terms that were customary in that age, usually three to six years. The most committed or specialized Canada merchants were those with commercial roots or relatives, or both, on the other side of the Atlantic: at La Rochelle, Bourgine, Charly, Fleury Deschambault, Pascaud, Simon Lapointe, and eventually Rodrigue and Goguet; at Bordeaux, Crespin, Descamps, Jung, Guillaume Pascaud, and eventually Trottier Désauniers; at Québec and Louisbourg, practically all shipping merchants, for they were legally confined to trade with French or West Indian ports.

Many of those who appear to have been committed to the Canada trade were also trading with Louisiana or the West Indies. Québec and Louisbourg carried on a considerable West India trade, as Jacques Mathieu has shown.[57] Descamps of Bordeaux and Dugard of Rouen sent nearly as many–sometimes more–ships to the West Indies as to Canada during the 1730s. Jung at Bordeaux and Bourgine at La Rochelle were deeply engaged in shipping to New Orleans during the 1740s. It is doubtful whether any but some of the smallest merchants limited themselves to the Canada trade.

The principal reason for this was that from the late seventeenth century French trade in West Indian sugar, indigo, coffee, rum, and some lesser products had grown so large that it had eclipsed the once-great Canadian fur trade. Students of the fur trade have always known this fact, but have seldom taken it into account, perhaps because it seems part of French imperial and Atlantic history rather than Canadian history.[58] The fish trade, always much greater than the fur trade, attracted hundreds of French ships, but most of them never visited New France, of which Newfoundland was not a part after 1713, and the Newfoundland fisheries had not been thought of in France as a North American trade at all.[59] In most years of the eighteenth century, dozens of ships were fitted out for Québec, but hundreds for Martinique, St Domingue, Guadeloupe, and the Newfoundland banks.

Louisbourg attracted much shipping after about 1730, but mainly as an intermediate port between France and the West Indian colonies. It had been built as a fortress, but by its commercial growth it drew Canada more and more into the orbit of the much larger and richer

[57] Mathieu, *Le Commerce*, e.g. pp. 224-5.

[58] But W. J. Eccles makes this very point in his article, 'A Belated Review of Harold Adams Innis, *The Fur Trade in Canada*', p. 421.

[59] Jean-François Brière, 'L'Armement français pour la peche à Terre-Neuve au XVIIIe siecle', Ph.D. thesis (York University, 1980), passim.

West India trade that was the principal interest of so many Canada merchants.

The growth of Louisbourg, fortress and trading centre, was part of the Anglo-French imperial rivalry leading to the mid-century wars. Another part was the increasing military and naval spending in Canada, and a third was the government contracts with such shipping merchants as the Beaujon and Gradis families of Bordeaux, Rodrigue of La Rochelle, and Trottier Désauniers of Québec. More and bigger ships moved in and out of Québec and Louisbourg during the twenty years of war from about 1743 to 1763 than during the thirty years of peace from 1713 to 1743.[60] In the history of diplomacy, the eight years from the Peace of Aix-la-Chapelle (1748) to the declaration of war in 1756 must be counted as years of peace, but the warlike preparations and the border raids in North America show them as years of 'cold war' between two periods of open warfare. The volume of French shipping did not decline in that interval but maintained the high level of the war years, and French military preparations aroused the anxiety of British ministers which led to a sudden attack on French shipping in summer 1755. During the last twenty years of New France, then, shipping to Québec and Louisbourg was at its peak partly because troops and supplies were sent and the Crown was spending more in Canada than ever before.

So great was the effect of imperial rivalry in those years that the community, so to speak, of Canada merchants was quite transformed, and this in three ways. First, many Huguenot firms large and small, and even some Jewish firms, took an increasing share of the trade. All sources show this increase to anyone who takes the trouble to identify Huguenots and Jews.[61] Secondly, the naval, military, and financial officials of the Crown at all the centres of New France were tempted to trade and to associate with merchants on an ever-increasing scale. These officials had always dabbled in transatlantic trade and intermarried with merchant families, but the ferment of the mid-century wars gave them more opportunities than ever before.

Thirdly, the old established Catholic families in the Canada trade were hard pressed to meet the new competition of Huguenots and officials. These Catholic families had inherited a favoured position in

[60] On this point, my lists agree in general with those of James Pritchard, 'The Pattern of French Colonial Shipping to Canada before 1760', *Revue française d'histoire d'outre-mer*, vol. lxiii (1976), p. 198.

[61] See below, ch. 7.

the Canada trade as a result of Louis XIV's policy of encouraging Catholic merchants and persecuting Huguenots. Closely associated with the Dutch, English, German, and English-American merchants, the Huguenots had aroused the hostility of the Bourbon government not only as heretics, but also as allies of foreign business interests. Under Louis XIV, therefore, Catholic firms took control of the Canada trade, but after imperial warfare broke out in 1743 some of the most established ones went bankrupt. Wartime needs forced the government to stop discriminating in their favour. In general, only those related to naval or financial officials, or associated with them, or those who bought royal offices, acquired government contracts, and made strong links with governing families, carried on successfully in the 1740s and 1750s.

The final result of imperial rivalry was the loss of Louisbourg to Great Britain in 1758 and of Canada and the rest of New France in the battles and negotiations of 1759-63. The trade between France and Canada ended in 1759–the last expedition from Bordeaux, in 1760, was disastrous–and those who had invested heavily in it, including several Huguenots, went bankrupt. The Crown added to the disaster by its reluctance to pay its debts to the merchants, by its suspension and depreciation of the Canada bills in which so many merchant fortunes were held, and by the *affaire du Canada* and the *affaire des Jésuites.* For merchants in the Canada trade, the complicated crisis of the conquest period marked much more than the end of the trade. It marked the end of an era, the end of Bourbon official society as they had known it.

2

The Merchant and his Family

TRADE between Canada and France was a family affair in the eighteenth century. Nearly every merchant was a family man in an age when the family was the main anchor, the principal source of security, for men, women, and children, especially in the mobile society of maritime trade. To identify trading families and related clans is to discover the purpose and meaning of merchants' lives. The family is the key to the world of the eighteenth-century merchant, because it was the object of his ambitions, his most intense loyalties, and all his labour, a hope of immortality in an insecure world. Hence the care with which he drafted and recorded the legal bases of family life, the marriage contracts, the wills, and the inventories of property.

Anyone about to embark upon the perilous Atlantic crossing made a will in which the poetry of eighteenth-century legal language had special meaning. 'Considering the fragility of this life, the certainty of death and the uncertainty of the hour of its coming. . .', reads the will of Pierre Lestage, a mariner from a trading family, about to leave Bordeaux for Québec in March 1759.[1] In the event of a man's death his property, listed item by item down to the last pair of shoes, was passed on to his heirs according to strict laws of inheritance. Marriage contracts as well as wills disposed of family property, both bride and groom bringing to the marriage, and so to their future children, whatever wealth they or their families could afford.

All families in that society were founded upon a pooling of property, but the merchant family was a business unit as well, almost a ready-made trading company. Unless a father had made a great fortune, he expected his sons to take up trade. In Jacques Savary's much-read handbook, *Le Parfait Négociant* (first published in 1675), merchants were advised to teach their sons commerce, modern languages, and history, but not to send them to college where they would meet proud noblemen disdainful of trade. 'For experience teaches us that the children whom fathers and mothers send to college to study Latin,

[1] ADG, Despiet (Bx.), 20 Mar. 1759.

grammar, rhetoric, and philosophy until the age of 17 or 18 years, are scarcely ever suitable for trade, and there will not be four out of thirty who will then devote themselves to the merchant's calling. . . .'[2]

Marriage alliances, the most vital decisions in merchants' lives, were usually made for business and social reasons, and they reveal more about merchant families than any other contracts. Formal partnerships, sealed by the notarized documents called *sociétés*, are also well worth knowing, but a partnership was brief, seldom lasting longer than a six-year term, and in any case it often followed upon a marriage or led to one. The most lasting and significant of them often turn out to be formal business arrangements among fathers and sons, widowed mothers and sons, or brothers and sisters. The firm of *La veuve Fesquet & fils*, a typical instance, was formed by a two-page contract of 14 July 1733 signed for four years by the widow and her two sons.[3]

We learn the meaning of such family partnerships in a will made out by Jacques Agard in favour of two sons who shipped merchandise to Québec in the 1740s under the name 'the heirs of Jacques Agard', according to their father's intention:

> . . . as it is in the interests of my heirs, all of whom I have brought up in trade, that my fortune (*mon cabal*) be kept whole and undivided, I desire my heirs, Pierre and Jacques Agard, to form an equal partnership (*société*) sharing profits and losses, and to bring all I leave them, without exception, to their partnership. I desire that Pierre Agard the elder shall have the power to sign and shall alone keep the funds (*la caisse*), from which Jacques Agard shall not be able to draw more than one thousand livres a year, for which he shall be debited, for his clothing, his belongings, and his other ordinary needs; that this partnership, under the name 'les héritiers de Jacques Agard', shall last until the said Jacques Agard, my second son, has reached the age of thirty years; that he may not renounce or dissolve it before he reaches that age. But in case he does renounce it or give cause by his own fault for its dissolution, I declare that the general provision I have made for him [in this will] shall be annulled and he shall be reduced to a claim of not more than 30,000 livres for all his paternal, maternal, and fraternal rights. . . . I likewise desire that Pierre Agard . . . may not dissolve the said partnership before Jacques Agard, his brother, has reached the age of twenty-five years. . . . I exhort my said heirs in their trade to take the advice of their brother-in-law, Sieur Jacques Legris, and of Sieur Sainerie, who will not refuse it because of the friendship there has always been

[2] Jacques Savary, *Le Parfait Négociant*, new ed. (Geneva, 1752), livre i, ch. iv, p. 15.
[3] ADG, Bernard (Bx.), 14 July 1733.

between us. I exhort them also, if any legal matters come up, to take the advice of Monsieur Riche, *avocat au Parlement*, which I always found good.[4]

The unwritten assumption in this will was that each of these sons would eventually take his own share of the heritage, and form a more lasting partnership in marriage with the daughter of another family, just as their sister, Marthe Agard, had gone away in June 1733 with a dowry of 10,000 livres to marry Jacques Legris. Marriage was the principal business partnership in Bourbon France, in merchant circles at least. A parent might sign a legal partnership document, that is, *une société*, with the children; brothers, sisters, and cousins might sign a partnership document binding them together in trade for a stated term of years; but husband and wife did not sign such a document because their marriage contract was itself a partnership in business as well as in life.

A Bordeaux merchant, Étienne Caussade, showed this relationship on the first page of his accounting *Journal* for the years 1741 to 1762. He began with a short prayer and then continued, under the date 2 March 1741, 'I declare that this day I celebrated the sacrament of marriage with Demoiselle Anne Guinlette, widow of the late Sieur Arnaud-Blaise Descamps, bourgeois and *négociant* of this town, and that to pursue the trade I propose to take up I have for my entire capital the sum of 115,250 livres. . . .'[5] He recorded his marriage and his business prospects in the same breath. In the list of capital assets that follows, he includes the value of his and his new wife's shares in various ships, as well as the 50,000 livres his father promised him in the marriage contract, signed only the previous week, and the 30,000 livres the bride and her father brought to the marriage along with various property. Two-fifths of his father's contribution was 'as gratuity and reward for all the services the Sieur future husband has rendered to [his father] Sieur André Caussade in the conduct of his vessels'.[6] Half of the wife's dowry her father simply transferred from her first marriage with Descamps, and the other half was the round sum of 'her savings and the profits she has made in her own personal trade (*son commerce particulier exercé pour son compte*) since the decease of the late Sieur Descamps'. She also possessed a great deal of property, including the jewels Descamps had given her 'for the children she had

[4] ADG, Faugas (Bx.), 12 Aug. 1746; St Pierre (Bx.), 21 June 1733, marriage of Marthe Agard and Jacques Legris.

[5] ADG, 7 B 2363, *Journal* 1741 to 1762, 179 fols.

[6] ADG, Bernard (Bx.), 24 Feb. 1741, marriage contract.

by him' worth 2,200 livres: a string of pearls, a diamond cross ('*une Charlotte*;), and a ring of seven diamonds. The inventory of business assets she drew up with the help of Descamps' clerk, her cousin Jean Lugeol, shows store-rooms filled with hundreds of sacks of ginger, cotton, and coffee, and hundreds of barrels of flour, wine, fish oil, and sugar, and bales of hides and furs.

As the business of Descamps' widow shows, a wife was not always a silent partner in these merchant marriages, but sometimes played a part in the family firm, even when she had not been brought up in a merchant family but was, like Madame Descamps, a surgeon's daughter. It was easy to develop such an interest because the counting-house and some of the store-rooms were usually in the family dwelling or next to it. Descamps and his wife lived in a house on the fossées des Salinières, rented from the widow of a Huguenot merchant, Jean Testas, with the counting-house on the second floor containing all the books and other records.[7]

To take another case, when in 1707 Anne Busquet, daughter of a merchant of La Rochelle, married Pierre Charly, the couple settled at La Rochelle in a house big enough to contain various store-rooms for their bales and boxes of merchandise ready for sending to Canada, and the hides and furs received from Pierre Charly's family and friends in Montréal.[8] For more than thirty years after his death in 1726, she carried on the Canada trade as *la veuve Charly* without even the help of sons–they appear to have had none–such as assisted Pascaud's widow at La Rochelle. Not all merchants' wives were business partners. When Jean Gatin died at Québec in 1733 the store-rooms in his house, rue du Cul de Sac, were full of merchandise, but his widow declared herself unable to read or write and ignorant of her husband's business, 'having had only the management of his household and not being capable of settling any accounts'.[9] Most merchants, however, seem to have regarded their wives as business partners. 'Thank God I have a wife endowed with some ability who will make the best of whatever reaches her', wrote Jean-François Jacquelin of the Canadian wife he left at Québec when he went to La Rochelle in 1756 on business and was caught by the war.[10] In general, a merchant who went

[7] ADG, Lamestrie (Bx.), 22 Feb. 1731.

[8] A. D. Ch. Mar., Guillemot (LR), 24 May 1707, marriage contract; St Jean du Perrot (LR), 13 July 1726, burial of Pierre Charly.

[9] ANQ, Barbel (Que.), 14 Apr. 1733, inv.

[10] AN, 62 AQ 31, Jacquelin (LR) to Dugard (Rouen), 25 Mar. 1758.

away on business or was dying had enough confidence in his wife to leave her in charge of their affairs by notarized power of attorney, and he preferred her to any other. She was his partner in business as well as in marriage. Her interests were the same as his and she could be counted on to do her best for their family.

Parents negotiated marriages for their sons and daughters, and merchants over thirty years of age their own marriages, with as much care and deliberation as did the royal families whose alliances were matters of war and peace. 'I married a daughter of Saubat Balanqué of Cape Breton, who has brought me goods and good character,' wrote the merchant, Étienne Cabarrus of Bayonne to his brother Léon at Louisbourg. 'That was what I was looking for and I may say that she has succeeded in winning the friendship of all of my family. That is enough talk about women. . . .'[11] This marriage, like all others, was first legalized in a contract that was the result of a long process in which many factors were weighed and discussed: not merely the sum of the dowry, but the family wealth behind it and the connections to be made in business circles, in official and perhaps noble circles, the law courts, the army, and the Church. What anxiety lies behind the following note of permission, notarized, signed by the Intendant Bégon, and sent to La Rochelle: 'I the undersigned, François-Mathieu Martin Delino, first councillor in the Superior Council of Québec, permit my son, Charles Delino de Balmon, to marry on condition that there shall be no reproach in the family of the young lady he takes; signed at Québec, this 26 October 1721'![12] Being a major step for the family, a marriage alliance might be cancelled by an agreement of the two families at any time before the consecration by a priest. On 13 December 1746, the Beaujon and Rodier families signed a marriage contract between Jean-Nicolas Beaujon, son of a merchant of Bordeaux, and Thérèse-Magdeleine Rodier, daughter of another merchant related to a *premier commis* in the ministry for marine and colonies.[13] The contract was signed by dozens of relatives on both sides, but a few weeks later it was cancelled for reasons we can only guess at.

A flourishing family being the sign and fruit of success, the dissolution of a family was a tragic result of failure, usually by death or

[11] PRO, HCA 30: 264-5, letter of 1757 undated.

[12] A. D. Ch. Mar., Fleury (LR), 3 Aug. 1722, reg. and followed by a marriage contract of Charles Delino and the daughter of a noble family.

[13] ADG, Parran (Bx.), 13 Dec. 1746, marriage contract.

bankruptcy. Ten years after Simon Pierre Thiollière and his wife died at La Rochelle in the early 1740s, a son on a sugar plantation at Cayes in the West Indies was writing sadly to his sister about 'your memory and that of my brother, all that remains of a dispersed family', and agreeing to the sale of family property in France.[14] When a merchant died, the courts appointed a legal guardian (*tuteur*), sometimes the widowed mother but more often a relative or friend, to manage the affairs of the children. Not everyone took such duties seriously. The tragic case of the Revol family shows what might happen. Pierre Revol, son of an attorney to the Parlement of Grenoble, had been sent to Canada as a punishment for salt-smuggling, but here he made a fresh start and in 1744 married Charlotte Roy, daughter of a prosperous *habitant* and merchant at Beaumont.[15] The family was dogged by trouble. In 1756, he went bankrupt; in 1757, while he was away in Gaspé, his wife had a notorious affair with his friend, Alexandre Dumas; and in 1759, he died at Gaspé.

His wife and children might have had some help from relatives at Louisbourg, Gabriel Revol and his wife, Geneviève Allemand, but as it happened they both fell ill and died in October 1758, leaving five children of their own, on board a British ship, *The Charles*, taking them to France after the fall of Louisbourg.[16] The first guardian appointed for Pierre Revol's children, Jean Corpron, soon returned to France, settled at Nantes, and in January 1761 passed the duties of guardian on to Jean-Élie Dupuy of La Rochelle. This was just as well because Corpron was arrested a few months later and eventually sentenced in the *affaire du Canada.* The Revol children were not yet settled, however: four years later, Dupuy passed their guardianship on to Joseph Brassard Deschenaux, an unscrupulous naval scrivener who had served as temporary naval treasurer at Québec and as secretary to the Intendant Bigot. We do not know how the Revol children fared thereafter, but already they had been thrown upon the mercy of men apparently too busy with their own affairs to take care of the children of a broken family.

One of the functions of marriage alliances between merchant families was to establish a branch of the family firm at another port. Prosperous enough for such marriages were the Le Moyne family of

[14] A. D. Ch. Mar., Guillemot (LR), 2 Apr. 1743, inv., 4 Aug. 1753.

[15] ANQ, Louet (Que.), 16 Feb. 1744.

[16] A. D. Ch. Mar., Delavergne (LR), 9 Jan. 1759, inventory made aboard *The Charles* on 5 Oct. 1750. A. D. Ch. Mar., Tardy (LR), 19 Jan. 1761, 13 Apr. 1765.

Rouen and the Pascaud family of La Rochelle, both with roots in Canada, who in 1730 arranged a marriage between Étienne-Claude Le Moyne and Susanne Pascaud. The Widow Pascaud seems to have been in the stronger position for she drove a hard bargain, putting up a dowry of only 50,000 livres to the 75,000 livres Étienne Le Moyne promised for his son. In addition, Le Moyne *père* promised 'to associate the said Sieur his son with himself as an equal partner in the trade he carries on and will continue to carry on, and this for a period of three years to begin on the day the marriage is celebrated, on the terms that shall be settled between them by the *acte de société* they shall sign for this purpose'.[17] The son promptly settled near his wife's family at La Rochelle where he carried on trading until his premature death on 16 May 1745. Meanwhile, in 1732 his elder brother, Pierre-Jacques Le Moyne, had married into a famous family of merchant bankers, the Le Couteulx family, originally of Rouen but well established in Paris and other cities; and Susanne Pascaud's sister, Henriette Pascaud, had married Guy-Guillaume Mahy de Cormeré who had connections in the West India trade.[18] Already the Pascaud and Le Moyne families were reaching into the ranks of the nobility, and in the next generation they were to add further alliances with noble merchant families at other towns.

One of the Pascaud alliances shows how the strength of family feeling sometimes brought two branches of the same family together. In 1747, the Widow Pascaud contrived to arrange a marriage between her daughter, Anne-Marie Pascaud, and Jean-Charles Pascaud de Poléon, an army officer from an old noble branch of the family that had acquired the barony of Pauléon, Poitou, in 1635.[19] Their common name was one of the cards in the widow's hand which she played to advantage in bridging the social gulf between her family and the Baron de Pauléon's. It was not uncommon for two branches of the same family to negotiate a marriage alliance. Two branches of the Irish family of Butler, established at La Rochelle and later to be related to the Pascaud family, made a marriage in the late seventeenth century.[20] Marguerite Bonfils married Hellies Bonfils in 1712; two branches of

[17] A. D. Ch. Mar., Desbarres (LR), registers, 10 June 1730; St Barthélemy (LR), 2 July 1730, 3 E 578.

[18] AN, MC, Morin (Paris), 19 May 1733; on the Mahy de Cormeré family see my *The Single Duty Project* (London, 1964), index, p. 209.

[19] A. D. Ch. Mar., Desbarres (LR), 1 Jan. 1747, marriage contract; notes Garneau.

[20] A. D. Ch. Mar., *Rivière et Soullard* (LR), 13 June 1709, fol. 52-3, marriage contract of Jean Butler, son of Jean and of Marguerite Butler.

the Desclaux family arranged a marriage between a pair of first cousins, as did two branches of the Dupuy family; Jean Jung de Saint Laurent married the widow of his cousin, Jean Jung, in 1718, becoming thereby the stepfather as well as the second cousin of her son, Jean Jung the younger. Other examples would not be hard to find.

Ties of blood counted for a great deal in that society, and were sometimes convertible into cash or power. In Nicolas Beaujon's will, he left 20,000 livres to a certain Marie Beaujon of Montauban 'who for some time has been claiming to be a relative of mine'.[21] Relatives had strong claims on each other and tended to trust each other because they were thought to be engaged in a common family enterprise. Whenever possible, the Canada merchants employed their own relatives as clerks, partners, and correspondents, and the great majority of firms were family firms. Loyalty and trust, supreme elements in all business relations, were doubly vital in the seventeenth and eighteenth centuries when cash was scarce and trade depended on a sophisticated network of credit. The wealth represented by the credit note, the bill of exchange, the bill of lading, or the statement of account was thought to be more secure if the signature were that of a relative. Certainly a merchant could expect little or no loyalty on the part of his fellow citizens, who were normally his competitors no less than the merchants of other towns. When a merchant went bankrupt, most of his creditors–including those whose failure of confidence had led to the collapse of his credit and the demand for immediate payments by all the other creditors far and near–were men of his own town.

Only members of his own family might be expected to stand by him. His wife, by agreement between them, would probably have already obtained a legal *séparation des biens* so that they might both live on her property after his assets had been disposed of by his creditors. Failing this recourse, he was at the mercy of his creditors, who customarily and legally formed an association to make his debtors pay and, if they were charitably inclined, to agree upon a small sum to keep for his livelihood. For instance, the Widow Lapointe at La Rochelle was left 12,000 livres at her bankruptcy in 1764, and early the next year Pierre Boudet was permitted to keep an income of 600 livres a year.[22] When the creditors could see no fault in the bankruptcy but only misfortune,

[21] AN, Y 62, fol. 62, Beaujon's will, 10 Jan. 1787.

[22] A. D. Ch. Mar., Tardy (LR), 9 Mar. 1764; and 31 Dec. 1764 to 16 Jan. 1765, *abandon de biens.*

they often made an agreement to give up a part of their claims in return for a firm undertaking to repay the rest over a fixed term of years. Pierre Mandret agreed in April 1728 to repay half of his bottomry loans and one-fifth of his other debts in four years; Pierre Gorsse undertook in 1741 to repay one-fifth of his debts and Armand Nadau in 1749 to repay four-fifths of his.[23] Creditors were not, then, entirely heartless and greedy during this period, but none could be counted as if they were members of the family, that soundest and most stable of business units in the eighteenth century. The more sons, daughters, nephews, and nieces the merchant could marry off to other merchants, the greater were his chances of security and success.

Merchant families spread and ramified as far as they were able, and the large clans they formed afford clues to the business associations and the geographical movements of certain merchants. Again and again investigation shows that a merchant went to Québec in the footsteps of a relative in a previous generation. The Bonfils living as a merchant at Québec in 1715 was the son or nephew of another who had been in the Newfoundland fishing business in the 1660s and 1670s. Pierre Pigneguy (1717-72), who made at least six voyages to Canada in the 1730s, was a cousin of Arnaud-Blaise Descamps, a Bordeaux merchant in the Canada trade and a nephew of Jean Pigneguy, who had traded to Canada in the previous generation in partnership with Jean Crespin. Further back still we find another relation in the Canada trade during the 1660s and 1670s: Jacques de Lamothe, who had spent many years at Québec.[24] Many such family traditions could be traced in the archives, and they are clues to the business life of the time.

Whether or not a French merchant had a family connection with Canada, he was unlikely to go there except in need. Established or successful merchants seldom if ever crossed the Atlantic. Bernard Cardenau, Joseph-Abraham Dérit, Pierre Glemet, Jean Grelleau, François Havy, and many others were sons of small-town shopkeepers or officials who went out to seek their fortunes.[25] Jean-André Lamalétie came from Bordeaux in 1741 as the younger son of François-Louis Lamalétie who had gone bankrupt in 1729 and was devoting what money he had to the career of an elder son in the navy.

[23] ADG, 7 B 403, 409, 415.

[24] J. F.Bosher, 'French Colonial Society in Canada', *Transactions of the Royal Society of Canada*, 4th series,vol. xix (1981), pp. 161-3; ADG, 7 B 405.

[25] These and other merchants in the trade with Canada are listed in Tables 2, 5 and 11.

Several came to Québec as the sons of manufacturers looking for markets: Pierre-Antoine Moufle from the cloth-making town of Beauvais, Texandier and Veyssière from Limoges, Dumas and Rauly from Montauban. Daniel Augier (1727-?) settled at Louisbourg in 1750 as the son and agent of a family of brandy merchants at Tonnay-Charente on the Charente River between Rochefort and Cognac. Others gravitated to Canada through the fur business: Jean Fournel (1705-32), the son of a merchant tanner of Agen, Luc Schmidt and Sacher from German families of furriers. The merchants who came to Canada were characteristically of humble origin.

It is therefore wrong to think of the Canada merchant as belonging to a class of merchant capitalists. The traditional idea of such a class rarely takes into account the penniless adventurers, ambitious shopkeepers, and capable sea-captains who found the means to send a few ships and shipments across the Atlantic. Yet a great deal of the Canada trade was done by such men, much more than is generally appreciated. Even some of the reputable established merchants were of humble origins. For example, the Pascaud family, though it could boast of royal offices and noble connections by the middle of the eighteenth century, went no further back than Antoine Pascaud (1665-1717), a village strap-maker's son from the Saintonge, who emigrated to Canada in his youth as a common *engagé*, and married an innkeeper's daughter, the capable Widow Pascaud of the years 1717-51 at La Rochelle. The Gradis fortune, too, some 162,000 livres by 1728, no less than 400,000 livres by 1751, had been built up by David Gradis since 1695 when his father, Diego Gradis, had sent him to Bordeaux with a mere 5,000 livres. Michel Rodrigue, a substantial merchant of La Rochelle who dispatched many ships to New France, and was able to buy an office of *Trésorier de France* in 1766 and to marry his daughters to minor noblemen, was the son of a Portuguese fisherman and sea-captain who settled at Louisbourg. Jean-Isaac Thouron and Pierre Boudet, who traded with Canada from La Rochelle on a large scale in the 1740s and 1750s, were the sons of small-town shopkeepers. Many more began in the same humble way and disappeared from trade after only a few years, or simply never prospered.

All these would have been astonished to hear themselves described as a class of bourgeois capitalists, and now, as then, it would be a mistake so to describe them. Some lived and died in wealthy bourgeois families; others did not. The merchant's place in the social hierarchy of Bourbon France is difficult to establish. That they were of the urban middle class, between the nobility and the peasantry, is not hard to believe if we ignore the noble rank of some merchant families and the humble origins of others. To describe them as bourgeois capitalists, however, would be misleading because only those with formal letters of bourgeoisie (*lettres de bourgeoisie*) were then accepted as bourgeois. Merchants were customarily distinguished from the bourgeoisie in that age, because most bourgeois were not merchants. As for the capitalists of Bourbon France, these were usually financiers who had made their fortunes by gathering, investing, and spending government funds, and were a very different group of business men from the merchants and bankers in the transatlantic trades. Even the port merchants and bankers accustomed to lending to the shipping merchants in the form of bottomry loans, or the Paris bankers who offered their credit, were seldom engaged themselves in the shipping trades. Conversely, few of the Canada merchants had capital to lend or to invest other than the credit they afforded each other in their mutual current accounts or in their insurance policies. The Canadian Intendant, Hocquart, reported that most merchants at Québec possessed too little money to trade without borrowing.[26] At Bordeaux even successful shipping firms such as *Gradis & fils, Beaujon & fils, Paul Penettes* or *Louis Granié* lent only a few thousand livres, and only rarely.[27] The usual lenders were families with fortunes from the fishing or West Indian or Iberian trades of earlier generations: Mercier, Griffon, Dubergier, Caila; Portuguese Jewish families, Fernandes, Pereire, or Peixotto; families with royal offices like Jean Dupuy, a *conseiller du Roi*; or widows with funds to invest. Table 1 shows bottomry loans to Canada merchants at Bordeaux for vessels about to depart for Québec. Such data show that most of the Canada merchants cannot be described as capitalists except in a loose and inaccurate sense, and in Bourbon France that abused term usually referred only to office-holding financiers.

The Canada merchants can more accurately be described according to their towns of residence, as 'merchants of Québec' or

[26] AN, Colonies C[11A] 64, fol. 106; Hocquart's opinion was general in the colony and concurs with our opinion that prosperous merchants rarely stayed in Canada; Jean Hamelin, *Économie et société en Nouvelle-France*, 3rd ed. (Québec, 1970), p. 136. The usual practice of borrowing by bottomry loan (*à la grosse aventure*) for an expedition to Canada also tends to confirm this view; 'utilisent cette forme de crédit, ceux qui ne peuvent faire autrement', as Charles Carrière judiciously argues ('Renouveau espagnol et pret à la grosse aventure (Cadix, 2e moitié du XVIIIe siècle)', *RHMC*, vol. xvii (1970), p. 246).

[27] See Table 1, 'Fifty Bottomry Loans in the Canada Trade at Bordeaux'.

Table 1. Fifty Bottomry Loans in the Canada Trade at Bordeaux

Notary and date	Ship	Destination	Sum in livres	% Interest	Borrower	Lender
Len. 11-7-09	*La Belonne*	Québec	1 000	65	Pierre Plassan	Jean Partarrieu
Len. 27-3-11	*Le Neptune*	Québec	?		Pierre Plassan	Lopez
Len. 26-3-14	*St Jérome*	Québec	1 129	25	Pierre Plassan	Lopez
Ber. 25-1-17	*St Laurent*	West Indies	1 000	25	Jung de St Laurent	*Veuve* Mathieu Clermon
Ber. 11-4-17	*La Providence*	Québec	1 500	25	Pierre Lamarque	Philippe Fernandez
Bed. 1-4-19	*La Polly*	Québec	1 500	25	Noel Nouguès	Mercier *père et fils*
Ber. 1-4-18	*La Polly*	Québec	1 000	25	Jacques Richard	Jean Dupuy
Bed. 8-3-17	*N. D. de Bon Secour*	Île Royale	1 000	25	Jacques Richard	Raymond Dubergier
Lam. 29-4-18	*La Polly*	Québec	1 000	25	Dupont de Bayonne	Martial Mercier
Ber. 8-4-19	*La Polly*	Québec	1 000	25	?	?
Ber. 8-4-19	*La Polly*	Québec	1 000	25	Noel Nouguès	Jean Dupuy (*cons. du Roy*)
Lam. 13-4-19	*La Polly*	Québec	1 000	25	Noel Nouguès	Raymond Dubergier
Ban. 26-5-21	*La Vigilante*	Québec	2 000	28	Noel Nouguès	Paul Griffon
Ber. 9-3-23	*N. D. de Bon Secour*	Que. & I. R.	2 000	?	?	?
Ber. 9-3-23	*N. D. de Bon Secour*	Que. & I. R.	2 000	?	Hugues Grangent	Paul Penettes
Lam. 30-4-23	*La Marie Joseph*	Que & Mart.	2 000	25	Jacques Leclerc	Paul Griffon
Lam. 2-4-24	*N. D. de Bon Secour*	Que. & I. R.	1 200	22	Antoine Nouguès	Raymond Ferbos
Ber. 4-5-25	*Les Trois Amis*	Québec	400	30	Jacques Sourcebille	Jean Mercier *fils ainé*
Ber. 7-5-25	*Les Trois Amis*	Québec	1 000	30	Doneu, Heliot & Graves	Jean Mercier *fils ainé*
Ber. 8-5-25	*Les Trois Amis*	Québec	200	30	Pierre Sorbe	Mathieu Risteau
Ber. 21-5-22	*La Marianne*	Que. & I. R.	1 500	15	?	?
Ber. 23-3-26	*Le Postillon Marin*	Que. & Mart	400	20	Alexis Douteau & J. Bonnefort	*Veuve* Touges
Par. 22-4-31	*Le Revanche*	Île Royale	2 800	7·5	?	?
Ber. 12-8-27	*La Mutine*	Que. & I. R.	600	25	Guillaume Fieuzol	Pierre Gorsse
Ber. 8-4-27	*N. D. de Bon Secour*	I. R.	2 000	25	B. Larreguy	Mercier *père et fils*
Par. 11-4-31	*Le Revanche*	Île Royale	1 500	17	?	?
Lam. 4-5-29	*La Louise*	Que. & I. R.	1 500	18	Jean Jung	Odet Couderc
Lam. 4-5-29	*La Louise*	Que. & I. R.	1 500	18	Jean Jung	Clément Dubergier
Lam. 24-5-29	*La Louise*	Que. & I. R.	300	22	Pierre Mesgrier	Jean Mercier *l'ainé*
Lam. 24-4-31	*L'Hirondelle*	Québec	1 000	23	Pierre Gorsse	Claude Mercier

Lam. 26-4-30	*L'Hirondelle*	Québec	1 500	23	Pierre Gorsse	Claude Mercier
Lam. 26-4-31	*L'Hirondelle*	Québec	2 000	23	Pierre Gorsse	Claude Mercier
Ber. 21-5-32	*La Marianne*	Québec	1 500	15	Pierre Sorbe	Nicolas Bensse
Barb. 1-5-32	*La Marianne*	Québec	1 800	22	Pierre Sorbe	Jacob Fernandès
Par. 7-3-33	*La Suzanne*	Que. & W. I.	2 000	20	Louis Parent	Joseph Pereire & Co.
Par. 7-3-33	*La Suzanne*	Que. & W. I.	2 000	25	Louis Parent	Jean Lafore *fils*
Par. 20-5-34	*Le Montréal*	Québec	5 000	14	René Legardeur de Beauvais	Jean Mercier *l'ainé*
Par. 4-5-36	*Le Brillant*	Québec	15 000	9	Simon-Pierre Thiollière	Jean Beaujon
Par. 16-2-37	*Le Luxembourg*	Québec	3 000	16	Ch. La Richardière Petiot	Jean Mercier *l'ainé*
Par. 27-5-39	*Le Prospérant*	Québec	800	20	René Ricoeur	Jean Mercier *l'ainé*
Lag. 22-6-42	*Le St Joseph*	Québec	1 200	30	Martin Larreguy	Pierre Rocaute
Lag. 16-3-43	*L'Intrigant*	Québec	12 000	14	Jean Jung	Christophle Caila
Fran. 29-4-47	*L'Aymable Marguerite*	Que. & W. I.	20 000	14	Jean Lafore	Martin Zachau
Man. 2-6-50	*Le St Pierre*	Que. & W. I.	6 000	22	Pierre Depé	Pierre Trottier Désauniers
Perr. 24-3-51	*L'Achille*	Que. & W. I.	12 000	14	Thomas Oualle	Peixotto
Perr. 20-5-51	*L'Aimable Catherine*	Que.	1 200	18	Guillaume Quesnel	Isaac Sasportes
Par. 16-2-52	*Le Tonnant*	Île Royale	6 000	20	Pierre Douezan	Antoine Groc
Perr. 22-2-52	*Le Saige*	Que. & St Dom.	1 000	25	Raymond Mandary	Jean Barreyre *l'ainé*
Par. 20-7-52	*Le St Espirit*	Île Royale	6 576	16	Pierre Camefrancq	Dupeyrat & Moras
Par. 20-7-52	*Le St Espirit*	Île Royale	3 268	16	Pierre Camefrancq	François-Xavier Dupeyrat
Lav. 19-3-53	*Le Fidelle*	Que. & W. I.	9 100	20	Michel Bouscaillou	Dehoste & Co.
Perr. 27-6-53	*Le Joseph*	Que. & I. R.	11 000	12	Cadet et Massot	David Gradis *et fils*
Lav. 18-4-53	*N. D. de Grace*	Que. & W. I.	2 000	22	Joachim Clemens	Louis Granié
Par. 1-4-54	*St Pierre le Victorieux*	Que.	1 200	14	Guillaume Noel	*Veuve* Jean Duffour *et fils*
Perr. 4-4-54	*Le St Jacques*	Île Royale	1 000	12	Jacques Ledos	Isaac Alexandre *et fils*
Perr. 23-5-55	*La Reine de France*	Que. & I. R.	10 782	12	Bertrand Lecombéry	David Gradis *et fils*

Notaries' names: Banchereau, Barberet, Bedout, Bernard, François, Lagénie, Lamestrie, Lenfumé, Lavau, Mansset, Parrans, Perrens, Séjourne *l'ainé*

Note

Many borrowers were ship's captains, but merchant-owners' names are cited herein when known.

'merchants of Rouen', but these terms too can be misleading. It is true that the Canada merchants in every French port tended to live close to one another, usually in the same parish. In lower-town Québec, in La Rochelle within ten minutes' walk of the *Bourse*, and in Rouen near the Seine, merchants were near one another. Even at Bordeaux, with a population as big as the French population of Canada, most lived in the parish of St Michel on a few streets not far from the docks: the rue de la Rousselle, the rue Neuve, the rue du Pont St Jean, or the rue des Fossés. As we walk through these narrow streets now, little changed since the eighteenth century, we can still see the store-room doors, big enough to admit horse-drawn carts through rounded arches in the stone walls of the houses. The houses of two, three, or four storeys were built against each other in a continuous line with an occasional alley a few feet wide leading darkly into a courtyard or over to the next street. These streets are silent now, but in the eighteenth century they were full of business people all crammed in together: the number of merchants who gave their addresses in those few streets is astonishing. If they did not meet at the *Bourse* (founded in 1717) where they went daily for news and conversation, they were likely to meet in the street or at a notary's office or at a mass in St Michel church or at a christening in St André's church.

The merchants of a town did much business together. Insurance policies for most ships were open to subscription up to the required sum, and might be underwritten by ten, twenty, or even more local merchants, each for a small sum of a few hundred livres. Later, if the ship were wrecked these sums had all to be collected, and if it returned safely a premium had to be paid to each underwriter.[28] Bottomry loans were commonly arranged between wealthy lenders and shipping merchants who needed cash for the customary two months' wages advanced to the crews of departing ships. Most ships were owned by several merchants, each holding a fractional interest–usually one-half, one-quarter, one-eighth, or one-sixteenth–that could be bought and sold on a market so lively that we can seldom be certain who owned a ship from one year to the next.

Cargoes to Canada were likewise nearly always made up of many consignments being sent by many different merchants to as many different customers. Merchandise was continually bought and sold;

[28] These and other business practices of the eighteenth century are explained in many books, such as Jean Cavaignac, *Jean Pellet, commerçant de gros, 1694–1772* (Paris, 1967), and Dale Miquelon, *Dugard of Rouen* (Montréal and London, 1978).

houses, shops, and farms changed hands; loans in the form of *rentes* were arranged. As cash was always scarce, payments were customarily made in the form of credit notes, current accounts, bills of exchange, and other forms of credit, so that a tissue of debtor-creditor relations bound the merchants of a town together. To this extent and in this sense, they may be treated as a group with common interests, in competition with the merchants of other towns. There is, then, a measure of truth in the usual historical account of trade in terms of 'merchants of Bordeaux' or 'merchants of Québec' and their doings.

These terms can be misleading, however, because few merchants were born in the towns where they lived; most moved about and had strong ties with relations and partners in other towns. Among the few 'merchants of Rouen' in the Canada trade of the eighteenth century were Étienne Le Moyne, born at Québec, Pierre Massac *l'aîné*, born at or near Bordeaux, Pierre D'Haristoy from a Bayonne family, and Guillaume France, possibly descended from a Portuguese Jewish family.[29] The more numerous La Rochelle merchants were nearly all from somewhere else, and the historian who, like John Clark, studies the old established families of La Rochelle is certain to miss the majority of families in the Canada trade.[30] At Bordeaux more merchants were from settled families, but there too the term 'merchants of Bordeaux' in the Canada trade can be misleading, as a review of the major shipping merchants shows. Table 2 shows where many of the Canada merchants came from.

The merchants at Québec, Montréal, and Louisbourg were even more mobile because many came out as agents of French firms and intended to return to France when they had made their fortunes. The resident merchants, especially those born in Canada, liked to think of themselves as established, and resented the intrusion of the *marchands forains* who came and went with the ships, but several such Canadians decided to settle in France once they had made enough money. And several younger Canadians moved to France to establish themselves in the Canada trade. The Canadian, Étienne Le Moyne, settled at Rouen sometime in the late seventeenth century. Fleury Deschambault, Simon Lapointe, Pierre Charly, and Michel Rodrigue, all Canadian born, went to live at La Rochelle. Pierre

[29] See Tables 2 and 3.

[30] John G. Clark, *La Rochelle and the Atlantic Economy during the Eighteenth Century* (Baltimore and London, 1981). Names such as Boudet, Grelleau, and Rodrigue do not even appear in the index. See Tables 2 and 3.

Table 2. Origins of the Principal Merchants in the Canada Trade at La Rochelle and Bordeaux

At La Rochelle	
Gabriel Admyrault père	Lavasseau-en-Poitou
Pierre-Gabriel Admyrault *fils*	La Rochelle
Pierre Blavoust	La Rochelle
Marguerite Bouat (*la veuve Pascaud*)	Montréal
Pierre Boudet	Caussade (near Montauban)
Hilaire Bourgine *père*	Poitiers
Charles-Polycarpe Bourgine *fils*	La Rochelle
Pierre Charly	Montréal
Charles Fleury Deschambault	Québec
Joseph Fleury Deschambault	Québec
Jacques Garesché	Nieulle (near Marennes)
Denis Goguet	Île de Ré
Jean Grelleau	Çorbarrieu (near Montauban)
Pierre Lamarque	Caudrot-en-Bazadois
Joseph Simon Lapointe	Québec
Jacques Leclerc *père*	Bayonne
Pierre Meynardie	Bergerac
Jacques Michel	Marseille
Nicolas Paillet	Marennes
Antoine Pascaud *père*	La Prade (near Aubeterre-sur-Dronne)
Antoine Pascaud *fils*	Montréal
Joseph-Marie Pascaud	Montréal
Étienne Ranjard	Châteauroux-en-Berry
Pierre-Jacques Rasteau	Marennes
Pierre-Isaac Rasteau	Marennes
Michel Rodrigue	Acadia
Jean-Baptiste Soumbrun	Misson (near Dax)
Simon-Pierre Thiollière	St Étienne-en-Forêt
Jean-Isaac Thouron	St Antonin-en-Rouergue
Jean Veyssière	Limoges
At Bordeaux	
David, Jacob, and Samuel Alexandre	Bayonne (or Portugal)
Jean Ancèze	Praissac-en-Agenais
Pierre Baour	Castres (Tarn)
Jean Beaujon	La Gruère-en-Condomois
Nicolas Beaujon	Bordeaux
Jean Crespin	Agen
Jean Delpech	Aubeterre-en-Agenais
Arnaud-Blaise Descamps	Barsac-en-Sauternais
Pierre Desclaux	Tonneins
Jean Domenget	Bergerac
Bernard Douezan	Sérignac-en-Brouillois
Durand Doumerc (father of Pierre)	Toulouse
Dubergier	Bordeaux
Jean-Patrice Dupuy	Bordeaux
Jacques and Joseph Féger	Le Tréguier (Bretagne)
Foussat	Lauzerte or Moncesson (near Moissac)

Pierre Garrisson	Montauban
Pierre Gorsse	Bordeaux
David and Abraham Gradis	Portugal
Louis Granié	Béziers
Joseph Grateloup	Dax
Antoine Groc	Castelnaudary (Languedoc)
Jean Jung de Saint Laurent	Fleurance (Gers)
Jean Jung (1698-1753)	Québec
Pierre de Kater	Amsterdam
Jean-André Lamalétie	Bordeaux
François Lartigue	Bordeaux
Pierre Lartigue	Bordeaux
Jean Liquart	Bordeaux
Pierre Mandret	Île Dieu
Antoine Marsal	Moissac
Amand Nadau	St Martin-de-Mascrac (Puynormand)
Guillaume Pascaud	La Prade (near Aubeterre-sur-Dronne)
Arnauld Pigneguy	Barsac
Louis Pourcin	Bordeaux
Mathieu Rocquier	Tonneins
Jean-François Rosier	Bordeaux
Sageran	Vacquay (near Clairac)
François Solignac	Lectoure (Leytoure)
Pierre Texandier	Limoges
Pierre Trottier Désauniers	Québec
Abel Vernhès	Montauban

Trottier Désauniers retired to Bordeaux in 1747 and died there ten years later. The Canadian-born merchant, Jean Jung, had been brought to Bordeaux as a child by his Canadian mother, and there they had stayed. Charles-Denis Perthuis settled in Paris as a merchant and died there on 30 November 1749. In 1746, Guillaume Delort, *conseiller au conseil supérieur de Louisbourg*, was living at Aignan-en-Armagnac with enough money to lend 25,000 livres to the Jacobin fathers of Bordeaux.[31] These examples show that 'Canadian' merchants returned to France without difficulty; it was, after all, their homeland in a deeper sense than we are sometimes ready to admit. Home is where the heart is, and many a Canadian born and bred has felt at home in France, in England, or in Scotland near the bones of his ancestors.

Furthermore, all merchants had agents or 'correspondents' at other towns, and many had formal partnerships or family relations which committed them to close collaboration with outsiders. For example, during the 1750s Pierre Boudet of La Rochelle, who had been in the

[31] ADG Guy (Bx.) 5 Nov. 1746, *procuration*.

The Port of Bordeaux. *Engraving from a painting by Joseph Vernet*.

Canada trade since the 1730s, had current accounts with dozens of merchants at other towns, including relatives.[32] Every bankruptcy revealed, as Boudet's revealed in 1764, a ramifying set of debtor-creditor relationships with merchants in many towns in France and abroad. Table 3 shows the range of Boudet's current accounts and principal correspondents. Many merchants traded with distant relatives in family firms to which they were committed by the strongest loyalties of the age. Knowing that Jean Crespin came from Agen and traded with his brother at Bordeaux and his father and brother-in-law at Agen, how could anyone regard him as a 'merchant of Québec' except in a superficial sense, even though he lived at Québec for about forty years?

To cite another example, various members of the Meynardie family can be found living as merchants at Bordeaux, *c.* 1720-50, at Petit Gouave in St Domingue during the 1720s, at Québec and La Rochelle in the 1750s, and at Bergerac throughout the century. They were all close relatives in correspondence with one another, and only in a very limited sense could any of them be thought of as belonging to one town rather than another. Their family came first with them and took precedence over the town where they happened to be living. Other very different families remained for generations in one town, held municipal or ecclesiastical offices or bought royal offices. Such, for instance, was the Lamalétie family of Bordeaux, boasting letters of bourgeoisie dated 11 October 1659 and 15 June 1720 and a coat of arms.[33] This family, at least, we might hope to label 'merchants of Bordeaux' with some confidence–until we discover Jean-André Lamalétie, the *secrétaire du roi* of the family, who made his fortune in Canada where he married and lived from 1741 to 1758 as a *greffier de la maréchaussée* and a 'merchant of Québec', as I have myself described him. On close acquaintance, most merchants in the Canada trade turn out to belong to families more than to towns, and we neglect their families at our peril.

The town of Montauban is an exception to this general rule in that its many families in the Canada trade were all, or nearly all, related. Furthermore, Montauban, with its woollen industry, was one of the

[32] See Table 4, mostly drawn from A. D. Ch. Mar., Tardy (LR), 31 Dec. 1764 and Delavergne (LR), 8 Feb. 1766.

[33] J. F. Bosher, 'A Québec Merchant's Trading Circles in France and Canada: Jean-André Lamalétie before 1763', *Histoire sociale* (Ottawa), vol. ix (1977), pp. 24-44; and Pierre Meller, *Armorial du Bordelais*, vol. ii (Bx., 1906), p. 281.

Table 3. Pierre Boudet's Current Accounts and Correspondents

Nicolas Beaujon	Paris banker
Behic	Bayonne
Jean Boudet	Rotterdam
Chabbert & Banquet	Paris bankers
Gabriel Da Silva	Bordeaux
Depeuille	Paris banker
Veuve Desbrières & Fils	Paris bankers
Pierre Desclaux	Bordeaux
Jourdain *Frères*	Amiens
La Gravere (married Marie Boudet)	Bordeaux
Pierre Le Moyne	Rouen
Mariette *père et fils*	Montauban
François Amy Miron	Orléans
François Mounier and Jean Grelleau	Québec
Salle & Cie	Paris
Jean-François Sellon	Paris banker
Valentin Sechober (?) and Jerome-Frédéric Silber	Nuremberg
Pierre Touche	Marseille

In addition, suggestive bundles of letters were found at his death as follows:

341 letters dated 1753-9 from Nicolas Beaujon of Paris
72 assorted letters from Canada dated 1751-3
259 letters from *Chabbert & Banquet*, Paris bankers, 1749-64
138 letters from Da Silva of Bordeaux, 1750-2
364 letters from Depeuille, Paris banker, dated 1739-57
156 letters from *Veuve Desbrières & fils*, Paris bankers, 1753-7
72 letters from *Desclaux & fils*, Bordeaux, dated 1752-6
12 letters from Jean-Laurent Forst of Nuremberg
115 letters from Nicolas Grignon of Marennes, Saintonge, 1750-9
68 letters from *Larquier jeune & compagnie* of Nîmes, 1751-4
147 letters from Le Moyne of Rouen, 1751-9
42 letters from Montaudouin of Nantes
(and others).

great centres of their trade. Merchants of Québec such as Joseph Rouffio, Antoine Malroux, or Alexandre Dumas, all born at Montauban, could sensibly be grouped as 'merchants of Montauban', for some purposes at least, whereas the birthplace of most other merchants is of little significance. All the same, Montauban families such as Dumas and Serres established branches at Bordeaux and intermarried with other families there. In the end, even merchants of Montauban are best studied in families.

The case of merchants from Montauban introduces another binding force in the Canada trade: practically all the Canada merchants there were from Protestant families. As we sort out the merchants according to their family and commercial affiliations we discover that Catholic families tended to intermarry and so did families of New Converts or Huguenots. Certain families remained Protestant, even when they conformed to Catholic practices in order to avoid persecution, and merchant families kept a lively sense of their own religious and social identity because of the importance of personal trust in eighteenth-century business. 'The trade of the ancien régime', writes Jean Meyer, 'rested above all on the credit of persons.'[34] Historians agree on this point. As Charles Wilson explains,

> Wherever possible a blood relation was appointed to take charge of important business. Beyond this, personal relationships between merchants were supremely important in an age when personal contact was the chief guide in regulating credit transactions; and since the whole of this international trade was carried on by credit, it may be said that the personal recommendation stood as the foundation of all international trade at this time.[35]

A merchant preferred to deal with people of his own family, of his own nationality, and of his own religion. Catholic, Protestant, and Jewish merchants traded freely together, but they seldom formed partnerships and even more rarely intermarried. Merchant families tended to persist in the same religion as their forefathers. Religious groups were, then, more persistent and fundamental than we are accustomed to think, and any social history of the Canada merchants must take them into account. The social history of Roman Catholic merchants is different from the history of Protestant merchants, and the two must be considered separately in order to make sense of their differences.

[34] Jean Meyer, *L'Armement nantais dans la deuxième moitié du XVIIe siècle* (Paris, 1969), p. 113.

[35] Charles Wilson, *Anglo-Dutch Commerce and Finance in the Eighteenth Century* (Cambridge, 1941), pp. 28-9.

II

Bourbon Official Society

3

The Roman Catholic Majority

FOR thirty years after the Peace of Utrecht (1713), most of the Canada trade was in the hands of Roman Catholic merchants. The greatest of these belonged to families with members on both sides of the Atlantic, such as Pascaud, who sent more than two dozen vessels, Fleury Deschambault, a prosperous and well-connected trading family, Jung and Lapointe who each dispatched a score of ships and many shipments on other men's vessels, Charly, who sent shipments annually, and Bourgine who sent at least ten vessels in this period. Many others traded for shorter periods or on a smaller scale. Pierre Lamarque, for example, sent out at least five vessels in the years 1727-33 and Simon-Pierre Thiollière at least seven vessels in the years 1730-9.[1] All of these were Catholic. Until the 1730s and early 1740s very few Protestant merchants were in the Canada trade, and their business amounted to only a tiny fraction of the total.

Merchants in the Canada trade were more religious than we are inclined to recognize, trained as we are to filter out religious elements and to focus upon the harbingers of our own secular view. Watched, guided, and served from birth to death by a numerous and influential clergy, merchants normally tried to live up to the Church's expectations. They would often write a prayer on the first page of a new ledger, instruct a ship's captain to assemble the crew for prayers morning and night, or set aside money for the Church in one of the clauses of a formal partnership agreement. 'And so that God will be pleased to bless this partnership [*société*],' runs the 14th clause of Michel Rodrigue's agreement with Pierre-François Goossens, 'the sum of 300 livres shall be distributed to the poor, to wit, 200 livres by Rodrigue and 100 livres by Goossens.'[2] Merchant post-mortem

[1] Lamarque's vessels included *Le Postillon*, 90 tx., in 1727, 1729, 1731, and 1733, and *Le Ville-Marie*, 200 tx., in 1731; Thiollière's included *Le Saint Antoine*, 100 tx., in 1730, 1734, 1735, *La Marie-Madeleine*, 130 tx., in 1732, *La Nouvelle France* in 1733, *Le Brillant*, 300 tx., in 1736, and *Le Saint Pierre*, in 1739.

[2] AN, MC, LXXXIII 415, 22 July 1750, *société*, clause 14; for another example, J. F. Bosher, 'A Québec Merchant's Trading Circles in France and Canada: Jean-André Lamalétie before 1763', *Histoire sociale* (Ottawa), vol. ix (1977), p. 33.

inventories everywhere list religious books, pictures, and other possessions. At Montréal, Louise Dechêne tells us, one-third of the merchants' dwellings were decorated with religious themes.[3] Many served as churchwardens, like Simon Lapointe in 1741 in the parish of St Jean du Perrot near the port in La Rochelle, and Jean-Baptiste Amiot at Notre Dame in Québec. Many rented pews in churches, like Arnaud-Blaise Descamps who paid 30 livres for a pew in St Michel, Bordeaux, and made a formal request to the archbishop for another in the parish church of St Vincent-de-Barsac where he was born. The ambient pressures on New Converts were heavy: when the Bordeaux Jewish merchant, David Gradis, received a black slave from the firm of *Gradis et Mendès* of St Pierre de Martinique, he made a formal declaration to the authorities of his intention to bring the slave up in his service as a Roman Catholic in conformity with a royal declaration that was to be renewed on 15 November 1738.[4]

Everywhere there were religious feasts and fasts to be observed. In Canada, fifty-nine fast days called for light meals and abstinence from meat and dairy products. Some thirty-three feast days were celebrated until 1744 when these were reduced to fourteen, all in addition to the usual fifty-two Sundays.[5] Grand processions of clergy, officers and soldiers, merchants and other notables, and common folk went around the town from church to church on occasions such as the feast of the Virgin Mary described in detail by the Swedish traveller, Pehr Kalm.[6] The church bells rang and all bystanders knelt upon the ground while the statue of the Virgin was passing. This was only one of ten special feasts celebrating this cult, including the feast of Our Lady of Victory introduced at Québec by Bishop Saint-Vallier in 1694 'for the most remarkable victory and protection that we have received from the most Holy Virgin against the English heretics'.[7] Even at sea, a merchant remained within the orbit of the Church for at French ports the *Confrèrie du Saint-Sacrement* recruited ships' officers for training courses in maintaining the Roman Catholic faith and combating the Protestant heresy so common among the mariners of Normandy and

[3] Louise Dechêne, *Habitants et marchands de Montréal au XVIIe siècle* (Paris and Montréal, 1974), pp. 457-9.

[4] ADG, 6 B 1195, 9 June 1729.

[5] C. Jaenen, *The Role of the Church in New France* (Toronto, 1976), p. 153.

[6] Jacques Rousseau and Guy Béthune, ed., *Voyage de Pehr Kalm au Canada en 1749* (Montréal, 1977), fol. 743.

[7] Gustave Lanctot, *Une Nouvelle-France inconnue* (Montréal, 1955), p. 49.

the south-west.[8] Louis XIV and Colbert had signed a series of contracts in 1683-7 wherein Edmé Joly, supérieur général de la Congrégation de la Mission, undertook to provide chaplains (*aumôniers*) on naval vessels and wherever else sailors might need them. These contracts were printed and circulated among the naval authorities, and freshly printed copies were sent to Rochefort in 1755.[9]

Merchant families usually had relatives in holy orders. Bourgine, for example, had at least four such relatives: René Hilaire Bourgine, a canon of the La Rochelle cathedral (who lent him 8,000 livres for business purposes); Hilaire-Polycarpe Massé, a parish priest at Ars-en-Ré; Jean-René Massé, a parish priest at Gué d'Allère; and Louis-Clerc-Simon Huret Soudinère, rector of the university of Poitiers. Pierre Charly had no less than four sisters in Canadian religious communities; Guillaume Estèbe had a brother, Antoine, in the priesthood;[10] the Jung family were well rooted in the Canadian clergy; Joseph Féger, of the well-known Féger brothers at Bordeaux, was a priest; Michel Rodrigue of Louisbourg and La Rochelle put his son Paul into the priesthood; Charles Fleury Deschambault of La Rochelle had a brother, Jacques, who served as a missionary in Acadia; Durand Doumerc of Bordeaux, who had two sons in maritime trade, put another, Jean-Baptiste, into the priesthood, wherein he already had a relative, André Doumerc. He also put his eldest daughter into a convent. A thorough search would turn up clerical relatives in practically every Catholic family.

Clerical relatives in Canada sometimes drew the attention of French merchants otherwise likely to have little or no interest in the colony. During the Seven Years War, the great merchant family of Magon at St Malo was continually anxious about a brother serving as a Sulpician missionary in Canada. This was François-August Magon de Terlaye (1724-77), variously referred to as the abbé de Terlaye or the chevalier de Terlaye. His merchant brother at St Malo, Luc Magon, often asked for news of him or sent him letters, tobacco, and candles through other firms sending ships to Canada, such as Auger of Bordeaux who was sending two ships to Québec in April 1758. On 31 October 1759, having recently learned of the defeat on the Plains of Abraham, Luc Magon wrote to *Josias Cottin & Co.* of London, 'We fear

[8] André Corvisier, ed., *Histoire du Havre et de l'Estuaire de la Seine* (Toulouse, 1983), p. 126.
[9] Arch. de la Marine, Rochefort, 1 E 153, fols. 505-8.
[10] ADG, Guy (Bx.), 28 Aug. 1769.

that his zeal may have taken him to Québec during the siege, and God grant that no accident has befallen him in any event. We do not doubt that he has remained in that country and we take the liberty of sending a letter for him attached herewith.'[11] Such letters as this, expressing concern for the missionary brother, often dealt with marine insurance and other business which Magon carried out for various Canada merchants.

What distinguished the Catholic families from the families of New Converts or Protestants was their place in the official society of the Bourbon monarchy. Only Catholics could obtain royal offices, royal appointments, military and naval commissions, or financial and ecclesiastical posts; and only the families of Catholic merchants, as a general rule, intermarried with families of officials, officers, financiers, magistrates, or clergy. Occasionally a Protestant family had a relative in the army, as the Dumas family had a cousin, Jean-Daniel Dumas, who came to Canada in 1750 as an officer in the colonial regulars, but this was unusual. Catholic merchants were, as a matter of course, part of the social fabric of the monarchy. Protestant merchants were not. Here was a fundamental difference between the two religious communities in the Canada trade.

Royal discrimination in favour of Roman Catholics was part of a Bourbon policy that can be traced back to Louis XIII and his minister, Cardinal Richelieu, who in the second quarter of the seventeenth century began to rely on the clergy to assist in maintaining order and obedience throughout the realm. Richelieu, the founder of the Bourbon absolute or administrative monarchy, used the Gallican Church as one of the pillars of royal power, almost as a department of state. Louis XIV took this policy further. Modern historians have not always recognized the clergy as a force for public order, but statesmen and political thinkers in the age of New France never failed to do so. As Rousseau, Necker, and other eighteenth-century thinkers reflected, the State had been relying on the established Church to teach people to obey their rulers and to be content with their lot.[12]

The police forces were astonishingly small, the army seldom called on for police duty, and yet 'between 1660 and 1788 calm reigned in French cities,' writes Jean Meyer. 'Never had they been more

[11] A. D. Île et Vilaine, 1 F 1897, no. 56, Magon papers, Magon to Auger, 31 Mar. 1758, Magon to Gallé (LR), 25 Aug. 1758, and Magon to *Cottin & Co.*, 31 Oct. 1759. Two Magon brothers entered the priesthood; Jean Magon de la Balue became a big financier in Paris; and Luc Magon de la Blinaye remained at St Malo as a merchant.

[12] Henri Grange, *Les Idées de Necker* (Paris, 1974), pp. 517-50.

tranquil.'[13] Among the reasons for this was the continuous exhortation and advice of some 30,000 clergy working under their bishops, or under the heads of their regular orders, nearly all chosen by the Crown. Their powers legal and spiritual were greater than a twentieth-century mind can easily appreciate except by making comparisons with the powers of the Communist parties of Soviet Russia and the Republic of China. Their wealth, including revenues from the tithe and from landed property amounting to perhaps 10 per cent of the realm, was much greater than clerical wealth in Protestant countries, where princes had confiscated Church property during the Reformation.[14] All this wealth and power was devoted during the Counter-Reformation of the seventeenth and early eighteenth centuries to converting men everywhere to the Roman Catholic faith. The reigning Bourbon family, and the ruling classes that served them, were soon enlisted in support of missionary work among the heathen overseas and among the Protestant heretics at home. The missionary orders–Capuchins, Jesuits, Recollets, Ursulines–were established at La Rochelle and elsewhere in the south-west of France as well as in Canada. Louis XIV supported Catholic missions the world over and declared war on the Protestant Churches in France and abroad.

Colonies of French merchants overseas were subject to the combined surveillance of clergy and officials whose common purpose endured through their many quarrels. 'The great fear of the French monarchy', writes a student of merchants in the Orient, 'was to see its nationals abroad escape from its control', and it counted on the clergy to help enforce its will. 'That association of religious power and monarchical power is a perfect reflection of the doctrine of royal absolutism in which religious unity was the guarantee of order and of political unity in the kingdom.'[15] Nowhere did French merchants feel the power of Church and State more than in Canada, where missionaries had been sent in the course of a vast official campaign sustained by the royal government as well as by the Church authorities in Paris and in Rome.

The clergy were not incidental to the French empire; they were a

[13] Jean Meyer, *Études sur les villes en Europe occidentale*, vol. i (Paris, 1983), ch. 8; T. J. A. Le Goff and D. M. G. Sutherland, 'The Revolution and the Rural Community in Eighteenth-Century Brittany', *Past and Present*, no. 62 (1974), p. 97.

[14] Georges Lefebvre, 'Répartition de la propriété et de l'exploitation foncière à la fin de l'ancien régime (1928)', *Études sur la Révolution française* (Paris, 1954), p. 206.

[15] J. P. Farganel, 'Les Comportements religieux des négociants marseillais au Levant, 1685-1739', *Annales du Midi*, vol. 95 (1983), p. 188.

vital element in it. Missionaries in New France were notoriously working with the native tribes as agents of the Crown as well as the Church. The feast of St Louis on 25 August associated Louis XIV and Louis XV with their predecessor, St Louis IX, thereby celebrating the united authority of Church and monarchy.[16] Some 40 per cent of the clergy's revenues in Canada were state subsidies, and Louis XIV and Louis XV took personal interest in the parish priests.[17] This royal support for the Canadian clergy reflected clerical power at the court of Versailles, still great in the eighteenth century even though the passions of the Counter-Reformation were waning.

Until the nineteenth century, the official missionary campaigns of the Roman Catholic clergy were much greater than any Protestant missions. As a result, the clergy in Canada held over 10 per cent of seigneurial lands in 1663 and over 25 per cent by 1763. 'All in all', writes R. H. Harris, 'the Church controlled a little more than a quarter of the conceded land, and because much of it was located close to a town, approximately a third of the population of the colony lived on this land.'[18] It is scarcely surprising that by 1760 there were 140 Canadian churches and chapels. The Swedish traveller, Pehr Kalm, was impressed by the many Church properties in town and country, especially at Québec where he remarked no less than seven churches for a population of less than 8,000, and large stone residences, the biggest and best, where religious orders lived. 'I think three hundred families could lodge in the Jesuits' building which now houses only ninety *pères*,' he recorded in August 1749.[19]

The Canadian clergy's total revenues, some 100,000 livres early in the century, of which the biggest shares went to the seminaries, the hospitals, and the Jesuits, do not convey a proper sense of their place and power in Québec society. Nor do the modest official revenues of the Bishop of Québec (much lower than those of all but the poorest French dioceses), because a missionary diocese cannot fairly be compared with a metropolitan one, and because the Bishop was in fact wealthy.[20] Continually advised and consulted by the Secretary of State

[16] A. J. B. Johnston, *Religion in Life at Louisbourg 1713–58* (Montreal and Kingston, 1984), pp. 13-15.

[17] Guy Frégault, *Études sur le dix-huitième siècle canadien* p. 106.

[18] Marcel Trudel, *Les Débuts du régime seigneurial au Canada* (Montréal, 1968), p. 52; R. H. Harris, *The Seigneurial System in Early Canada* (Madison, 1968), p. 43.

[19] J. Rousseau and G. Béthune, *Voyage de Pehr Kalm*, fols. 718 and 773.

[20] Guy Frégault, *Études*, (Montréal, 1968), p. 105; Claude Lessard, 'L'Aide financière de l'église de France à l'église naissante du Canada', *Mélanges d'Histoire du Canada*

for the Marine and Colonies, he ranked with the Governor and Intendant as an authority in the colony. He had much prestige in governing circles and influenced the entire population by continually advising his parish priests on many matters sacred and profane.[21] In short, as every student of New France may see for himself, the clergy had great power and wealth, but so they did in old France as well.

One of the reasons for the Church's power was the enormous part the clergy played in government administration. Practically all of what we now call social services were performed by the clergy; who were responsible for all hospitals, including naval and military hospitals; provisions for the numerous poor and destitute; homes for foundlings and for the aged, inspired by St Vincent de Paul in the era of Canada's birth; schools, universities, education at every level, even the courses in 'hydrography' taught to mariners in the ports. Perhaps most of all, the clergy offered every Catholic a measure of reassurance or spiritual support that enabled people to carry on in continual danger of death by disease, childbirth, war, poverty, even starvation; in short, circumstances worse than those that have driven so many twentieth-century people to the cynicism and suicidal despair expressed by the writers of our time.

In other ways, too, the clergy provided 'parental' care for French and Canadian society, a type of care repugnant to the liberal principles of England, Holland, the United States of America, and post-revolutionary France, but which offered a vocation in Bourbon France for tens of thousands of 'fathers', 'mothers', 'sisters', and 'brothers' of the cloth. What is now called *l'état civil* was in fact an *état ecclésiastique* almost entirely managed by parish priests. All babies were baptized Roman Catholic by law, even Protestant and Jewish babies, usually a few hours after birth by a priest, but sometimes hastily *ondoyé* as they died, by a nurse or relative. Each baptism was recorded in the parish registers with the names and sometimes the occupations of two godparents. Copies of the act in the registers were subsequently sent by the parish priest on request, this being the only proof of identity. We find these *extraits de baptême* with the applications for sea-captains' and pilots' licences and for venal offices of *secrétaire du Roi, trésorier de France*, and others.

français offerts au Professeur Marcel Trudel (Ottawa, 1978), pp. 162-82; *Almanach royal*, Paris, 1753, pp. 48-55.

[21] H. Tetu and C. O. Gagnon, *Mandements, lettres pastorales et circulaires des éveques de Québec* (Québec, 1887).

Sometimes identity seems to be established in the French empire by a notarized *attestation* with the corroborating signatures of respectable witnesses. Guillaume Estèbe, for instance, appeared before a Bordeaux notary on 21 September 1760 to declare that 'on leaving Québec for France he provided himself with baptismal copies (*extraits de baptême*) for his children, but was taken on the way, in October 1758, by the British, who seized all his papers, notably the said copies. He kept a little book, however, in which he recorded the birthdate of each of his children, and therefore now declares and certifies'[22] that his sons, Jean-François Estèbe and Henry-Albert Estèbe, both destined for military careers, were born on 24 June 1738 and 23 December 1739 and baptized at Notre Dame de Québec. Two well-known merchants, Joseph Perthuis and J. A. Lamalétie, signed as witnesses. As such examples show, the attestation was merely an affirmation of baptism and not a way to escape the official hand of the Church.

Death as well as birth was managed by the clergy. After the sacrament of extreme unction, a Catholic merchant might die in peace, and his death and burial would be recorded in the parish registers. This was the official record and all others, such as the notarial certificates of death, were merely copies of it. In an age when Roman Catholics wished to be buried as close as possible to the altar in the church, and most common mortals were squeezed out into the churchyard or nearby graveyard, merchants usually had sufficient wealth and social standing to find graves somewhere in the Church, a privilege guaranteed for members of the 'merchants' guild' at Montréal and elsewhere. Many bought family chapels or tombs in their parish churches. Wills provided for hundreds of masses to be said for departed souls: Jacques Agard, a typical merchant at Bordeaux, left 100 *louis* to the St Louis Hospital at Bordeaux and 200 *louis* to other religious orders with a request for 300 masses.[23] Whatever provisions were made in a will, they expressed that blend of law and religion characteristic of a monarchy with an established Church. For instance, the merchant Jean Crespin left a will at Québec on 18 November 1704 before setting sail for Bordeaux 'considering that there is nothing more certain than death nor more uncertain than the hour of its coming, especially on the voyage to France on which he is about to embark. He has every reason to fear the dangers of the sea which are only too frequent in this season when life is exposed to risk at every moment; which gives him

[22] Guy (Bx.), 21 Sept. 1760, *attestation.*
[23] ADG, Faugas (Bx.), 6 June 1746, *testament.*

cause . . . to put his affairs in order and to dispose of the little property it has pleased God to give him. . . .'[24]

The paternal authorities of Church and State also offered Catholic merchants advantages seldom extended to merchants suspected of latent heresy. The clergy were considerable customers in the transatlantic trade. Many clergy appear in the passenger lists.[25] More important, a sample of clerical orders, taken from the cargoes seized on prizes of war, shows a tendency to patronize certain Catholic merchants who appear to have had standing orders or agreements with clerical authorities.[26] These appear in Table 4. C. P. Bourgine, Étienne Ranjard, and François Gazan of La Rochelle and Jean Jung of

Table 4. Some Shipments to Clerical Customers

1. From Bordeaux on *L'Aimable Gracieuse*, 1744:
   Jean Beaujon sent cloth to Valérien Gauffen, *commissaire provincial des Récollets*; the Jesuits sent a mixed shipment to the Jesuits; Jean Jung sent paper and pepper to Mme Ste Hélène, *dépositaire des pauvres*; Guillaume Pascaud sent brandy and powder to Tonnancourt, *chanoine*.
2. From Bordeaux on *Le Fortuné*, 1747:
   Jean Jung sent cloth, groceries, prunes, etc. to Mme Ste Hélène, *supérieure*, and cloth, knitted wear, paper, etc. to Mme de l'Enfant Jésus, *dépositaire*.
3. From La Rochelle on *Le St Victor*, 1748:
   André Gazan sent almonds, raisins, olive oil, etc. to the Ursulines, and another such shipment to the Jesuits.
4. From La Rochelle on *Le Grand St Ursin*, 1756:
   Étienne Ranjard sent tiles to the Ursulines of Québec; Bourgine sent nails and dry goods to de Villars, superior of the Jesuits at Québec; *La Veuve Charly et Compagnie* sent nails, paper, cloth, etc. to Tonnancourt, *chanoine*.
5. From La Rochelle on *La Saintonge*, 1756:
   La Veuve Charly sent a mixed shipment to Tonnancourt, *chanoine*.
6. From Bordeaux on *La Providence*, 1757:
   Jean Latuilière sent olive oil to the Mother Superior of the Hotel-Dieu at Québec.
7. From Bordeaux on *La Renommée* and *Le Superbe*, 1757:
   Abraham Gradis sent oil and food to the Bishop of Québec.
8. From La Rochelle on *Les Deux Frères* and *Le Grand Gédéon*, 1758:
   Étienne Ranjard sent wine, flour, and other food to the Ursulines, and dry goods to R. P. de Ganor, *procureur* of the Jesuits.
9. From Bordeaux on *Le Berger*, 1758:
   Jean-François Dumolin sent wine and food to Chambon, director of the seminary at Montréal.

Sources

PRO, HCA 32: 96 pt. 1, 112 pt. 2, 157, 169, 182, 195, 236 pt. 1, 238 pt 2, 246.)

[24] ANQ, Chamballon (Que.), 18 Nov. 1704, *testament*.
[25] For example, for Bordeaux see ADG, 6 B *45-*52.
[26] PRO, HCA 32, see Table 4.

Bordeaux were the principal ones. Other evidence supports this conclusion. Bourgine and Ranjard were both patronized by the Jesuit de Sacy, *procureur général des missions de l'Amérique méridionale*, to whom Bourgine owed nearly 40,000 livres in 1745.[27] Unlike the West Indian Jesuits, the Canadian Jesuits seem to have done little or no trade themselves, but remained clients of certain merchants. The nuns of the Québec hospital, too, ordered a great deal of their food and other supplies from Jung and Bourgine with whom they maintained a steady custom.[28] In 1730 the Québec seminary had debts of more than 100,000 livres principally owing to Bourgine, Jean Crespin, Jean Fornel, Charles Perthuis, and other Catholic merchants.[29] Then, the Québec merchant Louis-Joseph Godefroy de Tonnancourt (1712-84) became apostolic syndic for the Recollets of Trois Rivières in 1738, and received many shipments of goods from the Widow Charly of La Rochelle, a relative of the Charly family of Montréal with all its ecclesiastical connections.[30]

Catholic merchants were permitted to buy royal offices and to benefit by such official contracts and other favours as influential friends might obtain for them. Almost as a matter of course, merchant families intermarried with families of office-holders and minor noblemen. Let us take the example of Charles Fleury Deschambault (1674-1742), the son of a judge at Québec, settled at La Rochelle as a merchant with the functions of *commissionaire des missions étrangères*, director at La Rochelle for the official Company of the Île St Jean (Prince Edward Island), and Coast Guard Major for the province of Aunis. A younger brother, Joseph Fleury de la Gorgendière (1676-1755), was the Québec agent-general for the Indies Company; an elder brother, Jacques Fleury Deschambault (1642-1715), had gone to Acadia as a missionary; a sister, Charlotte (1683-1755), married the Intendant of New France, Rigaud de Vaudreuil, and another married the naval treasurer's agent at Québec, Thomas-Jacques Tachereau. In an age in which all power and influence was to be used for the advancement of the family, an awesome accumulation of both was at the disposal of Charles Fleury's son, Louis-Charles, who was received as a sea-captain in 1729 at the age of twenty-four on condition that he

[27] A. D. Ch. Mar., Guillemot (LR), 1 July 1745, *abandon de biens*.

[28] François Rousseau, *L'Œuvre de chère en Nouvelle-France* (Québec, 1983), pp. 130-40.

[29] Noel Baillargeon, *Le Séminaire de Québec de 1685 à 1760* (Québec, 1977), pp. 270, 312.

[30] A. D. Ch. Mar., Goizon (LR), 20-3 Mar. 1759, *inv. après décès*, and DCB vol. iv, p. 304.

command only his father's vessels until he had reached the age of twenty-five and put in five years of sea-time.[31]

Charles-Polycarpe Bourgine, to take another example, was not so well placed, but nevertheless held the office of *juge garde de la monnaie* (a magistrate with authority over the mint) at La Rochelle, as did his son-in-law, Pierre Blavoust, after him. Blavoust, a considerable Canada merchant for a few years, was himself related to a Provincial War Commissioner in the Generality of La Rochelle and to a permanent town councillor and *juge consul* at La Rochelle. With these relatives and his own considerable ecclesiastical connections, Bourgine had no difficulty in borrowing 9,000 livres from the naval treasurer's agent at La Rochelle.[32]

A more remarkable example of a Catholic merchant winning social advancement in the course of Canadian trading, with all the commercial benefits to be expected, is the career of Antoine Pascaud (1665-1717). The son of a village tradesman of Saintonge, he was distantly related to the noble Pascaud de Poléon family. These well-connected relatives may have assisted or patronized him, for when he went to Canada in about 1685 he was able to form a lasting business association with the widow and sons of a rich and prominent Québec business man, Charles Le Moyne. This became a family relationship in 1730 when Pascaud's daughter married Étienne-Charles Le Moyne at Rouen. By that time, Antoine Pascaud had long since died, after moving with his family to La Rochelle in about 1709, but his widow was able to arrange this and other valuable marriages for her six children. This she was able to do partly because she, too, was well connected, her brother, François-Marie Bouat (1676-1726), being the *lieutenant général des affaires civiles et criminelles* at Montréal, whose daughter, her niece, married the *procureur du Roi et lieutenant général* at Trois Rivières in 1733. The Pascaud family prospered, like so many Catholic families, by the help of powerful relatives. It was no wonder that in 1723 and 1727 the two sons married into the prosperous Irish Catholic family of Butler, settled at La Rochelle, which had a trading partnership with the Intendant at Québec, Michel Bégon de la Picardière. In 1747, a daughter married none other than an heir of the noble Pascaud branch, Jean-Charles Pascaud de Poléon, and the family's aspirations now had no bounds. The Canadian-born sons, Antoine (1697-1758) and Joseph-Marie (1704-67), were appointed one

[31] A. D. Ch. Mar., B 5970, 19 Apr. 1729.
[32] A. D. Ch. Mar., *Rivière et Soullard* (LR), 9 Sept. 1740, fol. 64.

THE FLEURY DESCHAMBAULT FAMILY

(Roman Catholic)

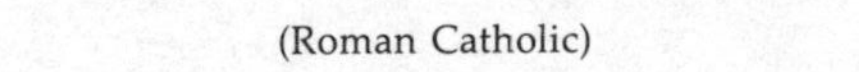

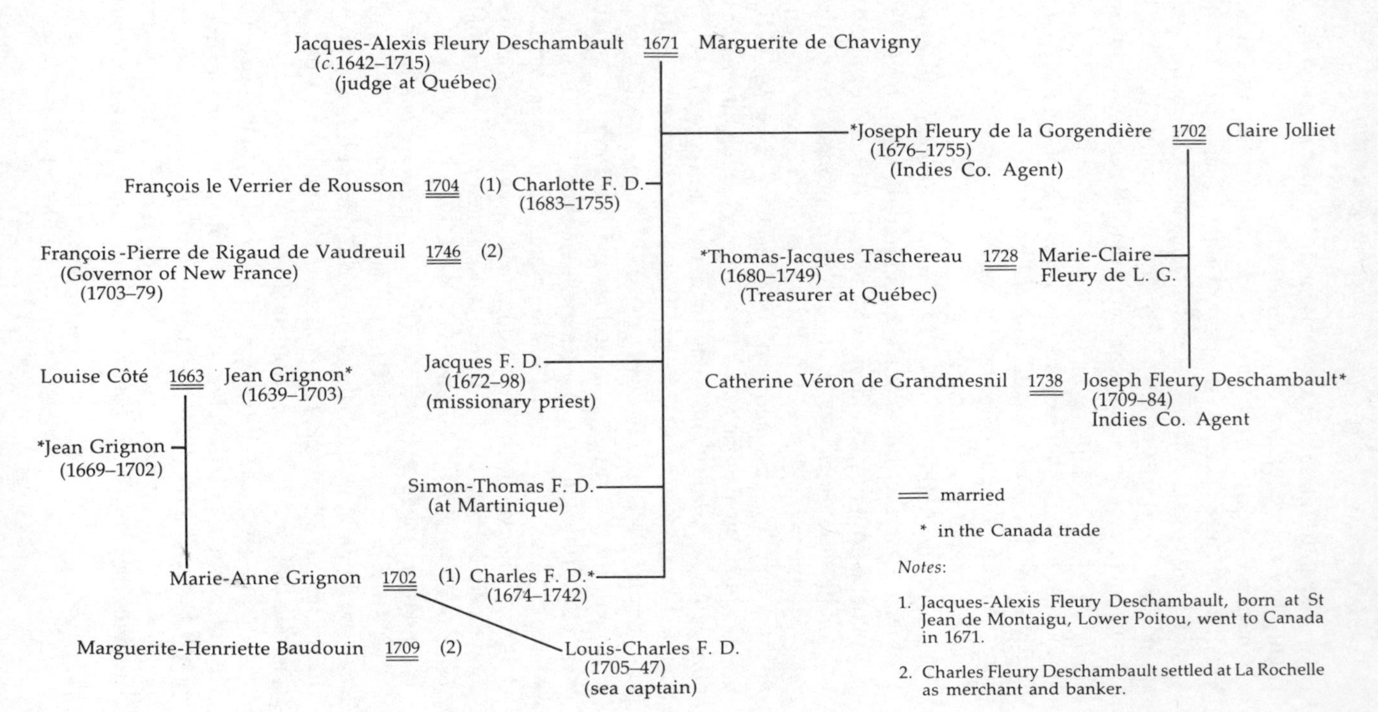

Notes:

1. Jacques-Alexis Fleury Deschambault, born at St Jean de Montaigu, Lower Poitou, went to Canada in 1671.

2. Charles Fleury Deschambault settled at La Rochelle as merchant and banker.

THE PASCAUD CLAN

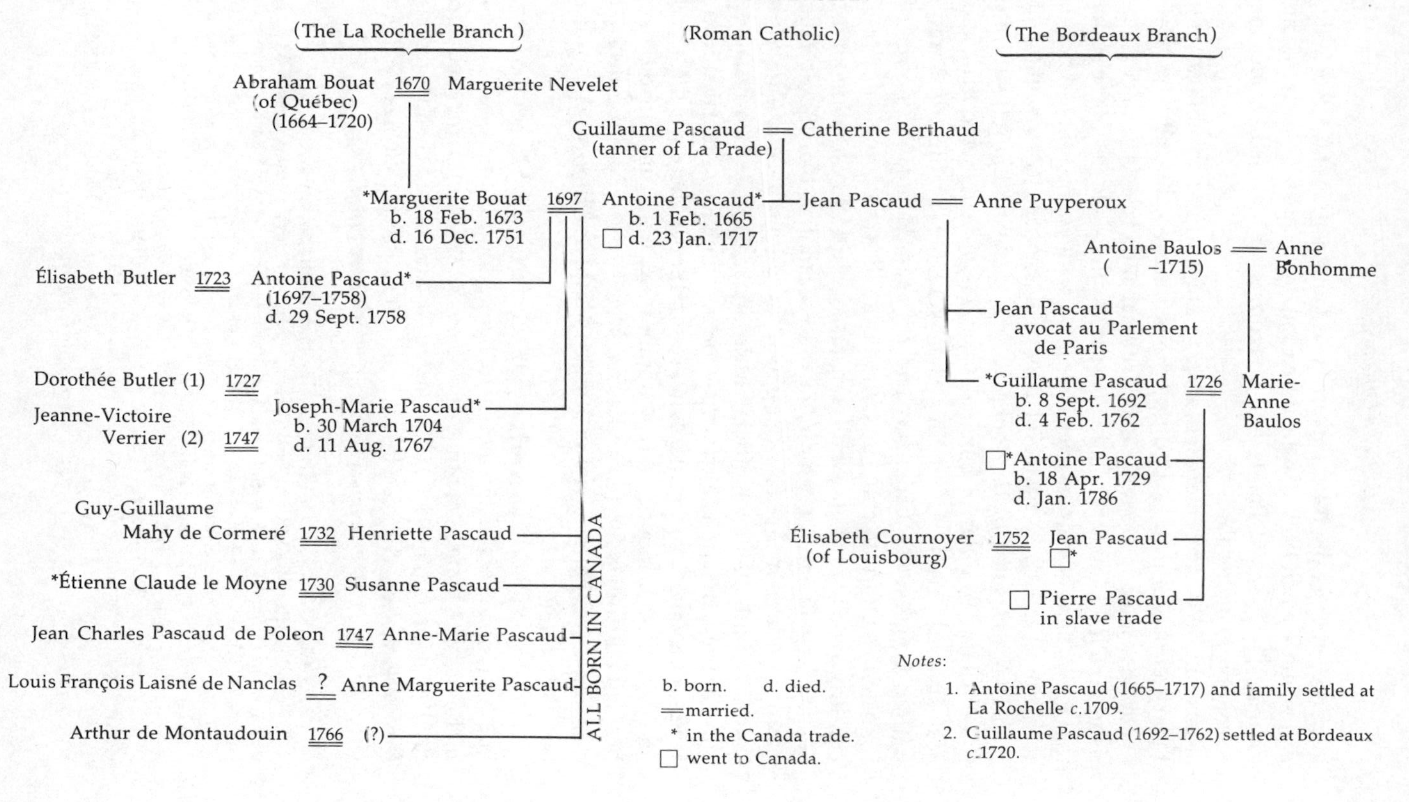

after the other as the official Deputy of Commerce for La Rochelle, and went to live in Paris. By the time Canada was lost to Great Britain in 1763, the Pascaud family had abandoned the Canada trade and moved on to higher things.

Few of the Canada merchants began life with the advantages of a Fleury Deschambault, a Bourgine, or a Pascaud, but all who were Catholic could hope to make use of official and ecclesiastical connections. And it was in their relations with the official classes of the realm that they had an advantage over their Protestant competitors. When in 1707 Pierre Charly, a native of Montréal, married the daughter of Jean-Blaise Busquet of La Rochelle, he was allying himself with the principal Catholic clan of Canada merchants with all their official and ecclesiastical relations.[33] In this clan were the families of Aramy, Gitton, Grignon, Le Gaigneur, and Viennay-Pachot, the flower of Louis XIV's efforts to cultivate Catholic families at La Rochelle. If the majority of rich merchant families there were still Protestant under the cloak of a simulated Catholicism, only Catholics like these could aspire to offices in the *Présidial* court, the Admiralty, the *Juridiction consulaire*, and other such official institutions.[34] In 1714 Charly gained another useful relation at Québec when his wife's sister married Jean-Jacques Catignon, son of the King's storekeeper there. In the 1740s and 1750s, the Widow Charly was importing furs from Canada for a big Catholic firm of fur buyers, *Le Duc, Morel, et Florée*, which consisted of Nicolas-Michel Le Duc of Rouen, Mathieu Morel of Abbeville, and Pierre-Thomas Florée of Paris.[35]

The career of Le Duc (1673-1752), whose father, Michel Le Duc, had been a successful fur merchant before him, is that of a Canada merchant who bought an office of *secrétaire du Roi* in 1741, married into the Rouen branch of the Le Moyne family, and so laid the foundation for noble careers for his children. His son, Pierre-Nicolas Le Duc (1725-66), became a magistrate in the Parlement of Paris in 1751.[36]

[33] A. D. Ch. Mar., Guillemot (LR), 24 May 1707, marriage contract.

[34] Francine Miot, 'La Révocation de l'Édit de Nantes et les Protestants jusqu'à l'Édit de tolérance (1787) en Aunis et en Saintonge', thesis of the École des Chartes, Paris, n.d. (see A. D. Ch. Mar., 4J 2995), p. 71; Claude Epaud, 'Le Commerce maritime de la Rochelle en 1720', mémoire de maitrise (Poitiers, 1975), pp. 31 ff.; *Calendrier des armateurs de la Rochelle* ... (Bibl. mun. de La Rochelle, Pér. 680), printed annually from 1748, listing office-holders; Clark, *La Rochelle and the Atlantic Economy* pp. 95-6.

[35] Marriage of Jean-Jacques Catignon and Marie-Anne Busquet, 8 Mar. 1714 (A. Godbout, *Émigration rochelaise en Nouvelle-France* (Québec, 1970), p. 42.

[36] A. D. Ch. Mar., Tardy (LR), 6 Mar. 1751, *procès-verbal*; Desbarres (LR), 8 Mar. 1747, *procès-verbal*; AN, V^2 41, 1741, Le Duc's file for *secrétaire du Roi.*

To take an example at Bordeaux, the very successful A-B. Descamps traded in the 1720s and 1730s with a relative, Jean Crespin, a merchant of Québec who held the post of colonel in the militia from 1713 and served as a councillor in the Superior Council from 1727. Descamps also traded with Pierre Trottier Désauniers and with Charles Perthuis *père* whose three sons were soon to include two councillors on the Superior Council and an attorney at the *Prévoté de l'Amirauté* court. Désauniers owed his fortune in trade partly to his relationship with the rich and influential Charest family of the immense Lauson *seigneurie*, partly to a marriage with the daughter of Martin Chéron, a councillor in the Superior Council, and partly to a government contract of 1745 to build fortifications at Québec.

The story of many other trading careers, probably of every successful Catholic merchant in the Canada trade, is similar to these. J. A. Lamalétie of Bordeaux and Québec benefited by association with his brother and brother-in-law who were naval *officiers de plûme* in the colonies, military and naval families being useful business links in the French empire.[37] One of the most successful of Canada merchants, Denis Goguet from the Île de Ré, early in his career married the daughter of Joseph Duburon, *officier des troupes de la marine*, then posted at Detroit, and at about the same time was commissioned as the official *receveur des droits de son Altesse, Monseigneur l'Amiral.*[38] Michel Rodrigue had a partnership with Michel de Gannes de Falaise (1702-52), an officer in the colonial regulars, and married one of his daughters to Charles-François Dupont Duchambon, a captain in the Foix regiment and a native of Louisbourg. Nicolas Larcher, the son of a paper merchant of Paris, built up a successful shipping business at Louisbourg in the 1750s in association with the naval commissioner there, Jacques Prévost de la Croix. Jean-Nicolas Bome, a Montréal merchant, made a second marriage with the daughter of Claude Torillon, a naval officer in Canada.[39] There were many other mutually useful marriage alliances between families of merchants and military officers.

As must now be apparent and as French statesmen complained, Roman Catholic merchants coveted royal offices and honours, regarding trade as no more than a means to the prestige and security of office.

[37] Bosher, 'A Québec Merchant's Trading Circles', pp. 179-201.

[38] ANQ, Jean de Latour (Que.), 18 Nov. 1738, marriage contract; Barolet (Que.), 23 Apr. 1743.

[39] A. D. Ch. Mar., *Rivière et Soullard* (LR), 8 Jan. and 1 June 1736, marriage contract.

Protestant and Jewish merchants did not, unless they were ready to convert, because by law they could not. In France, a successful Protestant or Jewish merchant became a rich banker in a big city with international interests, whereas a successful Catholic merchant more often became a landed seigneur with an ennobling office of *secrétaire du roi, trésorier de France*, or some other. In any event, he planted his feet on the first rung of the ladder of nobility, adopted the title of *écuyer*, and began to cast about for noble families poor enough to need alliances with a rich merchant. The Intendant at Bordeaux complained of the merchants there, 'as soon as they have a hundred thousands crowns, they quit commerce to become *secrétaires du Roi* or to give such offices to their children'.[40] As a consequence, Catholic merchant families tended to be poorer than Protestant families because those that became well-to-do moved up the social scale and began to turn their backs on trade.

The Pascaud and Goguet families of Québec and La Rochelle are good examples. Having acquired royal offices and the post of Deputy of Commerce for La Rochelle, the Pascaud brothers began to move out of the Canada trade in the 1750s. A changed attitude is already apparent in 1747 in the documents concerning their sister's marriage to a nobleman. The text of the marriage contract makes their Montréal-born sister a 'native de Paris, paroisse Saint Germain de l'Auxerois', adds the fashionable 'Louis' to their father's humbler name, and describes him as 'banquier en cette ville', as does the power of attorney carried by the bridegroom's brother, the abbé de Poléon, when he came to arrange the marriage.[41] Joseph-Marie Pascaud had married a rich merchant's daughter in 1727, but his second wife (1747) was the daughter of Étienne Verrier, *écuyer, Chevallier de l'Ordre militaire de Saint Louis*, Chief Engineer at Louisbourg. One of his daughters by the first marriage, Marguerite-Victoire, married Claude-Pierre Marion de Givry of Nevers, *écuyer, mousquetaire de la première compagnie de la garde ordinaire de Sa Majesté*, and the other, Antoinette-Auguste, married Arthur Montaudouin, *écuyer*, of the famous Nantes family. One daughter by the second marriage, Marie-Victoire, married a certain Despiaux, *écuyer avocat au Conseil du Roi et secrétaire du Roi à Paris*,

[40] Cited in Christian Huetz de Lemps, *La Géographie du Commerce de Bordeaux* (Paris, 1975), p. 99; this point has been developed at length by R. B. Grassby, 'Social Status and Commercial Enterprise under Louis XIV', *Economic History Review*, 2nd series, vol. xiii (1960), pp. 19-39.

[41] A. D. Ch. Mar., des Barres (LR), 7 Dec. 1746 and 1 Jan. 1747.

and another, Victoire-Félicité, married Joseph-Denis Goguet, later ennobled by royal letters of nobility of 11 March 1784.

Goguet was the son of the family friend, Denis Goguet, who in 1750 had bought a royal office of *trésorier de France* and was also marrying his daughters into noble families. In 1760, one Canadian-born daughter, Thérèse-Angélique Goguet, married Joseph-Louis Faure from Paris, *receveur des tailles de l'élection de Saintes*; in 1768 another, Marie-Elisabeth, married Pierre Navarre, *écuyer, Seigneur des fiefs de Saint Simon, Mareuil etc., trésorier de France* et La Rochelle; and in 1770 yet another, Jeanne-Louise, married Nicolas-Marie Gomé de la Grange from Metz, *écuyer*, governor of the town of Thouars in Poitou, all three of these marriages with dowries of 50,000 livres.[42] The Goguet and Pascaud families were ceasing to be merchants and becoming nobles, as all or nearly all Catholic merchants hoped to do.

Even such fortunate merchants as those in the Pascaud-Goguet clan were, let us remember, still only at the bottom of the imposing hierarchy of nobility. Nobody knew or knows now how many nobles lived in the France of Louis XV, but serious estimates range from 150,000 to 250,000. Among their many ranks and gradations, order of precedence was difficult to establish, then as now, but noblemen rose in a steep pyramid according to antiquity and prestige, titles and royal favour, property and wealth. The sparse and struggling nobles of Canada are no guide to the metropolitan nobles who lived closer to the royal family, the fountain of titles, favours, and employment on which they had come to depend during the previous two centuries. The King could confer nobility on commoners for various reasons, and in the eighteenth century he conferred it on merchants and others who merely bought offices and waited for a specified number of years. There were more than 4,000 ennobling offices, mostly those of magistrates in various courts of law, which the Crown had created and sold little by little over the previous three centuries. These included, according to a list drawn up by the Finance Minister in 1784, some 900 *secrétaires du Roi* and 740 *trésoriers de France* in the *Bureaux des finances.*[43] Many great families had risen through these offices.

Offices were gateways to the upper classes for the sons of families patronized by great noblemen, for employees in the French ministeries and tax farms, for the employees of naval and colonial treasurers, and for successful merchants and their sons. They were

[42] A. D. Ch. Mar., Delavergne (LR), 10 Dec. 1760 and 4 June 1770.

[43] Jacques Necker, *Des Finances de la France* (Paris, 1784), vol. iii, pp. 145-6.

also parts of the monarchy's political and administrative system. The King and his ministers counted on the loyalty and service of families that rose into the nobility or even families that hoped to do so. There was no organized 'service class' of the Prussian or Russian types, but in a less formal way many noble families had a similar relationship with the French monarchy. At the top, the thirty Councillors of State serving in the royal councils sometimes came from the same families for several generations: Phelypeaux, Colbert, Chauvelin, Estrées, Turgot, Feydeau, and others. Lower in the social scale, it was mainly from the rising families of office-holders that the Crown chose the scores of Intendants of Finance who served from the sixteenth century to the eighteenth, the hundreds of Intendants of Police, Justice, and Finance posted in the provincial capitals, and the many Intendants of the Marine posted at Rochefort, Brest, Toulon, Québec, Louisbourg, Plaisance (until 1710), and other naval bases.[44]

Very few of the rich merchants in the transatlantic trades, or even their sons, reached these upper ranks of society, but they had places in the same social and political hierarchy. Normally they entered the ranks of judicial or financial officers in provinces where their descendants might hope to rise further. Table 5 lists Canada merchants who purchased royal offices. Some of the magistrates in the *parlements* of Bordeaux and Rouen came from merchant families. At least five Bordeaux *parlementaires* in the late eighteenth century were from families that had earlier engaged in the Canada or Newfoundland trades.[45] That Catholic oligarchy of established families at St Malo, ennobled mainly in the 'explosion of Malouin capitalism' after 1689, had built its fortune on the Atlantic trades, including those of Québec and Newfoundland.[46] A few of the great Farmers General and Receivers General of Finance were from merchant families. Lower in the social scale, many a Catholic merchant at Québec and Louisbourg began his family's ascent with his own appointment as councillor in the Superior Council. Of the thirteen

[44] Françoise Mosser, *Les Intendants des Finances au XVIIIe siècle* (Geneva, 1978); Michel Antoine, *Le Conseil du Roi sous le règne de Louis XV* (Geneva, 1970), ch. 3, and *Le Gouvernement et l'Administration sous Louis XV: Dictionnaire biographique* (Paris, 1978); Jacques Aman, *Les Officiers bleus dans la marine française au XVIIIe siècle* (Geneva, 1976).

[45] These were Dubergier, Feger, Latouche-Gauthier, Minvielle, and Saige (William Doyle, *The Parlement of Bordeaux and the End of the Old Régime 1771–90*, London, 1974, pp. 316-23).

[46] André Lespagnol, 'A propos des élites urbaines dans l'ancien régime: l'exemple de Saint Malo au XVIIIe siècle', *Bulletin de la Société d'Histoire moderne* (Paris), 15e série, no. 9, 73e année (1974), pp. 2-12.

Table 5. Some Royal Offices Purchased by Men in the Canada Trade

Auger, Jean	Secr. du Roi	?
Beaujon, Nicolas	Rec. Gen. des Finances	1754
	Secr. du Roi	1766
*Bigot, François	Secr. du Roi	1754
Cabarrus, Dominique	Secr. du Roi	?
Depé, Pierre	Secr. du Roi	?
Desclaux, Pierre	Controleur en la Chancellerie près la Cour des Aides de Guienne	?
*Dupuy, Jean-Patrice	Trés. de France	1764
*Estèbe, Guillaume	Secr. du Roi	1759
Gauthier de la Touche, Pierre	Trés. de France	?
*Goguet, Denis	Trés. de France	1759
Gorsse, François	Secr. du Roi	?
Granié, Louis	Trés. de France	1754
*Jung, Jean	Garde marteau des eaux & forêts	1749
*Lamalétie, Jean-André	Secr. du Roi	1775
Lartigue, François	Officier garde laisse des grands levriers pour le loup en la grande louveterie de France	1745
Le Duc, Nicolas-Michel	Secr. du Roi	1741
Le Moyne, Étienne-Charles	Secr. du Roi	1734
*Pascaud, Antoine	Secr. du Roi	1723
*Pascaud, Joseph-Marie	Trés. de France	1758
*Rodrigue, Michel	Trés. de France	1764
*Trottier Désauniers, Pierre	Secr. du Roi	?
*Varin, Jean-Victor	Secr. du Roi	1758
*Veyssière, Pierre	Trés. de France	1748

* lived in Canada at some time.

Louisbourg councillors not appointed *ex officio*, six were merchants.[47] These are named in Table 6.

At a humbler level, the office of notary, formally closed to Protestants like all offices, assisted many a merchant family by providing capital funds as well as influence in the local business community. At La Rochelle, two merchants in the Canada trade, Pierre Veyssière originally from Limoges and S. P. Thiollière originally from St Étienne-en-Forêt, married the daughters of the prominent and related notarial partners, Rivière and Soulard, whose copious minutes record much of La Rochelle's business with Canada during the first third of the century. Veyssière and Thiollière, who had both spent years in Canada, became more and more involved in the official

[47] See Table 3; Christopher Moore, 'Merchant Trade in Louisbourg, Île Royale', MA thesis (Ottawa University, 1977), p. 120 note.

Table 6. Merchants in the Superior Councils at Québec and Louisbourg

Québec: All Roman Catholic	*Date of Appointment*
Charles Aubert de la Chesnaye (1632-1702)	1696
Jean-Antoine Bedout (1700-?–	1752
Jean Crespin (*c.* 1664-1734)	1727
François-Étienne Cugnet (1688-1751)	1730
François Daine (1695-1765)	1722
Guillaume Estèbe (1701-?)	1736
Guillaume Guillimin (1713-71)	1744
François Hazeur (1638-1708)	1703
Henry Hiché (1672-1758)	1754
Charles Macart (1656-1732)	1704
Mathieu-François Martin de Lino (1657-1731)	1719
Joseph Perthuis (1714-82)	1747
Louisbourg: All Roman Catholic	
Andre Carrerot (*c.* 1696-1749)	1735
Guillaume Delort *père*	1735
Guillaume Delort *fils*	1755
Louis Delort	1750
Nicolas Larcher (1722-88)	1755
Philippe Le Neuf de Beaubassin	1755
Pierre Martissans	1755

Catholic society of La Rochelle. One of Thiollière's sons became a priest. In 1748 Veyssière bought a royal office of *trésorier de France* as did his brother-in-law, Jean-Baptiste Thiollière, who in 1745 had married the daughter of Jacques Leclerc *père*, frequently elected *consul de la Juridiction consulaire*, a post open only to Catholics. By that marriage, Thiollière acquired another link with a notary, Grozé, whose daughter was Leclerc's second wife, and a brother-in-law, Jacques Leclerc *fils*, who was living as a merchant at Québec.[48]

Not all Roman Catholic merchants were successful in the Canada trade, quite the contrary in fact. But even humbler ones, such as Simon Lapointe of La Rochelle, who brought only 3,000 livres to a marriage to which his bride brought no more than 8,000 livres, lived in the same social hierarchy of officials, financiers, military officers, and others who formed the *cadres* of the French monarchy. Throughout the age of New France, Roman Catholic merchants and their families belonged to an official or approved society from which Protestants and Jews were excluded. Protestants and Jews could live in France,

[48] A. D. Ch. Mar., Guillemot (LR), 18 Sept. 1718.

and even in the French colonies, by conforming to Catholic practices, even pretending to be Catholic, and by good fortune and the tolerance of certain royal officials. They could not marry into official French society without in fact becoming Catholic themselves, and they could seldom obtain royal offices, appointments, contracts, or the other favours that the Crown reserved for Catholic merchants. In this sense, then, there was an official Bourbon society to which the Canada merchants belonged, but only if they were Roman Catholic.

4

Naval Officers in the Canada Trade

THE officers of the French army and navy were nearly all noblemen, though of widely different ranks, and the rest aspired to noble rank for themselves or their children. The noble ideals of the Middle Ages, still recognized in the eighteenth century, inspired a contempt for buying and selling, much as the Christian idea of chastity inspired a certain contempt for love between the sexes. As the clergy forswore sexual life, denying themselves even the pleasures and powers of the family in that age, the nobility forswore commercial life, as, for instance, when an applicant for the ennobling office of *secrétaire du Roi* submitted letters affirming that he had never kept a shop or worked as a retailer or a pedlar.[1] A shopkeeper was held to be socially inferior, somewhat like a domestic servant, and indeed French style-manuals for writing letters have expressed this inferiority even down to the twentieth century![2]

On the other hand, the occupation of the wholesale shipping merchant, *le négociant*, posed a problem for the eighteenth-century nobleman, as it had come to be so widely respected that the Crown had declared it to be compatible with nobility. This was regarded in some quarters as a dangerous permissiveness, and debate on the question of *la noblesse commerçante* rang through the century.[3] Though the Church would not allow its clergy to marry, as Protestant Churches did, the Crown, impressed by Dutch and English maritime trade, would allow and even encourage its noble families to trade as *négociants*, a term coined late in the reign of Louis XIV to distinguish the independent, respectable wholesaler from the inferior retailer or

[1] AN (Paris), V^2 series.

[2] For example Louis Chaffurin, *Le Parfait Secrétaire: Correspondance, usuelle, commerciale et d'affaire* (Paris, Larousse, 1954), pp. 14-15: 'A un fournisseur, on dira, *Recevez, Monsieur, mes meilleures salutations . . .*'.

[3] R. B. Grassby, 'Social Status and Commercial Enterprise under Louis XIV', *Economic History Review*, vol. xiii (1960), pp. 19-39; G. Richard, 'Un essai d'adaptation sociale à une nouvelle structure économique: la noblesse de France et les sociétés par actions à la fin du XVIIIe siècle', *RHES* vol. xl (1962), pp. 484-513; Abbé Coyer, *La Noblesse commerçante* (Paris and London, 1756).

purveyor. Dealing in ships, cargoes, and bills of exchange with distant fellow-*négociants* was not like exchanging goods for coins over the counter or supplying clothing, crockery, and food to a noble household. Noblemen, especially poor ones, were tempted to trade, and in Canada they usually did.

By giving its blessing to wholesale trade the Crown had undermined the noble sense of honour that might have discouraged trading in military and naval circles. The ethics of *dérogeance*, the loss of noble rank through ignoble behaviour, were waning in the eighteenth century. Opportunities to trade were many in a colony, even a relatively poor colony such as Canada. The stable class of noble magistrates, *la noblesse de robe*, were less tempted by trade than by the business of government financing because they were not posted at coastal and colonial ports or western fur-trading posts; nor were they asked to direct supplies of hardware, clothing, food, and munitions to imperial outposts.

Then, an officer's expenses in moving from one posting to another in the French empire were not regularly or systematically met, because of deficiencies in the financial system and the ancient idea that a gentleman was to be rewarded but not paid and should be ready to meet his own expenses in the King's service. Only the common soldier (*soldat*) was to be paid (*soldé*). 'The governor of Montréal', observed the traveller, Kalm, in 1749, 'has had no lodgings from the King and nothing is rented for him; he must procure and rent lodgings for himself. The King has no house which belongs to him here, except the prison.'[4] Salaries were so inadequate in general that the temptation to trade was strong. Few would disagree with Bigot's estimate of the situation: 'The King paid the people he employed in his service in the colonies so much below what their labour, their services and their station required that it would have been impossible for him not to give them tacit permission to trade, even to trade with him, provided they did it in an upright manner without abusing their authority.'[5]

i. Officiers de Plûme

Officers went into trade according to their opportunities, and those closest to transatlantic trade were the *officiers de plûme* at Atlantic ports like Rochefort and Québec; that is, the Intendants, commissaries,

[4] Jacques Rousseau and Guy Béthune, ed., *Voyage de Pehr Kalm au Canada en 1749* (Montréal, 1977), p. 521, fol. 904.

[5] *Mémoire pour Messire François Bigot, seconde partie* (Paris, 1763), p. 17.

scriveners, and storekeepers. These had been distinguished from the *officiers d'épée* or fighting officers in the seventeenth century, and a serious rivalry had grown up between the two branches of the service, evident in the frequent quarrels of governors and Intendants at Québec.

In the eighteenth century, the six governors in office between 1703 and 1760 were all career naval *officiers d'épée* except the first and the last, the Rigaud de Vaudreuil, father and son, who were *officiers d'épée* in the colonial regulars, the *troupes franches de la marine.* Of the four Intendants between 1710 and 1760, all, except Dupuy who stayed only three years, were career *officiers de plûme*, and it is a gross error to describe them as 'civil authorities', an English term that cannot be accurately applied to any authorities in the absolute monarchy of France. Bégon (1710-26), Hocquart (1729-48), and Bigot (1748-63) at Québec and the two Le Normant de Mésy, father and son (1719-39), and Prévost de la Croix (1749-58) at Louisbourg were all career naval officers in that part of the service responsible for administering naval bases and ports, ships and supplies, materials and personnel–doing practically everything, in fact, except fighting, planning strategy, or commanding warships, troops, and ceremonial occasions. Under the Intendant's command were the scriveners (*écrivains*) of the navy and the locally commissioned King's storekeepers (*gardes-magasin*), all with opportunities for dealing in government merchandise as well as buying and selling like ordinary merchants.

At Louisbourg, Jacques Prévost de la Croix, grandson of a successful merchant banker, son of a financier in Brittany, was appointed financial commissary on 1 January 1749. He had a suspiciously close business relationship with such merchants as Nicholas Larcher, the Rodrigue family, Michel Daccarrette, and the treasurer's agent, Jean Laborde. Furthermore, Prévost's wife was a daughter of the Carrerot family of naval storekeepers at Plaisance and Louisbourg, and so also related to the Delort family of merchants at those ports.[6] In 1747, when Prévost was still serving as a scrivener at Québec, he was sent a shipment of goods by a financier, Joubert, the Director of the *aides* taxes at Rochefort.[7] In 1758, Prévost was specified as business agent at Louisbourg for one of Gradis' ships, *Le Mercure* of Bordeaux, whose

[6] T. A. Crowley, 'Prévost de la Croix, Jacques', *DCB*, vol. iv, pp. 643-6.
[7] PRO, HCA 32: 149 pt. 1747, *Le Rubis.*

captain was instructed by Abraham Gradis to deliver the cargo to Prévost and to ask him to arrange a cargo for St Domingue.[8]

Michel Bégon, appointed Intendant at Québec in 1710 and, in addition, *commissaire général de la Nouvelle France* in 1716, had a business partnership for many years with Jean Butler, a merchant of La Rochelle with whom he traded on such a scale that other merchants complained, and the Minister in France ultimately recalled him to face legal charges.[9] His successor, Claude-Thomas Dupuy, who was not a naval officer, was soon recalled because, he wrote, 'I could not work in Canada to the satisfaction of a dozen persons who rob the Crown there and exhaust (*épuisent*) the colony with greater assurance and impunity than is done in any other place in the world.' United by ties of kinship and a friendship based on trade, he continued, these men formed a complete system from distant trading posts, where they placed their friends, to the King's vessels.[10]

It is customary to regard Dupuy's complaints as suspect because he was himself under a cloud of ministerial disapproval, being in financial difficulties and at loggerheads with the Governor, but he was only responding to the corruption of the Canadian administration as might be expected of a commissioned *maître des requêtes* from the mainstream of the Intendants of Police, Justice, and Finance not used to the ways of the naval and colonial service. Even Gilles Hocquart, Dupuy's successor, lamented the corruption rampant in the colony. 'In my time,' wrote the merchant, Havy, recalling his years at Québec from 1730 to 1755, 'Monsieur Hocquart, then our Intendant, often used to say, Poor King, how thou art robbed!'[11] If Hocquart himself was in business, he was discreet about it except for his investments in the Forges Saint-Maurice, but it is hard to believe that he was not somehow involved in the extensive trade of his subordinates.

The scrivener, Jean-Victor Varin de la Marre, for example, corrupt, rich, and ultimately disgraced, was sent to Canada with Hocquart in 1729–on the same ship, in fact–and became financial commissary at Montréal in 1747 on Hocquart's recommendation. 'I know that of the twenty-eight years he stayed in Canada he served eighteen years under

[8] PRO, HCA 32: 219; *Le Mercure de Bordeaux*, 150 tx., bound for Louisbourg and seized on 17 Mar. 1758.

[9] Adam Shortt, ed., *Documents* vol. i, pp. 231-3.

[10] Jean-Claude Dubé, *Claude-Thomas Dupuy, Intendant de la Nouvelle-France, 1678–1738* (Montréal, 1969), p. 290, quoting letters of May, Sept., and Oct. 1728.

[11] 11 AN, 62 AQ 31, Havy to Dugard,22 Dec. 1758.

your orders,' the Minister remarked to Hocquart when asking for his opinion in 1758.[12] Varin was arrested three years later and convicted of fraud and corruption during Bigot's term of office as Intendant, but he and his partners in crime, the storekeepers Estèbe and Martel de Saint-Antoine, and the merchants Lamalétie and Pascaud, had all been in the Canada trade during Hocquart's term of office. During an interrogation in the Bastille in 1761, Martel declared that his fortune of over half a million livres had come from twenty-eight years of trading and from his wife's dowry, but as his marriage contract does not mention even the 92,000 livres he was talking of, we may attribute his wealth to business.[13] By then, Martel had settled at Bordeaux with an office of *conseiller audiencier en la Chancellerie du Parlement* that he had bought in 1760 for 63,000 livres, a furnished house he had bought through a front man, his trading partner, Jean-Patrice Dupuy, for 100,000 livres, and investments like the 100,000 livres he asked Dupuy in 1760 to put into that part of the royal taxing services called the *régie des droits réunis.*[14]

Another naval storekeeper whom Hocquart patronized and promoted was Guillaume Estèbe who, like Varin and Hocquart himself, had come to Canada in 1729. Estèbe, too, made a fortune in trade and settled at Bordeaux as the founder of a noble family. In 1740, Hocquart recommended him for the post of storekeeper and wrote to the Minister, Maurepas, shortly afterwards: 'The Sieur Estèbe for whom you procured the post of storekeeper is a good acquisition for the service. I gave him the commission (*brevet*) for it, explaining on your behalf that it was on condition that he have no trade; he straightway got rid of whatever merchandise he had and promised me to conform exactly to your intentions.'[15]

[12] Arch. de la Marine at Brest, 1 E 148, Moras to Hocquart, 5 Apr. 1758.

[13] Bibl. de l'Arsenal (Paris), Bastille ms. 12, 142, fol. 352; Guy Frégault, *François Bigot, Administrateur français* (Montréal, 1948), vol. ii, pp. 88 ff. The Martels are difficult to distinguish one from another. Three were arrested in the *affaire du Canada*: Jean-Baptiste-Grégoire Martel de St Antoine (1710-67), his brother, Pierre-Michel Martel (1719-89), and a third who was 'formerly King's storekeeper at Fort Machault'. (See the printed *Jugement*... of 10 Dec. 1763.) Also in the family enterprise were two brothers, one a merchant at St Domingue who died early in 1760, and another who was a Jesuit priest in France (AN, Colonies B 112, Minister to R. P. Martel (Jesuit), 1 Mar. 1760). One of these may have been the Joseph-Nicholas Martel, a brother to whom J. B. G. Martel sold his Canadian fiefs of Saint Antoine and Kaskariset for 15,000 livres in 1764 (AN, MC, Étude XXX, 14 Mar. 1764.

[14] AN, MC, Étude XXX, 9 Feb. 1760, *société*; ADG, Guy (Bx.), 16 Feb. 1759, 7 June 1760, 11 Apr. 1768.

[15] AN Colonies Cÿ A 120, fol. 274, 3 Oct. 1741.

There is plenty of evidence, however, that Estèbe went on trading across the Atlantic openly and on a grand scale as a shipowner, merchant, and commission-agent in partnership with various French and Canadian business men. In December 1742, he and the former storekeeper, Foucault, became part-owners of *Le Saint Charles*. 140 tx., which their partner, Jean Jung, bought at Bordeaux for 6,600 livres and renamed *L'Intrigant de Québec* before sending her to Canada with a cargo in April 1743.[16] Jung and others sent Estèbe many consignments of goods on various ships during the 1740s. In 1746, Amand Nadau, a Bordeaux merchant, sent his ship, *La Légère*, to Québec with specific orders to his captain to deal only with Estèbe, and in 1748 *Doumerc & Rozier* of Bordeaux gave similar orders to the captains of *Le Saint François* and *Le Saint Victor*; and all these ships carried consignments of goods to him from other merchants.[17] Some biographers, such as Francine Barry writing in the *Dictionary of Canadian Biography* (vol. iii, p. 264), have concluded that Estèbe 'amassed most of his fortune in his last ten years in New France, during Bigot's term as intendant', but this dubious conclusion must have been based on a study of the *affaire du Canada*, which scarcely touched upon Hocquart's term as intendant. It is all too easy to forget that Estèbe was Hocquart's protégé first and Bigot's only later.

Estèbe took the storekeeper's post in 1740 from one of his friends and business partners, François Foucault, whom Bégon had appointed in 1715 and whom Hocquart, like Bégon, patronized 'as one of the most trustworthy and capable officials in New France'.[18] It was Hocquart who recommended Foucault for appointment to the Superior Council in 1733, for promotion to *écrivain principal* in the marine services in 1737, as manager of the royal shipbuilding industry in 1740, and as temporary Controller of the Marine to replace Varin in 1740 and 1747. Yet Foucault, like his friend Estèbe, was a busy merchant during his decade as King's storekeeper under Hocquart, and was deeply involved with the young Bordeaux merchant J. A. Lamalétie, who married his daughter in 1747. Others, too, who were

[16] ADG, 6 B 1305, *déclaration* of 1 Apr. 1743; 6 B 97, fol. 182; Lagénie (Bx.), 16 Mar. 1743; they each owned a one-third share. See also J. F. Bosher, 'A Québec Merchant's Trading Circles in France and Canada: Jean-André Lamalétie before 1763', *Histoire sociale*, vol. ix (1977), pp. 24-44.

[17] PRO, HCA 32: 127 pt. 1, 111 pt. 1, and 157; J. F. Bosher, 'Une Famille de Fleurance dans le commerce du Canada à Bordeaux: les Jung', *Annales du Midi*, vol. 95 (1983), pp. 40, 176.

[18] D. J. Horton, 'Hocquart, Gilles', DCB, vol. iii, p. 225.

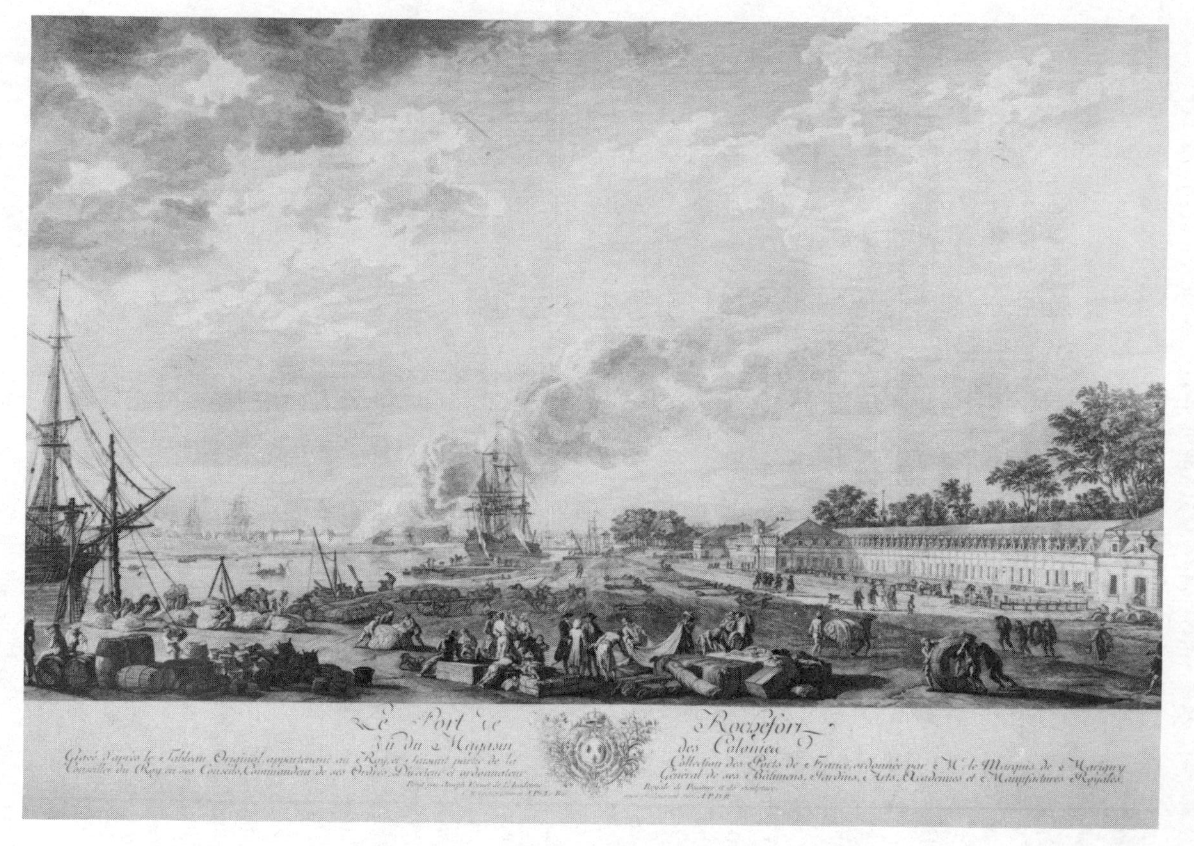

The Port of Rochefort seen from the colonial warehouse. *Engraving from a painting by Joseph Vernet*.

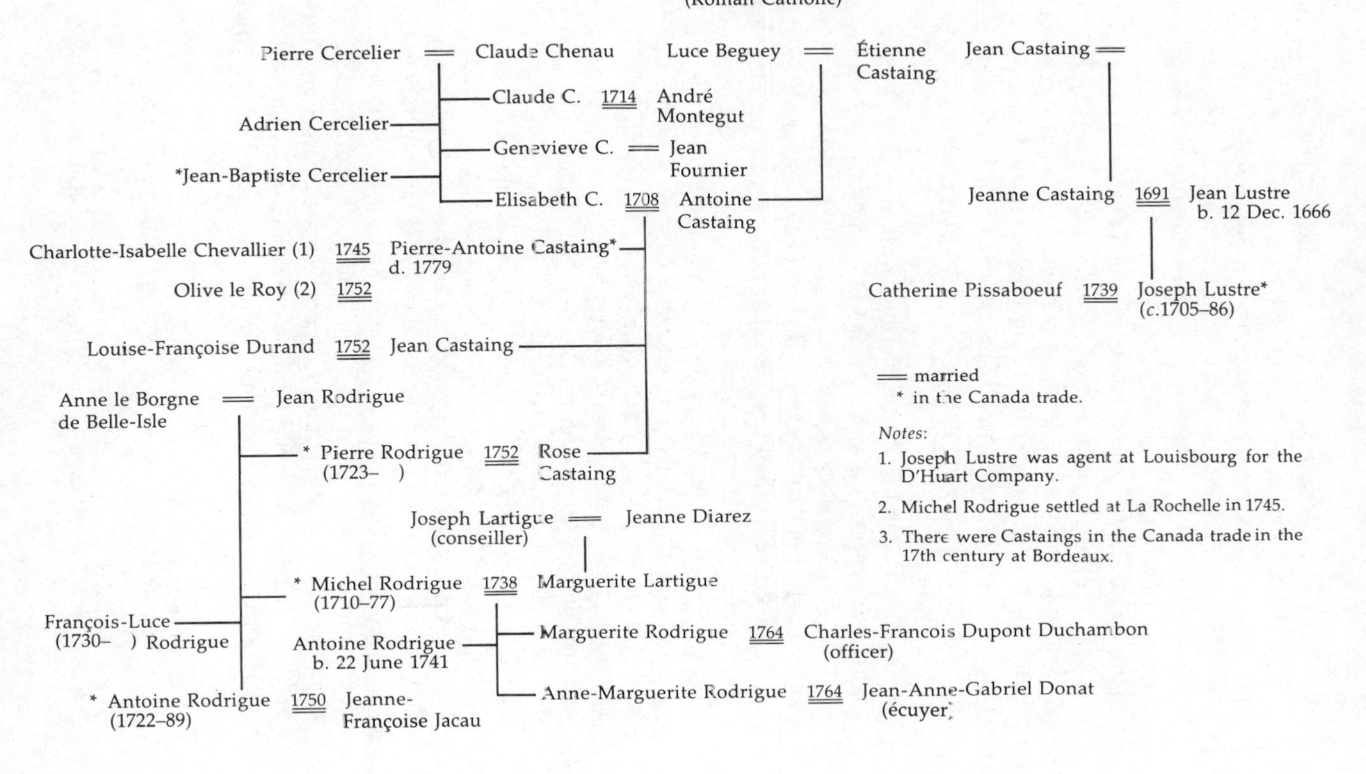
THE CASTAING—CERCELIER—LUSTRE—RODRIGUE CLAN
of Bordeaux and Louisbourg
(Roman Catholic)
Pierre Cercelier
Claude Chenau
Luce Beguey
Étienne Castaing
Jean Castaing
Claude C.
1714
André Montegut
Adrien Cercelier
Genevieve C.
Jean Fournier
*Jean-Baptiste Cercelier
Elisabeth C.
1708
Antoine Castaing
Jeanne Castaing
1691
Jean Lustre
b. 12 Dec. 1666
Charlotte-Isabelle Chevallier (1)
1745
Pierre-Antoine Castaing*
d. 1779
Olive le Roy (2)
1752
Catherine Pissaboeuf
1739
Joseph Lustre*
(c.1705–86)
Louise-Françoise Durand
1752
Jean Castaing
married
* in the Canada trade.
Anne le Borgne de Belle-Isle
Jean Rodrigue
Notes:
1. Joseph Lustre was agent at Louisbourg for the D'Huart Company.
2. Michel Rodrigue settled at La Rochelle in 1745.
3. There were Castaings in the Canada trade in the 17th century at Bordeaux.
* Pierre Rodrigue
(1723–)
1752
Rose Castaing
Joseph Lartigue
(conseiller)
Jeanne Diarez
* Michel Rodrigue
(1710–77)
1738
Marguerite Lartigue
François-Luce
(1730–) Rodrigue
Antoine Rodrigue
b. 22 June 1741
Marguerite Rodrigue
1764
Charles-Francois Dupont Duchambon
(officer)
* Antoine Rodrigue
(1722–89)
1750
Jeanne-Françoise Jacau
Anne-Marguerite Rodrigue
1764
Jean-Anne-Gabriel Donat
(écuyer)

convicted in the *affaire du Canada* had their start under Hocquart, notably Joseph Cadet, the infamous Purveyor General to the French forces in Canada from 1 January 1757, whom Hocquart engaged in 1745 to provide the meat required by the Crown.

Was Hocquart honest enough to keep aloof from the commercial life of his subordinates but too weak to stop it? Or cynical enough to be indifferent to it? Or stupid enough to be ignorant of it? Or cunning enough to profit by it in secret? Whatever the answer, there is no denying that *officiers de plûme*, storekeepers, and their subordinates traded during his term as Intendant just as they did during Bégon's, Dupuy's, and Bigot's terms. This was normal, it appears, and no different at other French ports on the Atlantic, especially among naval storekeepers.

The naval storekeeper at Bordeaux during most of the early eighteenth century, Adrien de Cercelier, who also served for many years as the *directeur des vivres de la marine* there, belonged to a large family of merchants that extended even to Louisbourg.[19] His father, Pierre de Cercelier, had been naval storekeeper before him, and his sister Geneviève married a naval scrivener. But one of his nephews, Pierre-Antoine Castaing, emigrated to Louisbourg about 1740, married into the Louisbourg merchant family of Chevallier, and traded there until the British invasions of 1745 and 1758. In 1752, Castaing's sister married Pierre Rodrigue, a merchant and sea-captain of Louisbourg, whose older brother was established as a merchant at La Rochelle with his wife, Marguerite Lartigue, sister of the Louisbourg naval storekeeper, Pierre-Jérome Lartigue. Also in 1752 Castaing's brother and partner, Jean Castaing, married Louise-Françoise Durand, and Castaing's cousin, Joseph Lustre, came from Bordeaux as local manager for the Baron d'Huart's fishing company.

Castaing and his relatives at Louisbourg seem remote from his uncle Adrien de Cercelier, the King's storekeeper at Bordeaux, until we learn that another uncle, Jean-Baptiste Cercelier, Adrien's brother, was a Bordeaux shipping merchant in the Louisbourg trade.[20] A network of family relations linked the naval storekeepers at

[19] This paragraph is based on many minutes in the notarial *études* at the ADG, especially in the *études* of Lagenie (Bx.), Lavau (Bx.), Guy (Bx.), and Roberdeau (Bx.).

[20] ADG, Lavau (Bx.), 25 Apr. 1749, 9 Feb. 1750, 4 Apr. 1750, 3 Feb. 1751, 10 May 1751, 7 Feb. 1752, being records of bottomry loans Cercelier made for *L'Aimable Marguerite* (1749 and 1750), *Le Saint Vincent* (1750), and *L'Amitié* (1751 and 1752), all at Bordeaux at 20% interest from Christophe Caila.

Bordeaux and Louisbourg with merchants in the Bordeaux-Louisbourg trade. We do not have precise knowledge of any business relations between the merchants and the naval storekeepers of the family, but they would have been unusual in that age if they had not done much business together.

The business networks of the later naval storekeepers at Québec and Montréal were, we may suspect, no more extensive than those of their predecessors, but they are better known, thanks to the official inquiries and trials of 1761-3 known as the *affaire du Canada*. The Québec storekeeper from 1755, Pierre Claverie, was a first cousin of a Montréal merchant who served there as naval storekeeper from 1 January 1757 to 8 September 1760, Jean-Pierre Labarthe, and also a nephew of the Receiver General of Finance for La Rochelle, Gratien Drouilhet. From 1 July 1755 Claverie and Drouilhet were trading in a joint-stock company with the adjutant at Québec, Michel-Jean-Hugues Péan, and a Montréal merchant, Louis Pennisseault, a company that dissolved when Drouilhet died in June 1756 and Claverie the following August. On 30 October 1759, La Barthe and Pennisseault formed another company with the latter's relatives at Montréal, Jacques-Joseph and Jean-Baptiste Lemoine Despins.[21]

Meanwhile, Claverie's successor, François-Joseph de Vienne, had long been a scrivener in the office of the marine at Québec, and he won the post of storekeeper in 1756 through the influence of his cousin, the famous Admiral Bougainville who was powerful enough to protect him from arrest during the *affaire du Canada*. We therefore have no official report of Vienne's trading, but he is known to have worked the seal fisheries of the Baie de Phélippeaux (Brador Bay) and to have owned more property than he was likely to be able to afford as a naval writer and storekeeper. In 1757, Abraham Gradis dispatched a load of wine, brandy, and various foodstuffs to him on *Le Superbe* of Bordeaux, and probably other shipments, too.[22]

The story of the ramifying business system built up by the last Intendant at Québec, François Bigot, has been recounted often

[21] Labarthe was a good friend of Estèbe who, in 1765, commissioned him 'to recover from the secretariat (*greffe*) of the commission established for Canadian affairs, all the monetary notes, bills of exchange, notes and all other papers concerning the Sieur Estèbe' (AD, MC, Étude XIII, 19 Jan. 1765, *procuration*). Estèbe had just been acquitted of charges against him in the *affaire du Canada* and was established at Bordeaux; Labarthe was established as a *négociant de Paris*.

[22] PRO, HCA 32: 246, bill of lading (*connaissement*).

enough not to need repeating here.[23] What does need repeating, however, is that Bigot's opportunities were greater than those of his predecessors, and that his depredations were exposed in the trials of the *affaire du Canada* because the government needed a scapegoat for its own military and financial failures. He had merely done what his predecessors in Canada had also done, but on a greater scale, and in the circumstances of the Seven Years War the results were disastrous for him. He wrote of himself in 1763:

> When le Sieur Bigot went to Louisbourg in 1739 as *commissaire-ordonnateur*, he found that the Controller of the Marine, the King's storekeeper, and all the other officers had ships at sea, all openly under their own names, and had priority to sell their goods to the Crown. In 1748, he found in Canada that the King's storekeeper at Trois Rivières was charged with supplying victuals to the service, and that establishment had existed in his family from father to son for eighty years. The storekeeper at Montréal had the supply duty in his jurisdiction (*gouvernement*) and kept it for a great many years. The one at Québec was also in trade, and he received many vessels on commission. The Crown was supplied in these vessels and even in the store of that individual. The principal scrivener acting as Controller of the Marine had been supplying flour for the service for several years . . . even when he had been King's storekeeper at Québec. All the *officiers de plûme* without exception were in business, either in the interior of the colony or overseas. The Minister was informed of this, and he could not have failed to be. Not only did common knowledge (*la notoriété*) tell him of it, but in 1740 he had sent a commissioner to Canada and expressly instructed him to gain a detailed knowledge of all this trade, and he did not disapprove of it, because he did not prevent it.[24]

In this matter, on which Bigot was certainly both well-informed and truthful, no clearer indictment could be desired.

ii. Officiers d'Épée

The fighting officiers of the navy and the colonial regular troops (*troupes franches de la marine*) were accustomed to profiting, like all officers everywhere in that age, from naval prizes and other wartime booty, but some of them were able to trade as well. The ships, forts, and companies of men under their command afforded opportunities to those with the right connections. Warships commonly took

[23] Guy Frégault, *François Bigot, Administrateur français*; J. F. Bosher and J. C. Dubé, 'Bigot, François', *DCB*, vol. iv; and J. F. Bosher, 'The French Government's Motives in the *affaire du Canada*', *English Historical Review*, vol. xcvi (1981), pp. 59-78.

[24] *Mémoire pour Messire François Bigot . . . Accusé*, seconde partie (Paris, 1763), pp. 9-12.

cargoes across the Atlantic. *Le Belliqueux*, for instance, a 1,000 tx. man-of-war, was carrying 200 bales of Canadian furs when captured in 1758, and *Le Chariot Royal*, a *flûte du Roi*, had a mixed cargo of goods, private and official, when taken in 1756 *en route* from Rochefort to Louisbourg.[25] The latter's captain, a Louisbourg man named Jean-François Large, had loaded a quantity of goods for himself and a business partner, a certain merchant of Rochefort, Lamontagne, whom he had met during his twelve-year residence there. This example seems typical, and we must be content with examples because there seems no hope of quantifying this type of trade. In any event, it would be a surprise to discover that a naval captain in that age did not use his authority to trade on his own account.

The trade of army officers in the colonial regulars is somewhat better known. Their best opportunities lay in the fur and supply trades at Canadian forts, especially the western outposts where a number of well-known military families had established monopolies by the eighteenth century. More than a dozen names recur in the records: Beaujeu, Céloran, Demuis, de Gannes de Falaise, La Corne, Laperrière, Marin *père et fils*, Mercier, Péan, Ramezay, de Repentigny, and Villiers.[26] The commanders of some forts farmed the trade out to merchants, such as Charly Saint Ange of Montréal who took over the Chagouamigan trade in 1749 for a lease price of 4,300 livres.[27] But certain military names recur in the records of transatlantic trade. The family of de Gannes, chevalier de Falaise, for instance, was trading on a considerable scale during the 1740s, as we discover from a flurry of legal papers that followed the death of François de Gannes, chevalier de Falaise (1677-1747), at Grenada.[28]

The family had evidently built up credit with a Bordeaux merchant whose family had long done business in Canada, Raymond Aquart, to whom they had been sending their cargoes of colonial goods, and on whom François de Gannes had been in the habit of drawing bills of exchange. For example, on 29 September 1747, he had drawn a bill at Québec for 2,000 livres to order of a merchant of Québec, Jean-Étienne Jayat, who on 31 October had endorsed it to Amand Nadau of

[25] PRO, HCA 32; 170 and 178 pt. 1.

[26] Marie-Noelle Baudouin, 'Les Postes de l'ouest à la Nouvelle-France', thesis of the École des Chartes, Paris (?1970), 271 pp.; Nish, *Les Bourgeois-gentilshommes de la Nouvelle-France*, chs. 5 and 9; *Le Rapport de l'Archiviste de la Province de Québec* (1927-8), p. 334.

[27] Baudouin, op. cit., pp. 105-52.

[28] ADG, Parran (Bx.), 23 and 29 Dec. 1747; 8 Jan., 10 Feb., and 9 Mar. 1748; Lagénie (Bx.), 19 Jan. 1748; and A. D. Ch. Mar., Desbarres (LR), 11 July 1748.

Bordeaux, who in turn had presented it to Aquart for payment on 29 December 1747–but Aquart would pay nothing until the late de Ganne's inheritance had been cleared up. Among the other merchants holding such suspended bills of exchange were such Canada merchants as Nicolas Beaujon and Gabriel Grateloup of Bordeaux, but a brother of the deceased, Charles de Gannes, chevalier de Falaise, Lieutenant of the Colonial Regulars in the Québec garrison, was at La Rochelle in time to lay claim to the inheritance for himself and another brother, abbé de Gannes. They both then sailed for Canada on Beaujon's vessel, *Le Marquis de Tourny*, early in 1748, leaving two prominent Canada merchants, Denis Goguet of La Rochelle and Jean Jung of Bordeaux, to act for them.[29]

We learn of another Québec officer's trade through the capture of six shipments sent to him in the years from 1744 to 1758. This was Eustache Lambert Dumont the younger, and the chance capture of some of his goods warrants a strong presumption that many other shipments reached him during those fifteen years, too many to be merely presents or personal orders. Besides, as Cameron Nish relates, he was a fur trader.[30] Until 1753, he dealt with Guillaume Pascaud of Bordeaux, who sent him soap, olive oil, and cloth in 1744, brandy and olive oil in 1746, and draperies in 1748.[31] Pascaud sent him enough goods to justify protecting himself with insurance for the voyage from Bordeaux to Québec, wisely as it turned out, for at least six shipments were captured during the mid-century wars.[32] Meanwhile, he had also worked for some years as 'commis du Sieur Thiollière'. In 1757 Pierre Desclaux of Bordeaux sent him wine and various other goods, and in 1758 Étienne Ranjard of La Rochelle sent him a shipment of dry goods.[33]

This is the proper context in which to view the notorious Péan, adjutant at Québec, whose wife was mistress to François Bigot, and who was convicted with Bigot and the others in the *affaire du Canada.* Much is known about Péan's trade because of the *affaire*, but he was merely a typical officer from a typical military family whom the Intendant befriended and who happened to be caught up in the post-war scandals

[29] PRO, HCA 32: 129, *Le Marquis de Tourny*, passengers listed.

[30] Nish, op. cit., p. 123.

[31] On *L'Aimable Gracieuse, La Légère*, and *Le St Victor.*

[32] ADG, Lagénie (Bx.), 1 Oct. 1744, concerning insurance bought SSP in 2 June 1744 for goods loaded on *La Gracieuse* of Bayonne, seized and taken to Bristol.

[33] On *La Minerve, La Nouvelle Constante*, and *Le Grand Gédéon.*

of 1761-3. The traces of his transatlantic trade in the British Admiralty prize papers turn out to be clues to a vast seigneurial and commercial empire founded by his father, Jacques-Hugues Péan de Livaudière (1682-1747), who commanded Fort Frontenac (1722-5), Fort Chambly (1727-9), and Detroit (1735), and acquired various Canadian fiefs. The father put one son, Michel-Jean-Hugues, into the colonial regulars, and the other, René-Pierre, into the navy; during the Seven Years War the one was adjutant at Québec and the other *commissaire de la marine* at Brest. Father and sons kept in touch meanwhile with relatives in Paris, particularly with Charles-René Péan de Mosnac, *maître ordinaire en la Chambre des Comptes de Paris*, who lived near many naval and colonial financiers in the parish of St. Eustache.[34] Péan de Mosnac was the family's business agent in Paris, and soon began to act for Bigot as well, investing money and finding suitable front men to conceal these investments. These connections, as well as the personal charms of Péan and his wife, induced Bigot to befriend the Péan family and to assist their business ventures.

Péan had a share in most of the enterprises promoted by Bigot, Varin, Bréard, and Cadet during the 1750s. He was joint owner with Bigot and Bréard of several vessels, including *Le Saint Maudet* and *L'Étoile du Nord*, of the infamous retail shop, *la friponne*, in Québec, and of a company for supplying food and munitions to western outposts. He had a large share in supplying wheat and flour to the troops, outposts, and towns, the sort of trade in which the Beaujon family had made their first fortune at Bordeaux. In this, he involved various storekeepers and merchants, such as Geraud, La Barthe (Labarthe), Claverie, and Corpron. In 1755 he joined in a transatlantic trading company with Drouilhet, Pennisseault, and Claverie, and when it collapsed the next year, he formed another trading company on 20 October 1756 with Jean Baptiste Martel and with a merchant of Bordeaux, Jean-Patrice Dupuy, who had spent some years at Québec.[35] In this company, called *Jean Dupuy fils et compagnie*, he held a 25 per cent share. At the same time, he bought a 20 per cent share of Cadet's supply-trade in which the Governor, Vaudreuil, and the Intendant, Bigot, were also shareholders. In 1759, he bought a share in

[34] But they do not seem to have had anything to do with the family of Péan de Saint Gilles, merchant grocer of Paris, *cirier ordinaire du Roy en la grande chancellerie*, with a candle-making business in Orléans (AN, MC, Étude XLI, 11 Dec. 1758).

[35] ANQ, Dulaurent (Que.), 11 June 1756, *dissolution de société*; ADG, Faugas (Bx.), 30 May 1768, *cession et dissolution de la sossiété (sic) de Péan et Dupuy.*

Le Colibry, 140 tx., from Abraham Gradis who had bought a 50 per cent share in her at Cadiz, and she reached Québec with a captured prize as well as her cargo of Spanish wines and liqueurs. These enterprises were profitable enough for Péan, like his partners, to have large sums to invest.

The variety of his investments, typical of the rich colonial trader at the time, reflects his quest for security and a gentlemanly life. At first, beginning about 1750, he bought a great deal of Canadian property in town and country, including all his brother's properties.[36] The last payment to his brother, of some 15,000 livres, was arranged by Péan de Mosnac, who had been receiving and cashing Péan's bills of exchange and other negotiable paper in Paris. Using Mosnac's services in 1756, he invested 202,500 livres in bonds (*rentes*) of the Estates of Languedoc, and then went on to invest unspecified sums in the Estates of Brittany, the loans of the clergy, the tax farms of the *gabelles* and the *aides*, certain loans of the Duc de Penthièvre, and other such *rentes.* All these investments were made for Péan in the name of a front man, Pierre-Charles Cordier, *bourgeois de Paris*, whose identity is revealed in only a few notarial acts.[37] As Péan did not live in Paris, Péan de Mosnac was empowered in 1757 to collect the returns on these investments, until January 1760 when Péan for some reason empowered a certain Nicolas-Félix Vaudive, a goldsmith's son and a *greffier de l'audience du grand conseil du Roi*, to make these collections. Meanwhile, François Bigot, whose fortune was bound up with Péan's, also used Vaudive's services, investing large sums in a similar range of loans, tax farms, and other enterprises.[38] They were both arrested and convicted of various crimes in the *affaire du Canada*, but even after paying 600,000 livres according to a court order of 1764, Péan was holding 491,167 livres in Canada bills in 1766, and he was wealthy enough to live as a seigneur at Orzain, near Blois, where the banished Bigot was allowed to visit him in 1771.[39] He had been more enterprising and colourful than most colonial army officers, but his business life had been essentially similar.

Chance discoveries in the archives offer tantalizing glimpses of officers' business lives never exposed in the *affaire.* A good example is

[36] AN, MC, Étude LVII 427, 13 Feb. 1758, *quittance*; *DCB*, vol. iv, pp. 615-16.

[37] Such as a *procuration* by the notary Charlier (Paris) dated 26 Nov. 1757 and 24 Jan. 1760 (AN, MC, Étude LVII).

[38] AN, MC, Charlier (Paris), 1 Dec. 1757; Nau (Paris), 7 July 1764, including 60 shares in the firm of *Banquet & Mallet.*

[39] AN, V7 365.

Laurent-François Le Noir de Rouvray, *écuyer*, who was wounded in Canada as an *enseigne* in the regiment of the Sarre under Bougainville's command, praised by Lévis, promoted to captain in the *Cents-Suisses de la garde du Roi*, named (like Péan) to the Order of St Louis, and sent (unlike Péan) to St Domingue for another ten years of military service.[40] In 1758 he and his brother, Jacques Le Noir, who was a Paris notary, and the naval treasurer at Montréal, D'Hauterive, ordered sixteen barrels of wine and sixteen half-barrels of brandy from the Bordeaux firm of *Lamalétie, Latuilière & Compagnie*, late of Québec, which duly sent off this shipment in spring 1759 on *Le Saint Augustin de Bilbao*.[41] The total value of this shipment, reckoned at prices current in Québec which took into account a freight rate of 250 livres per tx., was 72,450 livres, of which the brandy was worth 41,250 livres. Only a dispute, between the shipping company and its Canadian customers, which went before the court of admiralty in Paris, brings this transaction to our notice, and there must have been many others. In 1767, Le Noir de Rouvray was wealthy enough, in the suspended Canadian funds, to borrow 50,000 livres from Joseph Cadet, the former Purveyor General in Canada, on the security of ten *reconnaissances du Canada* with face values of 5,000 livres each, and a promise to repay in cash two years later if required to do so.[42]

The next year, he acquired a colonel's commission, the title of Governor of the town of Provins-en-Brie, and went to Cap Français, St Domingue, where he bought two plantations the Crown had confiscated from the Jesuits, for which he paid 800,000 livres. These plantations he worked with some assiduity, as we learn from a letter to the Minister of Marine and Colonies in 1772 wherein he proposed to hire a specialist in the current methods of inoculation against smallpox in order to protect his slaves from epidemics. 'For this purpose,' he wrote, 'I propose to bring to St Domingue a doctor well trained in this method who has had ten years of medical practice in Paris.'[43] Meanwhile, he commanded *le corps de chasseurs volontaires de St Domingue*, and was soon begging the minister for the rank of brigadier. We learn from his letters, however, that he was not asking for money and did not mind that he had not been paid during all his years in St Domingue. 'His fortune and especially his character', he wrote of

[40] AN, Colonies E 278, personal file.

[41] AN, Z[1D] 132 under date 1 June 1764; MC, Étude XIII, 21 Apr. 1763 and 11 Feb. 1765.

[42] AN, MC, Étude XIV 401, 25 Nov. 1767, *obligation.*

[43] AN, Colonies E 278; MC, Trutal (Paris), 18 Mar. 1768, *vente.*

himself, 'make him indifferent to all pecuniary favours, but he is much disgusted to see his juniors promoted and himself forgotten.'[44] Le Noir de Rouvray was only one of the many colonial officers who succeeded in business and escaped official censure.

Many other case histories could be added in developing the theme of naval and military officiers in the Canada trade; many have, indeed, already been told of officers at Louisbourg.[45] Clues to others in New France may be seen in the marriage alliances of officers' families with merchants' families: Fleury La Gorgendière, commander of the Temiscamingue post in 1725, was related to a merchant of La Rochelle, Fleury Deschambault; Pierre-Joseph de Céloron, Sieur de Blainville, commander at Michilimackinac (1737), Detroit (1941 and 1750), and Niagara (1744), married a merchant's daughter at Montréal, Marie-Madeleine Blondeau, and traded in furs and supplies at all his western postings. François Josué La Corne Dubreuil, commander at Kamanistiquia (1743) and Michilimackinac (1746-7), married into the prominent merchant family of Hervieux. Joseph Feré Duburon, an officer at Québec with a house on the Place Royale, married his daughter in 1738 to a successful merchant in the Canada trade, Denis Goguet, and so had a partner at La Rochelle when Goguet settled there in 1747. Taken together, these cases show that it was normal rather than exceptional for French officers to trade in the colonies, and that many were engaged in the Canada trade.

[44] Loc. cit.

[45] T. A. Crowley, 'Government and Interests: French Colonial Administration at Louisbourg, 1713-1758', Ph.D. thesis (Duke University, 1975), 441 pp.; Allan Greer, 'Mutiny at Louisbourg, December 1744', *Histoire sociale* (Ottawa), vol. 10 (1977), pp. 330-5; Nish, *Les Bourgeois-gentilshommes*, chs. 5 and 9.

5

Financiers and the Canada Trade

MANY a merchant in the Canada trade was related to government financiers, and all lived in the shadow of the financiers, whose wealth and influence were a permanent feature of Bourbon society.[1] As the term was then used (and as it is used in this book), it referred to men whose business was to collect, spend, or otherwise manage government funds. Foremost among them were the forty Farmers General of Taxes, who managed the huge company collecting the customs duties (*douanes* or *traites*) and the excise duties on alcoholic drinks (*aides*), and the revenues from the state salt and tobacco monopolies (*gabelles* and *tabac*).[2] A second group, nearly as rich and powerful as the Farmers General, were the Receivers General of Finances (*receveurs généraux des finances*), about fifty of them, who gathered the taxes imposed on property, persons, and revenues: the *tailles*, the *capitation*, the *vingtième*, and the rising surtaxes known as the *sous pour livres.*

Some fifty Treasurers General (*trésoriers généraux*) formed a third group, and these managed the spending of government funds at the centre, each man arranging the payments to be made for one of the spending departments, Crown commissions, sovereign courts, or other agencies. Among them were the two Keepers of the Royal Treasury (*gardes du trésor royal*), the two *trésoriers des parties casuelles*, who managed the funds received and paid out in the selling of royal offices and the paying of interest on the funds invested in offices, and the two Treasurers General for the Marine, to whom were added two Treasurers General for the Colonies in 1749. Somewhat lower in the scale were the *payeurs des rentes* who paid the interest on funds lent to the Crown in the form of bonds or *rentes* on the *Hôtel de ville.* Beneath these great financiers were large but variable numbers of lesser financiers.

[1] For a general account of the financiers see J. F. Bosher, *French Finances 1770–1795: From Business to Bureaucracy* (Cambridge, 1970), chs. 4, 5.

[2] The best accounts of the Farmers General are in George T. Matthews, *The Royal General Farms in the Eighteenth Century* (NY, 1958), and Yves Durand, *Les Fermiers généraux au XVIIIe siècle* (Paris, 1971).

Tax farmers, receivers, treasurers, and payers were listed by name in the semi-official *Almanach royal* and were recognizable by their functions, but many other financiers had government contracts or venal offices that defy classification except in the vaguest terms.[3] Some were sub-farmers (*sous-fermiers*) leasing from those who had leased from the Crown. Others were purveyors (*munitionnaires*) supplying armies and navies. But who were the many *intéressés aux affaires du Roi*, as they called themselves? What can be said of the *croupiers* who bought shares in a Farmer General's place, and the vast crowd of nameless people who contributed to the cost of the big venal offices and drew interest on their investment from the financiers holding these offices?

Most financiers paid for their offices with borrowed funds. Mouffle de Géorville, for example, a Treasurer General of the Marine in charge of colonial funding, employer of the treasurers at Québec and Montréal, borrowed most of the 800,000 livres that he eventually paid for his office from his brother-in-law, Aymard-Félicien Boffin, marquis de la Saône, baron de Chaste, etc., a lieutenant-colonel in a regiment of French guards.[4] Perichon, a Treasurer General for the Colonies, bought his office in 1758 from Tavernier de Boullogne for 660,000 livres, of which he borrowed 500,000 livres from a retired merchant, Thomas de la Porte of Paris.[5] The financiers were well anchored in the French ruling classes and held much of the debt that eventually brought the monarchy to the brink of revolution.

Throughout the age of New France they were the principal business men in Paris, and extremely powerful throughout the kingdom. Although they were quite a different social element from the merchants and bankers, they offered banking services to the public. A notice in the *Almanach royal* for 1753 (p. 328) read:

> The public should be informed that anyone with money to send to a town where there are Receivers General of the Tax Farms may go in the morning from eight o'clock until noon, and from three in the afternoon until seven in the evening, to the *Hôtel des fermes*, to the office of Monsieur Maizières,

[3] The *Almanach royal*, published annually from 1699, listed all the royal servants and officials of the kingdom; the volume for 1753, for instance, lists the great corps of financiers beginning on p. 318, and others that may be found through the index. It does not, however, list the hundreds of *sous-fermiers, traitants, intéressés aux affaires du Roi*, and purveyors (*munitionnaires*) speculating in royal government business.

[4] AN, MC, Étude XIV 382, *traité de la charge de trésorier général de la marine*, 1 Feb. 1764.

[5] AN, MC, Étude XXXIX 495, 29 Mar. 1764 and Martel (Paris), 13 Jan. 1758.

Receiver General of the said Farms, who will issue Rescriptions payable at sight on the above-mentioned Receivers General of the Farms, to whomever they may designate. These Receivers General will send funds at no cost to their correspondents in the various provinces of the kingdom.

The cashiers of the sub-farm for the *aides* and the *domaines* will do the same, this notice continued, and these services are of benefit to the Farms as well as to the public.

Agents for the big Paris financiers could be found in every provincial capital. At La Rochelle, for instance, a town of scarcely 10,000 inhabitants, there was a Director of the General Farms for the customs duties, the *gabelles*, and the *tabac*, a Receiver General of the General Farms, not to be confused with the Receivers General of Finance who also had an agent at La Rochelle, an agent for the Treasurers General for Marine and Colonies, more than one financier managing funds for the Church, and others besides.

None of the main royal taxes was collected in Canada, but the Farmers General employed an agent at Québec to collect import and import duties, and succession duties, for that part of the tax farms known as the *domaine.* The Indies Company, essentially a company of financiers rather than merchants, also employed an agent in Canada to manage their monopoly of the beaver trade. The principal financier at Québec, however, was the agent (*commis*) of the Treasurers General for Marine and Colonies. He provided a banking service for the Canada merchants by drawing bills of exchange on his employers in Paris.[6] Such bills were a common medium of payment among the Canada merchants.

In view of these banking services offered by financiers, it is essential to understand that financiers were fundamentally different from bankers, and *la finance* different from *la banque.* Financiers and their agents owed their authority and standing to the French government, or in some cases to a provincial or municipal government, and had little or no standing outside the French empire. Firmly tied to the government by contracts or venal offices, they dealt primarily in government funds and were supposed to serve government purposes. Private funds and transactions were, on the contrary, managed by

[6] John Keyes, 'Un Commis des trésoriers généraux de la marine à Québec, Nicolas Lanouillier de Boisclerc', *RHAF*, vol. xxxii (1978), pp. 181-202; J. F. Bosher, 'Government and Private Interests in New France', *Canadian Public Administration* (1967), pp. 244-57; Adam Shortt, ed., *Documents relating to Canadian Currency, Exchange and Finance during the French Period*, 2 vols. (Ottawa, 1925).

bankers (*banquiers*) who were basically merchants managing other people's business, advancing money, accepting and discounting bills of exchange and other commercial paper, disposing of enough credit and business connections to obtain whatever goods and services their clients required at home and abroad. Unlike the financier, the banker enjoyed whatever authority and standing he could command in the cosmopolitan world of trade centred more and more on Amsterdam, London, and Hamburg. Holding no office or contract with the government, a French banker was not confined to the French empire, and unlike the financier, he did not have to be formally certified as a Roman Catholic.

Many successful Huguenot merchants became bankers in Paris or in one of the French ports, usually disguised as conforming Catholics, of course, but dealing extensively with their Huguenot relations and friends in foreign business centres. There were also many Catholic bankers, but so many of them gave way to the temptation to become financiers, or to enter official French society by some other route, that as a group or class the remaining Catholic bankers were weaker, poorer, and fewer. Besides, Protestant families of bankers had the advantage of being at home in the vigorous, triumphant, expanding world of Anglo-Dutch Atlantic power. During the eighteenth century, a vast network of Protestant merchants and bankers grew up in the Atlantic world, a 'Protestant international', as Herbert Lüthy calls it, particularly strong in Amsterdam, London, Geneva, Hamburg, and such English colonial ports as Boston, Philadelphia and New York.[7]

In France the official Catholic financiers and the cosmopolitan Protestant merchants and bankers were different social groups. Commerce and finance had always been different and opposed interests in the French empire, and a glance at the history of the later eighteenth century shows an inherent rivalry between them. When in 1776 Louis XVI called on Jacques Necker, a Swiss Protestant banker, to direct the finances of the realm, the financiers felt threatened, and rightly, because Necker attacked them and their interests as far as he could.[8] The financiers and their friends defended themselves, but scarcely a decade after Necker's fell in 1781, the revolutionary National Assembly began to abolish financial offices and tax farms.

[7] Herbert Lüthy, *La Banque protestante en France de la Révocation de l'Édit de Nantes à la Révolution française*, 2 vols. (Paris, 1959, 1961).

[8] Robert D. Harris, *Necker, Reform Statesman of the ancien régime* (Berkeley, 1979); Bosher, *French Finances*, ch. 8.

The French Revolution promoted merchants' interests in France by destroying the financiers along with the monarchy and the Catholic Church. The society in which the official classes of New France had had their place was swept away, leaving the business of the Atlantic world to the merchants and bankers. That event lay in the future, but it shows the difference between financiers and bankers more clearly than does the history of the age of New France.

The characteristic differences between merchants and bankers, on the one hand, and financiers on the other, are expressed in the memoirs of Jean-Joseph de Laborde, a Bayonne banker who sent ships and food to Canada during the Seven Years War and became court banker in 1759. When he took charge of military financing in 1758, he did so as a banker intruding in government financing and believing he had 'toute la Finance' against him.[9] He refused to take an office of Farmer General or Receiver General until 1760, when he felt obliged to. 'I had been brought up in Trade,' he then wrote to his son. 'I had made a fortune in it and felt an extreme repugnance for every place in Finance. Not that they are not perfectly honest, but Trade and Finance never go well together. I have always maintained a most decided attachment to Trade. I beg you, my dear son, to love it always: it is the calling of a true citizen (*l'état d'un vrai citoyen*). A merchant who works on a grand scale stimulates all the various orders of the State by letting them gather the fruit of his labour. Agriculture, manufacturing, the artisans, the workers of every sort, all feel the workings of a merchant. I have had up to ten vessels at the fisheries in America, in the East Indies, in the West Indies and in Guinea. How many people employed! How much money distributed!'[10] How many other merchants of that period must have had the same thoughts!

They were the thoughts of a successful Bayonne merchant faced with the power of the Paris financiers and obliged to join them in spite of his scruples. At the root of his reluctance was the tendency, more and more resented by the French public, for the Bourbon financial system to corrupt those who worked in it.[11] Farmers General, Receivers General, and all the rest had always been widely hated and despised, the villains of many a play and fable, the 'capitalists' the French revolutionary governments were soon to sweep away. In that

[9] Yves-René Durand, ed., 'Mémoires de Jean-Joseph de Laborde, fermier général et banquier de la cour', *Annuaire-bulletin de la Société de l'Histoire de France, années 1968–69* (Paris, 1971), p. 146.

[10] Ibid., pp. 153-4.

[11] Bosher, *French Finances*, ch. 5.

part of their work, the revolutionary governments represented not only the merchants against the financiers but also the seaports and other commercial cities against Paris.

There were, of course, financial agents in the seaports and merchants in Paris, but each was a minority in the local business world. For Paris was more concerned with government finances than with trade, and the *Bourse* founded there in 1724 was chiefly a centre for financial speculation.[12] The reverse was true in the seaports where every local *Bourse* reflected the preoccupations of traders and bankers. This difference is clear in, for instance, the field of maritime insurance, so vital in all transatlantic trade.

Marine insurance at the seaports was an affair of the merchants themselves. An insurance policy for a ship or a cargo was hawked about the town or left at the *Bourse* for merchants to underwrite specified sums at a premium specified in the policy, and most of the underwriters were merchants or bankers. Not all can be identified, of course, but I have not yet read of a policy in the ports that was underwritten by a majority of financiers or any group but merchants, even when the owner of the ship was himself a financier.

For instance, in 1750, the naval treasurer's agent at St Malo, Jean-Baptiste Violette, sieur Dubois, dispatched his ship *L'Expédition*, 90 tx., under Captain Pierre Violette, 'to the coast of Newfoundland, to the region of Cape Breton, Québec, the coast of Canada and other spots and places on the said coast wherever the captain shall see fit to find dry or salt cod'.[13] For this voyage he insured the vessel for 10,000 livres for eight months at a premium of 7 per cent, and at least eight of the eleven underwriters–perhaps all of them–were merchants of St Malo. These are listed in Table 7. In any event, all the many marine insurance companies and *chambres d'assurance* founded at Bordeaux, La Rochelle, and Rouen were merchant companies.

Two of the three companies founded in Paris during the early 1750s were quite different, and probably typical of large Paris companies in general. Their history shows a serious rift between the merchants and bankers on the one hand and the financiers, officials, and *rentiers* on the other.[14] The *Chambre d'assurance et grosse aventure*, founded on

[12] George V. Taylor, 'The Paris Bourse on the Eve of the Revolution, 1781-89', *American Historical Review*, vol. 67 (1962), pp. 951-77.

[13] A. D. Île et Vilaine (Rennes), Pitot (St Malo,)9 Apr. 1750. See Table 1.

[14] J. F. Bosher, 'The Paris Business World and the Seaports under Louis XV: Speculators in Marine Insurance, Naval Finances and Trade', *Histoire sociale* (Ottawa), vol. xii (1979), pp. 281-97.

Table 7. Insurers of L'Expedition *of St Malo, en route to Newfoundland, Cape Breton, and Canada in 1750*

	livres
Pierre-Daniel Deslandes	1 200
Pierre Drake	2 000
Nicolas Gaillard	1 200
Jacques Porée, sieur De Coudray	600
Georges Dechais *et amis*	1 000
Jacques Meslé de Grandclos	500
Le Veuve, La Fontaine, Le Bonhomme et fils	500
René Le Gentil	1 000
Jean-Baptiste Magon de la Villehuchet	800
Nicolas Magon de la Villehuchet *fils*	400
Jean Nouet	800
Total	10 000

Source

A. D. Île-et-Vilaine, Pitot (St Malo), 9 Apr. 1750.)

29 January 1750, and the *Compagnie d'assurances générales maritimes et incendiaires*, founded on 27 September 1753, each with scores of shareholders, were soon dominated by the many financiers in them; and a group of eighteen merchants and bankers, most of them Protestant, then formed their own insurance company on 7 July 1755, excluding all financiers. Many other merchants remained independent of all three companies, underwriting such insurance policies as they judged likely to be profitable, and their names appear on certain Paris policies drawn up at the request of merchants in the seaports sending ships to Canada. Even these policies show the names of financiers such as Gabriel Prévost, *trésorier général des ponts et chaussées*, who in 1757 and 1758 underwrote at least forty policies on vessels bound for Québec or Louisbourg.[15] These are listed in Table 8.

In that age French merchants were in daily contact with financiers or their agents collecting taxes, duties, and tolls, making payments for the Crown, and even investing in trade. British and Dutch merchants, on the contrary, were not in the same position because financiers were fewer and less powerful in the 'republics' of Great Britain and the Netherlands, so few indeed that they scarcely affected trade, or even appeared as a social element at all.[16] This difference between France

[15] AN, Z^{1A} 915. See Table 2.

[16] Marcel Trudel, *Histoire de la Nouvelle-France*, vol. iii, 'La Seigneurie des Cents-Associés 1627-1663', tome i (Montréal, 1979), appendix A; Léonard Blussé and Femme [*Footnote continues on p.94.*]

Table 8. Investments in Marine Insurance, 1756–1758, by Gabriel Prévost, trésorier général des Ponts et Chaussées *(and related to Prévost de la Croix, the financial commissary at Louisbourg, 1749–48)*

Date of Policy	Vessel	Policy in the name of:	% Premium	Voyage
29-12-56	§*Escarboucle*	Gradis	36	?
3-1-57	*Printemps*	*Vve Tassin & fils*	28	Que.-St D.
14-1-57	*Aventurier*	Gradis	55	?
3-2-57	*Emeraude*	Dorn *fils*	60	Mars.-Que.-St D.-Bx.
23-2-57	§*Monplaisir*	R. Dufour, Mallet	35	Bx.-Que.
22-3-57	**Gracieuse*	Pascaud	40	LR-Que.
22-3-57	**Touraine*	Chevalier Lambert	58	LR-Que.-St D.
23-3-57	*Pénélope* cargo	J. F. Batbédat	35	Bx.-Louis.
23-3-57	**Fidelle*	J. F. Batbédat	35	Bx.-Louis.
25-3-57	*Mercure volant*	*Vve Tassin & fils*	35	Roch.-Louis.
25-3-57	**Mercure*	Batbédat	35	Bx.-Louis.
25-3-57	**Mentor*	Batbédat	32	Bx.-Louis
25-3-57	**Sauvage*	Noordingh-de Witt	42	Nantes-LR-Que.
25-3-57	§*Petite Suzanne*	Bouffé-Dangirard	40	LR-Que.
16-4-57	§*Victorieux*	J. F. Batbédat	40	Bay.-Que.
16-4-57	**Adour*	J. F. Batbédat	40	Bay.-Louis.
28-4-57	§*St Martin* cargo	Batbédat	40	Bx.-Louis.
7-5-57	§*Nouvelle Constante*	Grand & Labhard	78	Bx.-Que.-St D.-Bx.
2-6-57	§*Phaeton* cargo	Bouffé-Dangirard	65	LR-Louis.-St D.
13-7-57	§*Providence*	Bellivier	50	LR-either Que. or Louis. or Mart. (premium 4% less if Louis.)

29-7-57	§*Angélique*	*Delenc & Cie*	50	LR-Louis.
20-8-57	*Mentor*	J. F. Batbédat	70	Louis.-St D.-France
5-12-57	*Mercure*	Batbédat	40	Louis.-Bx.
9-12-57	**Amitié*	Batbédat	40	Louis.-Bx.
14-12-57	§*Lalouette* cargo	Batbédat	40	Louis.-Bx.
22-12-57	§*Sauvage* cargo (furs)	Chev. Lambert	40	Que.-LR
22-12-57	*Chouagen*	Mentz	20	Que.-LR
30-1-58	§*Catiche*	*Lafreté frères Daribert & Cie*	45	Bx.-Que.
7-2-58	§*Baleine* cargo	P. F. Goossens	50	Dunkirk-Que.
9-2-58	§*St Pierre* cargo	Goossens	50	Dunkirk-Que.
9-2-58	§*Annack* cargo	Goossens	50	Dunkirk-Que.
		(Goods in the above three ships worth 146 000 livres)		
25-2-58	*Orignal*	*Vve Tassin & fils*	50	Bay.-Que.
2-3-58	*Echope*	J. F. Batbédat	50	Louis-Bx.
4-3-58	§*St Dominique*	Trousseau & Montauban	55	LR-Que.
30-3-58	§*Deux Frères*	Batbédat	55	LR-Que.
30-3-58	*Fidelle frégate*	The Crown	25	Roch.-Louis.
8-4-58	*Paille en Cul*	Abraham	50	Louis.-Martinique
19-4-58	*Valeur*	Masson de Malboue	45	Bx.-Que.
29-5-58	§*Aimable Thérèse*	de Can	55	Bx.-Que.

* known to have arrived safely.
§ known to have been seized by the enemy.

Source

AN, Z^{1A} 915.

and the Protestant sea-powers we have seen in the field of marine insurance, but it is also visible in the monopoly trading companies, dominated by merchants in Britain and the Netherlands and by financiers in France.

The *Compagnie des Indes* and the Company of New France were dominated by financiers, whereas merchants formed controlling majorities in the English and Dutch East India companies, in the Hudson's Bay Company, and all or nearly all others in England and Holland. In the field of banking, to take another example, the French Crown depended for its short-term advances on its own financiers, whereas the British and Dutch governments borrowed from their central banks, the Bank of Amsterdam founded in 1609, and the Bank of England founded in 1694, both of them funded by merchants and bankers. The Bank of France was not founded until the year 1800, and in France during the eighteenth century there was no equivalent to it or to the private British country banks.[17] Again, financiers controlled the French customs duties and blocked all efforts to abolish the internal tolls and duties by resisting the pressure of merchants and reforming officials in the various council and committee meetings.[18]

Still another commercial activity of financiers was as supply-merchants or purveyors to the navy and naval bases in France and the colonies. Supplies of timber, hemp, and other stores from the Baltic, and foodstuffs or victuals, were normally contracted out to partnerships or (in the case of victuals) to a consortium of about a dozen financiers. A victualling company was called, like the General Farm of Taxes, by the name of the front man (*homme de paille*) with whom the partners each signed a contract for a term of three to six years. Thus, the naval victualling company was named Jacques Framéry (1742-7), Thomas Sauvalle (1748-50), Claude Fort (1751-6),and Nicolas Perny (1757-62), but some of the same partners were in them all, while others were descended from a previous generation of naval victuallers, and all were widely connected in official and financial circles.

Gaastra, ed., *Companies and Trade* (Leiden, 1981), pp. 28, 101; T. K. Rabb, *Enterprise and Empire: Merchant and Gentry Investment in the Expansion of England 1575–1630* (London, 1967); H. A. Innis, *The Fur Trade in Canada* (Toronto, 1956), pp. 70-4.

[17] J. H. Clapham, 'The Private Business of the Bank of England, 1744-1800', *Economic History Review*, vol. ii, (1949) pp. 77-89; D. M. Joslin, 'London Private Bankers, 1720-85', *Economic History Review*, vol. vii (1954), pp. 167-86; R. D. Richards, *The Early History of Banking in England* (London, 1929).

[18] J. F. Bosher, *The Single Duty Project: A Study of the Movement for a French Customs Union in the Eighteenth Century* (London, 1964), 215 pp.

Louis-Antoine Charlot de Charlière and his brother-in-law, Louis Miotte de Ravanne, for instance, both members of the Jacques Framéry company, had been in the naval victualling business since the 1720s or earlier, and had many relations among the magistrates, officers, and financiers of their time.[19] François-Marie Prévost (1697-1766) in the Nicolas Perny company was related, through his wife, Marguerite Fabus, to Michel-Henry Fabus (b. 1713) who was in business with his nephew, Jacques Prévost de la Croix (1715-91), naval Intendant at Louisbourg.[20]

Salomon Delahaye Desfosses (1691-1764), born at Louviers, was the son of a magistrate in the Parlement of Dijon, brother and father of Farmers General, and married to a sister of the Treasurer General of the *Maréchaussée* who brought him a dowry of 120,000 livres. He seems to have nothing to do with Canada until we discover that he was related to Nicolas-Félix Vaudive, a Paris merchant jeweller whom Bigot, Bréard, and other Québec officials employed to invest their ill-gotten profits during the Seven Years War.[21] Pierre Escoure (d. 1767) of Bordeaux, a member of the Perny company, had many maritime interests and in 1749 married the sister of the naval victuallers' director at Martinique, Laurent-Alexandre Dahon, who was at Halifax, Nova Scotia, in August 1759 for some reason.[22] These are only a few examples of that class of rich, powerful financiers in the naval victualling companies.

One of the most active in the Canada trade was Joseph-Michel Cadet (1719-81), Purveyor General to the French forces in Canada from 1 January 1757, according to a nine-year contract signed at

[19] AN, MC, Étude LVII 441, 26 Aug. 1760, inv., 478, 8 Apr. 1767; and *Mémoire pour les syndics des créanciers du feu Sieur (Claude) Miotte de Ravanne, Grand Maître des Eaux et Forêts de la Genté d'Orléans*. . . (1734), 39 pp. (BN, f° Fm. 11258); lists of members of some victualling companies are in AN, MC, XCI, 4 Aug. 1759 (Perny), AN, V^7 108 (Framéry), Arch. de la Marine at Rochefort, 1 E 171 (Honoré Chéris signed 14 Dec. 1762).

[20] AN, Y 11082, *scellés*, 10 Sept. 1766; AN, V^1 373, 1 Dec. 1752, *lettres de provision* for Fabus; AN, P 2843, 2 Aug. 1765, inv. on the Fabus bankruptcy; V^2 41, 30 July 1739, *Secr. du Roi* file; Bibl. de l'Arsenal, Bastille ms. 12,200, fols. 145-350, interrogation of Jacques Prévost de la Croix; Marc Perrichet, 'Plûme ou épée? . . .', *Actes du 91e Congrès national des Sociétés savantes* (Rennes, 1966), tome ii (1969), pp. 145-81.

[21] AN, MC, Étude LVII, 12 June 1755, *notoriété*, 29 July 1755, *partage*, 29 Oct. 1764, inv., 2 Apr. 1767, *partage*, 13 Apr. 1767, *compte*.

[22] AN, MC, Bronod (Paris), 16 and 17 Jan. 1749, marriage; Étude LXXIX, 21 May 1758, *transport*; ADG, Guy (Bx.), 12 Feb. 1761, Escoure's will; Parrans (Bx.), 9 Oct. 1759, Dahon's will; 13 Oct. 1759, inv. Escoure lived in Paris, rue des Bons Enfants, in the parish of St Eustache with the rest of the naval financing circle, but had much business with the victualling director at Bordeaux, Pierre Carcy.

Québec on 26 October 1756.[23] Cadet was the son of a humble Canadian merchant butcher and rose as a purveyor of meat to the forces under the Intendant, Gilles Hocquart, and then, in the post-war period after the Treaty of Aix-la-Chapelle (1748), as a shipping merchant on his own account. He offered his services as Purveyor General as early as 1754, and when the offer was accepted two years later was ready to provide the goods and the shipping necessary for supplying the colony from France. During the three years 1757-9, he imported food and other supplies to the value of several million livres, some of it on other men's ships and some on ships of his own. His agents at the French ports purchased ships and cargoes for him, secure in the knowledge that he, like any other government purveyor, paid out of a bottomless purse. No reliable list of his vessels has been compiled, but some of them are listed in Table 9.

Meanwhile, like all or nearly all the business men in the employ of the Bourbon monarchy, Cadet carried on trading on his own personal account, using the advantages he had as the official Purveyor General. His many private partnerships were typical of Bourbon official society, and but for the Conquest and the resulting *affaire du Canada* in which he was arrested and sentenced, Cadet might have established one of the those families of financiers so powerful in the French empire. Even so, he managed extremely well. He may have benefited by his mother's second marriage to Pierre-Joseph Bernard, the son of one of Maurepas' secretaries, and he certainly had the benefit of the Intendant's patronage. Whatever the reason, he survived the *affaire* and built up a business managing and selling large landed estates in France. His two daughters married into minor noble families and one of his sons was soon calling himself by the sonorous name of Joseph Cadet Deschamps, seigneur of Mondon.

The Canada merchants had to face the competition of purveyors such as Cadet and of other financiers who invested in trade. These investments were usually concealed by trading through a relative or a front man, so that we shall never know them all, or even be able to estimate the financiers' share of trade. Enough has been discovered, however, to warrant the claim that financiers, like smugglers, engaged in a great deal of it. For example, a monopoly of the fishing trade at Île

[23] J. F. Bosher, 'Cadet, Joseph-Michel', *DCB*, vol. iv, pp. 123-8; J. F. Bosher, 'The French Government's Motives', *English Historical Review*, vol. xcvi (1981), pp. 59-78; AN, MC, Étude XIV, 28 June 1781. Cadet's post-mortem inventory; other acts in the same étude; ANQ, Panet (Que.), *passim*; for Cadet's shipping see Table 4.

St Jean (Prince Edward Island), the Magdeleine Islands, and other islands near by, was granted in 1719 to a nobleman, Louis-Hyacinthe Castel de Saint Pierre, but financed by two Paris financiers. These were Jean-Marie Fargès, purveyor to the French army, and his son-in-law, Abraham Peirenc de Moras (1686-1732), prominent members of John Law's company and of the financial group behind the founding of Louisiana. The company of Île St Jean went bankrupt in 1724, but the Fargès-Peirenc de Moras clan prospered. A son, François-Marie Pereinc de Moras (1718-71), even ruled New France as Secretary of State for Marine and Colonies in 1757-8.[24]

The company for Île St Jean used the shipping services of the agent for the Indies Company, Joseph Fleury de la Gorgendière (1676-1755), who traded in partnership with his brother, Charles Fleury Deschambault. They sent *La Suzanne* of La Rochelle to Île St Jean until 1723 when they sold her to the Île St Jean company. The next year, on 24 May, they dispatched *La Marguerite* of La Rochelle (150 tx.) under Captain Testu de la Richardière from La Rochelle and she arrived at Québec on 5 August after calling at Île St Jean. The financial connections of their family were still strong twenty-five years later when a Fleury Deschambault was paying for imports from France with remittances drawn on two Paris financiers, Doutreleau, a Treasurer of the Chancellery living in the rue des Gravilliers, Paris, and Joseph Peschevin, a cashier with the Indies Company.

Another financier at Québec, the agent of the Farmers General for the *domaine*, was the promoter of a famous ironworks, the *Forges Saint-Maurice*, for which he borrowed heavily from Arnaud-Blaise Descamps and other French merchants in the Canada trade.[25] This was the well-known François-Étienne Cugnet (1688-1751).

Most of the port agents of the Treasurers General for Marine and Colonies were busy part-time merchants. In 1703, Jean Petit, agent at Québec, and Pierre Plassan, a merchant, formed a trading partnership with a capital fund of 15,000 livres, of which Petit immediately gave Plassan 7,189 livres in bills of exchange. After a year's profitable trading across the Atlantic, they raised their capital to 30,000 livres and

[24] D. C. Harvey, *The French Régime in Prince Edward Island* (New Haven, 1926), pp. 40, 51, 52; Lüthy, *La Banque protestante*, vol. ii, pp. 788-9; Guy Chaussinand-Nogaret, *Les Financiers de Languedoc* (Paris, 1970), p. 130; AN, P 2473, fol. 105, *lettres de provision de Secrétaire d'État*, 8 Feb. 1757.

[25] Nish, *Les Bourgeois-gentilshommes de la Nouvelle-France*, *passim*; and *François-Étienne Cugnet, entrepreneur et entreprises en Nouvelle-France* (Montréal, 1975).

Table 9. Some Ships in Joseph Cadet's Service

Year	Name	Tonneaux	Captain	Remarks
1752	*Joseph*	140	Maurice Simonin	owned with Nicolas Massot
1755	*Angélique*	90	Fr. Urbain Le Brun	owned with François Gazan
1756	*Madeleine*	80	Joseph Massot	paid 4 000 livres Can. for her 22-5-56
1756	*Rameau*	130	Beaurivage	bought 23-8-56 from *Mounier & Grelleau*
1757	*Madeleine*	80	Joseph Massot	
1757	*Saint Patrice*	290	Jean Desarnaud	
1757	*Cérès*	72		
1758	*Vénus*	200	Jean Carbonnel	bought 18-9-58 from Lamalétie for 12 750 liv.
1758	*Jazon*	300	Jacques Bertrand	
1758	*Amitié*	130	Michel Voyer	
1758	*Hardy*	140		bought 17-10-58 from *Imbert, Lannelongue & Gabarre* of Louisbourg for 7 500 liv.
1758	*Victoire*	150	Guillaume Hamon	bought 17-8-58 from Nicolas Massot
1758	*Foudroyant*	360	Raymond Laville	
1758	*Bonne Amie*	300		bought 9-8-58 for 50 000 liv. from *Rasteau & Bécard*

1758	*Cheval Marin*	360	Dominique Lafourcade	
1758	*Charmante Nanon*	350		bought 18-9-58 from Penne
1758	*Aigle*	340	Jean Douteau	
1758	*Toison d'Or*	300	Joseph Marchand	bought 18-9-58 from Lamalétie for 50 495 liv.
1758	*Légère*	330	J.-B. Cassemain	bought 6-10-58 for 40 000 liv. from *Rasteau & Bécard*
1758	*Nanette*	71	Voyer	
1758	*Sérieuse*	100		bought 1-11-58 for 8 800 liv. from Nicolas Massot
1758	*Espérance*			bought 9-11-58 for 12 900 liv. from Nicolas Massot
1758	*Amitié*	130	Michel Voyer	bought 9-11-58 for 9 600 liv. from Nicolas Massot
1758	*Héros*		Barre	
1758	*Colibry*	50		sold in France for 12 000 liv.
1759	*Quatre frères*	500	Fr. Géraud	bought for 130 000 liv. by Desclaux for Cadet
1759	*Aimable Nanon*	400	Martin Minbielle	new frigate
1759	*Soleil Royal*			
1759	*Maréchale de Senneterre*	550	Joseph Goret	
1759	*Machault*	550	Kanon	
1759	*Vénus*	200	Jean Carbonnel	
1759	*Victoire*	150	Guillaume Hamon	
1759	*Chézine*	430	Pierre-Nicolas Guyot	
1759	*Rameau*	120	Louis Nadeau	
1759	*Amitié*	130	Michel Voyer	

agreed that Plassan should sail to France to borrow more, if necessary, and to buy trading goods. 'And inasmuch as the said Sieur Petit does not want his name used on the invoices and bills of lading that the Sieur Plassan will draw up for the said merchandise', runs their notarized agreement, 'these papers will nevertheless be for the account and risk of the said company as well as for its profit, even though all is done under Plassan's name alone.'[26]

By 18 October 1705, when the partners again renewed their agreement, their joint capital stood at 44,378 *livres tournois*, and in 1708 after they had dissolved the partnership Plassan's summary of their investments showed a one-quarter interest in *Le Chamilly* sent to the West Indies, worth 13,000 livres; an investment of 3,500 livres for the purchase of cod at Plaisance, Newfoundland; a one-third interest in *Le Trident*, worth about 1,200 livres, bound for Newfoundland; a one-sixth interest and a one-thirty-second interest in *La Notre Dame des Victoires* and its cargo, worth altogether about 4,000 livres (of which half was insured); and furs and other goods worth about 5,000 livres that Plassan was planning to take to France.[27] The financier's role in this trade is not diminished by the revelation that Petit's brother, a *contrôleur des rentes de l'Hôtel de ville* in Paris, did business for them there, and that the early documents of the partnership were witnessed by Henry Hiché, a clerk at the King's stores in Québec, and by Étienne Marandeau, a *huissier royal* there. The worthy Petit was made a councillor in the Sovereign Council in 1718, and who would believe that he did not continue trading until his death in 1720?

His successor at Québec, Nicolas Lanoullier de Boisclerc, who also became the *contrôleur du domaine d'occident*, carried on 'a considerable trade in the French goods sold at Québec',[28] notably with his father and a certain Julien, both Paris merchants, with Le Moyne at Rouen, with Andrieu Cornet, a merchant at Amiens, the Pascaud family and Bourgine at La Rochelle, and the Mariette family of Montauban. Whether the next treasurer's agent, Thomas-Jacques Taschereau, also invested in transatlantic trade is not clear, but in the eighteenth century his investments in the *Forges Saint-Maurice*, and the enormous deficit discovered in his accounts when he died in 1749, intimate that he had commercial interests.[29] The last treasurer's agent, Jacques Imbert, was also engaged in trade, as wartime shipments to him show.

[26] ANQ, Genaple (Que.), 13 Nov. 1703, *acte de société*, and 16 Nov. 1704.
[27] Ibid., 12 Nov. 1708.
[28] Keyes, op. cit., p. 183.
[29] H. Provost, 'Tachereau, Thomas-Jacques', *DCB*, vol. iii, p. 616.

Five shipments, captured in 1757 and 1758, are a mere sample of his trade:

On *Le Berger* 6 barrels of wine worth 500 livres.
On *La Catiche* wine, ham, flour from Pierre Lartigue.
On *Les Deux Frères* dry goods from Denis Goguet.
On *La Légère* pork, ham, liqueur, marinated artichokes, and sausages, from Pierre Lartigue.
On *Le Superbe* two cases from Paris, sent by Gradis.[30]

Imbert's cashier at Montréal from 1753, Philippe-Antoine Cuny D'Hauterive, had an importing business on the side big enough to claim a loss of 200,000 livres' worth of imported goods in a fire of 1754, and to garner profits enough to invest in royal tax farms in France and to buy an office of *avocat au Parlement*.[31] The treasurer's agent at Louisbourg from 1749 to 1758, Jean Laborde, was a big shipping merchant there with investments in many vessels and cargoes, and various partners in France, notably the Bordeaux firm of *Cabarrus et Solignac* and an uncle, Michel-Henry Fabus, who traded with the West Indies during the 1750s while holding the financial offices of *trésorier général des Invalides* and *receveur général des Domaines et Bois* for the Generality of Paris. Fabus was married to a member of the great financial family of Le Riche.[32]

These treasurer's agents in Canada, it should be added, were not exceptional in the French empire. Many of their colleagues at French ports went into maritime trading, some on a large scale, and although we have no record of any such trade with Canada even by the agent at Rochefort, Bréard, brother of the naval controller at Québec, it would not be safe to assume that there was none.[33] As for the Treasurers General, the employers of all these agents, they made many commercial investments but any they may have had in the Canada trade were well concealed.[34]

[30] PRO, HCA 32:169, 178 pt. 1, 182, 212, 246.

[31] J. F. Bosher, 'Cuny Dauterive, Philippe-Antoine', *DCB*, vol. iv, p. 187.

[32] Bibl. de l'Arsenal, Bastille ms. 12,200, fols. 89 ff., 145 ff.; AN, V^1 373, *provision d'office*, 1 Dec. 1752.

[33] J. F. Bosher, 'Bréard, Jacques-Michel', *DCB*, vol. iv, pp. 90-2.

[34] Joseph de Saint Laurent (1707-73), a Treasurer General for the Marine who married a daughter of the Le Couteulx family of Rouen bankers, invested 12,000 livres in a company for trade with Martinique (AN, MC, Étude CXV 875, 20 Nov. 1773, inv.). Noel-Mathieu-Étienne Périchon (1698-1764), Treasurer General for the Colonies in office from 31 Jan. 1758, had many commercial investments such as the 30,000 livres he put into a one-tenth interest in a trading company in 1753 managed by Darragory of Santanders; an unspecified sum he had put into a trading company in 1750 that

The Receivers General of Taxes for the Generalities with major seaports in them had opportunities for seaborne trade, as two cases show. One is the case of Gratien Drouilhet, a Receiver General of Finance for La Rochelle since 1742, who formed a joint-stock company for trading to Canada by a private contract of 1 July 1755 and contributed 40,000 livres to its capital.[35] His three partners in the firm were his nephew, Claverie, an army officer, Péan, and a merchant, Pennisseault, all living in Canada. This firm lasted scarcely one season, for Drouilhet died on 30 January 1756. His heirs sold his office to a veteran of the Canada trade at Bordeaux, Nicolas Beaujon, who continued in it, at least for some years.[36]

Financiers of a lower order, almost a financial underworld, were always looking for profitable speculations in Bourbon France, and these too were attracted to the transatlantic trades, especially towards the middle of the eighteenth century when every port had families grown rich in the West India trade. A good view of these speculative activities appears in the history of an Atlantic fishing company founded in 1750 for a term of eight years by a certain Baron D'Huart, a military officer born in Luxemburg.[37] This company's vessels, registered at the fishing port of Les Sables d'Olonne on the coast of Poitou north of La Rochelle, made occasional voyages to Québec and many voyages to Louisbourg where the company employed a manager.[38] These are listed in Table 10. The Baron D'Huart spent seventeen months at Louisbourg in 1752-3 in the service of his company, during which he made an unsuccessful bid for the contract to improve the Louisbourg fortifications, and without some knowledge of his partners an observer would be inclined to see the company as an ordinary merchant venture.[39]

included David-Michel-Henry Fabus, Ferdinand Grand, and Jean-Paul Silvestre; the 8,000 livres invested in *La Maréchale de Saxe* (Captain Labadie) which *J. André Crapp et Compagnie* of Nantes sent to Angola in 1750; the 1,000 livres invested in a privateer, *Le Granville*, in the Seven Years War; and the one-fifteenth share (17,400 livres) in two 200-ton ships, *L'Angély* and *La Reine Anne*, he bought from *Eustache frères* of Le Havre in 1750 (AN, MC, Étude XXXIX 495, inv.). Among Baudard de Vaudesir's investments was a sum of 300,000 livres in a weapon factory at Charleville in 1763.

[35] ANQ, Dulaurent (Que.), 11 June 1756.

[36] AN, T 306, marriage contract, 21-2 Oct. 1753, listing Beaujon's investments in the Canada trade at the time.

[37] J. F. Bosher, 'A Fishing Company of Louisbourg, Les Sables d'Olonne, and Paris: *La Société du Baron d'Huart*, 1750-1775', *French Historical Studies*, vol. ix (1975), pp. 263-77.

[38] See Table 10.

[39] F. J. Thorpe, *Remparts lointains: le politique des travaux public à Terre-Neuve et à l'Île royale, 1695–1758* (Ottawa, 1980), p. 100.

Table 10. Vessels of D'Huart and Co. All sailings are from France to Louisbourg unless otherwise stated

Year	Name	Tonneaux	Captain	Remarks
1750	*Minerve*	200	Jean Derze	left Louisbourg 24 Nov. for France
1751	*Minerve*	200	Peneau	
1751	*Cibelle*	150	Biloneau	
1751	*Baron D'Huart*	180	Jacques Pigeon	
1751	*Vainqueur*	105	Jean Goulpeau	left Louisbourg 28 Oct. 1751, arr.at Bx. 2 Dec. with cod, fish oil, etc.
1751	*Hirondelle*	36		sailed to Gaspé
1752	*Minerve*	150	Marsan Sallaberry	
1752	*Vainqueur*	105	Jean Goulpeau	
1752	*Dibonne*	80	Gilles Texier	
1752	*Baron D'Huart*	110	Jacques Pigeon	
1753	*Vainqueur*	105	Jean Goulpeau	
1753	*Inconnu*	135	Pierre Bertaud	
1753	*Minerve*	150	Luc Salaberry	
1753	*Baron D'Huart*	110	Jacques Pigeon	
1753	*Vainqueur*	105	Jean Goulpeau	
1753	*Dibonne*	80	Gilles Texier	from Sables d'Olonne to Louisbourg to W. I.
1753	*Cibelle*			from W. I. to Louisbourg to W. I.
1753	*Héroclite*		Dominique Laisné for France (?)	fitted out at Louisbourg
1753	*Marie Jeanne*, schooner	60	André Collinet	built at Louisbourg for 3640 liv.; sailed to Québec and then to France
1753	*Victoire*, schooner			built at Louisbourg for 2351 liv.
1753	*Trompeuse*, schooner			bought at Louisbourg
1754	*Vainqueur*	105	Jean Laisné	left Louisbourg 17 Sept. 1754, arr. at Bx. 27 Oct. with dried cod and planks of 'sapin'
1755	*Minerve*	150	Pierre Darthiague	left Bx. in Mar. with a passenger, Jean Hiriart of Louisbourg
1755	*Dibonne*		François Maillet	seized and taken to England as a prize

Most of the partners were not merchants, however, but adventurers and ambitious financial speculators. Louis Le Tellier was an *entrepreneur des bâtiments du Roi*; Philippe Seichepine and Claude-Étienne Petin were clerks in the royal service for managing vacant ecclesiastical benefices (*les Oeconomats*) under the direction of one of the great financial speculators of the time, Marchal de Sainscy; Louis-Gabriel Laisné, a master saddler and coachmaker, was engaged with Seichepine in a brandy-tax farm in Artois; Barthelemy Crozat de Chabaudière had joined Seichepine, Pétin, and a certain François Chavigny in a company for managing and exploiting large estates near Brest; Jean-Baptiste Plagniole was an inspector of the Paris ports; Honoré-Henry Lejay and Philippe-Antoine Chainot held venal offices as *avocats au Parlement*; still others had joined Seichepine and Pétin in leasing the tax farm for the county of Olonne in lower Poitou.

Two of the leaders, Seichepine and Pétin, had an indirect acquaintance with New France through their employer, Marchal de Sainscy, who was a relative of Hugues-Jacques Péan de Livaudière, adjutant at Québec, and had sent his troublesome younger brother, Sébastien Marchal de Noroy, to stay at Québec with a merchant during the 1740s. But what characterizes the members of the *Société du baron D'Huart* is their wide-ranging speculations and the unscrupulous behaviour which prompted D'Huart to remark later that he had learned 'a great lesson which he will not forget, if some day he is obliged to find himself with financiers of the stamp of Pétin and the Sieur de Sainscy'.[40] High or low, financiers who invested in the transatlantic trades were always managing a variety of other enterprises. They did not live as merchants lived or make it their business to learn what merchants knew. Their principal sphere of interest was government finance.

Almost any sphere of French business might attract these financial speculators. Even the fur trade, for example, which we think of as the business of specialized merchants such as the Le Duc family at Rouen or the Charly family at Montréal, helped to build the fortunes of many a financier in the seventeenth century. The French companies selling Canadian furs in the reign of Louis XIV had members who were financial speculators.[41] A good example in our period is

[40] Bosher, 'A Fishing Company', p. 276.

[41] There is no study of them, but some of their names and activities are cited in Guy Frégault, *Le XVIIIe siècle canadien* (Montréal, 1968), ch. 5,'La Compagnie de la colonie'; and in Claude-Frédéric Lévy, *Capitalistes et pouvoir au siècle des lumièeres des origines à 1715* (The Hague, 1969), pp. 110-11 and ch. 3 *passim.*

René-François Gondot, who styled himself an *intéressé dans les affaires du Roi*, and who in 1751 formed a joint-stock company in Paris for the trade and manufacture of beaver and other hats. His partners were Jean-Joseph Tapret, *bourgeois de Paris*, and Marguerite-Louise Descordes, wife of a beaver manufacturer (*fabricant de castor*), Pierre Lartigue, who was to manage the manufacturing part of the business. Gondet was to contribute 24,000 livres to a total capital of 50,000 livres. Though neither a merchant, nor a specialist in fur, Gondot rose socially, as we find him in 1760 described as *écuyer* and a former War Commissioner.[42]

The influence of Paris financiers in the business of seaports and colonies was undoubtedly greater than these few examples might convey. Wherever there were financial families patient research in the archives is likely to discover family support for a business venture or powerful people in Paris ready to patronize an official turned part-time merchant. It is not easy to see how the Québec merchant bankers, Barthelemy Martin and Jean-Baptiste Tropez Martin, and the chief royal shipwright at Québec, René-Nicolas Levasseur, with whom they made marriage alliances, benefited by their connections with families of Farmers General and other financiers.[43] Nor has anyone accused Gilles Hocquart, Intendant of New France from 1729 to 1748, of taking commercial advantage of his powerful and close-knit family of noblemen and financiers, including two brothers, Jean-Hyacinth Hocquart, a Farmer General from 1721 to 1762, and Louis-Jacques-Charles Hocquart, a Treasurer General for Artillery and Engineering for thirty years.[44] Nevertheless, close study of the officials, financiers, and officers in that age shows that such men were exceptional indeed if they and their relatives did not dabble in trade.

[42] A. D. de la Seine, 3 B[6] 52, 1 Sept. 1751, *société; AN, MC, Étude LXXXIII 471, 17 Nov. 1760, constitution.* Étude CXVIII, 13 Nov. 1751, *quittance.*

[43] Bosher, 'The French Government's Motives', p. 68.

[44] Durand, *Les Fermiers généraux*, p. 377; François Bluche, *L'Origine des Magistrats du Parlement de Paris au XVIIIe siècle*, Paris et Île-de-France, Mémoires publiés par la Fédération ..., tomes v-vi, 1953-4, (Paris, 1956), p. 215; A. Deschard, 'Notice sur l'organisation du corps du commissariat de la marine française depuis l'origine jusqu'à nos jours', *Revue Maritime et coloniale*, vol. 60 (1879), p. 779; D. J. Horton, 'Hocquart, Gilles', *DCB*, vol. iv, pp. 354-65.

III

Atlantic Trading Society

6

The Huguenot Minority

THE religious identity of Huguenots is vital in the history of the Canada trade because Protestant and Catholic families remained largely separate, trading together but seldom forming partnerships or intermarrying. Protestants and Catholics were not merely different religious groups but also different social groups, each with its own history. Their recent histories were, moreover, sharply different. The Protestants had been persecuted on and off since about 1620, outlawed since 1685, and so deprived of the benefits of royal offices and other means of social progress, just as the Jews had been. Worse than that, unless they turned Roman Catholic or pretended to do so, they could not obtain passports for the colonies, enter any of the trades or professions, buy property, or marry.

Church and State went as far as to break up Protestant families. Sometimes the men were sent to the Mediterranean fleet as galley slaves, where many were still chained to their oars in the middle of the eighteenth century.[1] Sometimes the women and children were imprisoned in convents to be taught the Catholic religion. For example, in 1722 Susanne Oualle, aged fifteen, was imprisoned in the convent of the *Nouvelles catholiques de la providence* at La Rochelle by an official *lettre de cachet*.[2] Her father, Jean-François Oualle, tried to rescue her but could not, and in 1727 she became a nun under the name Sister Saint Laurent. By an order of 7 July 1730, a daughter of the Paillet family of Marennes and two daughters of the Monbeuil family of Cozes in Saintonge were imprisoned in the convent of Notre Dame at Saintes.[3] The parish registers at La Rochelle described Henriette-Esther Bonfils, at her baptism in 12 February 1722, as 'the natural [i.e. illegitimate] and posthumous daughter of Pierre Bonfils, *marchand banquier*, and of Susanne Tresahar', and she thought it

[1] Paul W. Bamford, *Fighting Ships and Prisons: the Mediterranean Galleys of France in the Age of Louis XIV* (Minneapolis, 1973), pp. 285-8; André Zysberg, 'La Société des galériens au milieu du XVIIIe siècle', *Annales ESC*, vol. xxx (1975), pp. 43-65.

[2] A. D. Ch. Mar., 4 J 7, notes Garnault, 'Oualle'.

[3] Victor Bujeaud, *La Chronique protestante de l'Angoumois aux XVIe, XVIIe et XVIIIe siècles*, n.d., n.p., p. 312.

necessary to explain in a letter of 1779 that all children of Protestant parents were so stigmatized in those earlier years.[4]

The 'New Converts' were watched by the clergy, by royal officials, and by zealous magistrates. At Rouen, for example, a *procureur général* of the Parlement compiled a list of New Converts on the basis of reports from parish priests, and sent it with comments to a minister of the Crown on 1 May 1736. Several New Converts, he wrote, are living with women to whom they are not married (i.e. in the Catholic Church), such as 'the Sieur Dugard, merchant, living in the rue des Charettes near the Cordeliers with Mademoiselle Laurent from the parish of St Eloy'.[5] In the same archival carton are lists of Protestant women and girls imprisoned in convents at Rouen. The mounted brigades of the *maréchaussée* in Saintonge, to take another example, were instructed by the Intendant at La Rochelle in 1750 to make frequent night visits to the villages near the coast, from which many mariners in the transatlantic shipping business came, and where 'the *religionnaires* assemble especially on Saturday or Sunday nights or on the eves of certain feast days'.[6] If these troops heard any singing or prayers, they were to enter, breaking down the door if necessary, and write down all names and addresses. Again, two Protestant merchants who went to Louisbourg from Tonnay-Charente in 1752 were closely watched and one, Élie Allenet, sent back to France by the Governor and Intendant for 'actions in matters of religion sufficient to have him brought to trial'.[7] At Québec, too, the authorities kept a close watch on New Converts, who were allowed to live there from about 1730 so long as they did not bring wives and have families, and lists of their names were sent to the minister at Versailles from time to time.[8]

As a result of persecution, the Huguenots developed a subculture of their own in which their collective memory of the injustices and brutalities they had suffered played a large part. Huguenots in general, indeed all Protestants everywhere, shared memories not only of the notorious massacre of St Bartholomew on 24 August 1572, but also of

[4] AN, Marine C7 289, personal file for Ruis Embito, her husband, naval intendant at Rochefort during the Seven Years War.

[5] AN, TT 264.

[6] E. Moutarde, *La Réforme en Saintonge: Les Églises réformées du Saujon et de la presqu'île d'Arvert* (Paris, 1892), documents, pp. 203-5. The villages named in these instructions were Mornac, Chaillevette, Vaux (home of the Bonfils family), Pelourdonnier, Coulonges, Breuillet, and St Augustin.

[7] Quoted in J. F. Bosher, 'French Protestant Families in Canadian Trade, 1740-1760', *Histoire sociale* (Ottawa), vol. vii (1974), p. 193.

[8] AN Colonies C11A, vol. 75, fol. 27; D2 C, vol. 53; D2 D, carton 1.

the more recent fate of refugees' relatives. 'One of my uncles was hanged,' the well-known Anthony Benezet of Philadelphia recalled. 'My aunt was put in a convent, two of my cousins died at the galleys, and my fugitive father was hanged in effigy for explaining the gospel differently from the priest, and was ruined by confiscation of his property.'[9] Certain notorious cases were known far and wide, such as that of the American Huguenot, Élie Neau, which made a sensation early in the century. Neau, a New York merchant, was captured by a French privateer on a business voyage to London in 1692 and sentenced to row in the galleys for the rest of his life.[10] He was soon thrown into a dungeon at Marseille, however, for converting a fellow galley slave to Protestantism, and then released in 1698 under the terms of the Treaty of Ryswick (1697), after the forces of William of Orange had won the first of the great Anglo-Dutch victories over Louis XIV. By the mid-1690s, Neau's experiences and prison letters had already caused an outburst of religious feeling among Huguenots and others in New York. In London and Rotterdam, books and pamphlets published his story and others like it.

The Neau Case at the beginning of our period and the Calas Case (1761-2) at the end of it showed then (and show now) that anti-Catholic feeling in the age of New France was no mere prejudice but founded upon real dangers. The Calas Case, like the Neau Case, was watched with intense interest throughout the Protestant world.[11] The story began about thirty years before Jean Calas came to public notice. In 1731, when he was living as a young merchant at Toulouse, he had married a cousin's daughter, Anne-Rose Cabibel, who had been born in London but taken back to live in Languedoc with her parents. Shortly after their marriage, this couple had been caught by the French authorities trying to flee to England with other Huguenots, but they had eventually settled down in Toulouse where they had brought up their family. Eventually one of their sons converted to Catholicism, and Jean Calas was arrested, tortured, and executed on 12 March 1762 for the alleged murder of another son who, it was said, also planned to become a Catholic.

It was not the trial and execution that shocked public opinion in Atlantic trading society; it was the family's pathetic helplessness in

[9] George S. Brookes, *Friend Anthony Benezet* (Philadelphia, 1937), p. 5.

[10] Jon Butler, *The Huguenots in America* (Cambridge, Mass., 1984), pp. 162 ff.

[11] Edna Nixon, *The Calas Case* (London, 1965); David Bien, *The Calas Affair* (Princeton, 1960).

official French society. One son had converted to Catholicism partly through the influence of a Catholic servant whom the family employed because it was illegal for them to hire a Huguenot or New Convert. Calas was tried with no proper legal counsel or defence, and twice tortured according to normal French practice to make him confess and to reveal the names of any accomplices. After his death, his family was dispersed and his daughters forced into the Convent of the Visitation at Toulouse where they were to be systematically converted under the direction of the well-connected Sister Anne-Julie Fraisse.

After Voltaire had taken up the case and dramatized it, many French Catholics adopted his humane view of it, but the response in Protestant circles was immediate because it was merely the latest case of so many over the previous two centuries and it occurred near the bicentenary of the slaughter of 4,000 Protestants at Toulouse in 1562. To help fight the case, the Huguenot Paris bankers, *Dufour et Mallet*, began to receive contributions of money from England as early as August 1762.[12] One of the Paris lawyers who took up the case under Voltaire's encouragement was a Mariette from the well-known merchant family of Montauban and Orléans. News of the affair was followed with indignant interest throughout the Protestant world while Voltaire's account of it, and his *Traité de la tolérance* (1762), were banned in France.

Most Huguenots did not suffer such a terrible fate as Calas or Neau. French clergy and officials varied in their persecuting zeal and towns in their religious composition. Consequently there was a shifting pattern of persecution and toleration which drove many Protestant families to move about. In 1757 a certain Mounier at La Rochelle informed his uncle at Québec that he had formed a partnership 'with Monsieur Moreau who came here to escape the persecution which the Subdelegate of St Maixent-les-Écoles makes the Protestants suffer there'.[13] The Mounier family itself had travelled a good deal to avoid persecution: to St Maixent, Geneva, Lausanne, Jarnac, Cognac, La Rochelle, and elsewhere. And such was the history of many Protestant families. Many of the Huguenots in the Canada trade came from inland towns of the south-west. To some of them, ports like La Rochelle and Bordeaux with their colonies of foreign Protestants were

[12] Randolph Vigne, 'The Killing of Jean Calas: Voltaire's First Huguenot Cause', *PHSL*, vol. xxiii (1981), p. 291.

[13] PRO, HCA 32: 253, *La Vainqueur*, M. Mounier (LR) to J. M. Mounier (Que.), 1 Apr. 1757.

havens, even stopping-places on the way to the safety of foreign ports like Amsterdam, London, or Hamburg.

Not all French ports attracted them. St Malo, 'that great centre of Irish emigration', never had a large Protestant community, foreign or French, and few if any Protestant merchants settled there in the age of New France.[14] After the middle of the seventeenth century, Malouin merchants withdrew from trade with the British Isles to concentrate on the Spanish trade and formed a community at Cadiz where they and Bayonne merchants were dominant.[15] They went on to specialize in the illegal trade with the Spanish Indies until English merchants drove them out of it in the eighteenth century. In wartime, they were famous for the privateers they fitted out to prey upon Anglo-Dutch shipping. The Newfoundland fishing fleet of St Malo, the largest in France, was the principal training ground for French sailors and much prized by the French navy for this reason.[16] If there was an Atlantic port that suited official French society, it was St Malo where the *Confrèrie du Saint Sacrement* had great success in recruiting ships' captains as informal chaplains, where Protestants and Jews rarely set foot, and where the clergy 'weighed upon political life'.[17]

Most of the Protestants in the eighteenth-century Canada trade survived, some even prospered, by the discreet use of several advantages. Some had friends or relations in high places who could speak for them, and there were always certain officials quietly well-disposed towards Protestants. Even in the worst century of Catholic persecution, about 1620 to 1720, royal officials seldom molested certain rich Huguenot business men whose fortunes and services were too useful to sacrifice. In Paris, Samuel Bernard and Barthelemy Herwart were only the most famous of many Protestant bankers who served the Crown at one time or another and escaped persecution. These in turn protected other Protestants in the seaports whose survival unmolested can scarcely be otherwise explained–such wealthy and successful merchant families as Desclaux and Jauge at Bordeaux, Delacroix and Garesché at La Rochelle, Dugard at Rouen,

[14] The phrase is Jacob Price's in *France and the Chesapeake* (Ann Arbor, 1973), p. 559; André Lespagnol *et al.*, *Histoire de Saint Malo et du pays malouin* (Toulouse, 1984), chs. 5 to 7; André Corvisier, ed., *Histoire du Havre et de l'Estuaire de la Seine* (Toulouse, 1983), ch. 4 by J. Meyer.

[15] Charles Carrière, *Négociants marseillais* (Marseille, n.d.), pp. 942-4.

[16] Lespagnol *et al.*, *Histoire de Saint Malo*, pp. 98, 105-7, 130; Peggy K. Liss, *Atlantic Empires: The Network of Trade and Revolution, 1713–1826* (Baltimore, 1983), chs. 1 and 2.

[17] Lespagnol *et al.*, *Histoire de Saint Malo*, ch. 7.

Feray at Le Havre, and many more. This social system (as it became) was strengthened by other successful merchants whose Protestant sympathies were concealed behind an official identity as New Converts. A certain useful ambiguity was cultivated by influential families such as Depont de Granges and Mouchard.

Certain government officials were in much the same ambiguous position and for much the same reasons. Jean Massiot, for instance, had converted or pretended to convert to Catholicism in the late seventeenth century and had been rewarded with a royal appointment as General Naval Commissary (*commissaire général de la Marine*) at La Rochelle which he continued to hold after the Peace of Utrecht. We are assured on all sides that Massiot had truly converted to Catholicism, and yet as early as 1691 several Catholic merchants in the Canada trade, Arnauld Péré, Jean Blaise Busquet, and Antoine Grignon, complained that he, like other New Converts, 'abused his power' to favour merchants of his own religion, that is, the Protestant religion.[18] They accused him of finding pretexts for holding up the departure of Catholic merchants' ships in order to give Protestant merchants an advantage in the race to be first at Québec and West Indian ports. Turning to another New Convert, François Mouchard, who sat on the Royal Council for Commerce as the official deputy for La Rochelle, we may ask how he viewed the Catholic monopoly of the Canada trade in 1718 while serving in the Indies Company 'for relations with Canada'.[19]

Repression of Huguenot families was normal but not universal because certain officials, even genuine Catholic officials, did not always enforce the law in all its rigour. For instance, at La Rochelle in 1716 the Intendant, François de Beauharnois, permitted the merchant Louis Allaire to bring his English wife and two daughters to France without converting to Catholicism, and in 1727 the Intendant, Amelot de Chaillou, allowed Jacques Garesché to go and live in Holland to learn foreign languages.[20] At La Rochelle the local authorities seldom forced shipping merchants to obey the laws requiring all children to be schooled as Roman Catholics.[21]

[18] AN, TT 263B, fols. 1056-73, *Mémoire des choses qui se sont passés et se passent contre les ordres de Sa Majesté* (31 May 1691).

[19] Marcel Giraud, *Histoire de la Louisiane française*, vol. iii (Paris, 1966), p. 28.

[20] Francine Miot, 'La Révocation de l'Édit de Nantes et les Protestants jusqu' à l'Édit de tolérance (1787) en Aunis et en Saintongue', thesis of the École des Chartes, Paris, n.d. (see A. D. Ch. Mar., 4 J 2995), p. 170.

[21] Clark, *La Rochelle and the Atlantic Economy during the Eighteenth Century*, p. 80.

Some families survived by what seems to have been a planned dispersion. Part of a family, even an entire branch, would flee to a Protestant country at some time between 1660 and 1760, leaving another part of the family in France as New Converts.[22] Those left behind were often able to retain or to win the management of the property left by the fugitive members of the family. The agency supervising confiscated property, the *Régie des biens des religionnaires fugitifs*, was centred in Paris under the direction of the *régisseur* who engaged a representative in each town or district where fugitive Huguenots left property. After the representative had compiled a list of properties, usually on a printed form recording the name of the parish, the name of the fugitive owner, the nature of the property, its annual yield, and any debts or charges on it, each property was then leased to someone willing to manage it for a fixed term of years. In many cases property was leased to New Converts, sometimes relatives of the former owners, sometimes members of families who may have become New Converts expressly to serve as property managers and trading partners to friends abroad.

This hypothesis–for such it is–would explain, for example, why a member of the Bonfils family at La Rochelle put in successful bids on property left by the fugitives Jacques Pagès and Daniel Paillet, or why Jeremie Frescarode, *négociant bourgeois* of Bergerac, put in a successful bid of 80 livres a year for the land and buildings of his uncle, Jean Frescarode, a Calvinist minister who had fled abroad earlier.[23] In 1724, a member of the Testas family was managing the property left in the Election of Condom, near Bordeaux, by Pierre, Jacob, and Jean Testas who had all fled abroad. In 1732-3, a certain Marthe and Marguerite Gorsse were managing the property of their fugitive relative, Abraham Gorsse.[24] It is possible, of course, that such New Converts were merely greedy profiteers, but this seems unlikely in view of their business with friends and relatives abroad. The Huguenots scattered about the Atlantic world maintained a freemasonry of mutual help and dependence which New Converts usually respected even while collaborating with Catholic authorities in France. Their cosmopolitan freemasonry was, indeed, one of the Huguenot merchants' greatest strengths in the transatlantic trades.

[22] Miot, 'La Révocation', p. 203; John Carswell, *The South Sea Bubble* (London, 1960), p. 5.

[23] AN, TT 40 B, *arrêt du Conseil*, 17 Mar. 1733; TT 416, *État des biens des fugitifs qui sont à donner*. . ., 26 Apr. 1717.

[24] AN, TT 27, *Compte rendu*. . ., and *Compte des restes*. . . .

Family property kept many Huguenots in France when they had every reason, as Protestants, to escape abroad with friends and relatives. In that age of hardship and poverty, houses, lands, and business assets were even more vital in the life of a family than they are today. Others were kept at home by strong links with their own communities in La Rochelle, Bordeaux, Montauban, Rouen, or Paris, and in many small towns, for whole communities conformed as New Converts and survived collectively. Furthermore, many of those in the eighteenth-century Canada trade came from modest families of shopkeepers and tradesmen who could not afford to emigrate or did not wish to take the risk. Most of the merchants from Montauban were in this class. So also were those from small towns who had taken up the Canada trade at one of the larger seaports: Aliés, Boudet, Grelleau, Meynardie, Paillet, and Thouron at La Rochelle; Derit, Dumas, Penettes, and Vernhès at Bordeaux; and Courrejolles at Bayonne.

As Frenchmen remaining in France, such Huguenots apparently hoped for an end to persecution, and not without reason. New Converts at the seaports, at Montauban, and in Paris enjoyed a certain modest immunity in the eighteenth century, especially after the Peace of Utrecht (1713), the death of Louis XIV (1715), and the subsequent friendship established between the regent Duke of Orléans and the British government. At La Rochelle, the rigours of official persecution began to soften in the 1720s. Among merchants, many Roman Catholics were evidently tolerant of New Converts, both Protestant and Jewish, with whom they did business daily. How otherwise could the Canada trade have been carried on by such notorious Huguenots as Robert Dugard at Rouen, Jean-Mathieu Mounier at Québec, or by such notorious Jews as David and Abraham Gradis at Bordeaux? It was in the interests of Catholics and Protestants to trade with one another, and trade encouraged a measure of toleration among merchants long before Church and State showed any signs of change.

Certain towns, especially the big cities of Paris and Lyon and the seaports, Bordeaux, La Rochelle, Le Havre, Marseille, and Rouen, offered Huguenots an unusual measure of safety because of their mobile populations, their ancient communities of Protestant merchants from the Netherlands, England, and Germany, and their cosmopolitan traditions. The civilizing influences of trade and travel, observed by political thinkers such as Montesquieu of Bordeaux, were most felt at the Atlantic seaports.[25] In the maritime trades, Jews, Catholics, and Protestants traded with one another just as they all traded with Muslims and various African and Asian merchants at oriental ports. At La Rochelle, by the middle of the century merchants even had a reading room at the *Bourse* where they could find foreign journals such as *La Gazette d'Amsterdam, La Gazette de Leyde, Le Journal Hélvétique*, and *L'Encyclopédie de Pellet*.[26] Bordeaux may have had a similar arrangement, as the first news of a certain ship lost to the enemy in 1747 reached the city in an issue of the *Gazette d'Utrecht* dated 9 June 1747.[27] Authorities at the seaports were often reluctant to threaten Protestant merchants, knowing that so much overseas trade was in their hands. Their very numbers afforded a certain safety in the eighteenth century, for they tended to encourage and protect one another, and this was true at old Protestant centres such as Montauban and Nîmes as well as at seaports.

A measure of informal religious toleration grew up here and there after the War of the Austrian Succession (1743-8). At La Rochelle a Calvinist consistory quietly revived in March 1755 in the form of a small committee of merchants able to lead the Protestant community, and it included such Canada merchants as Élie Bonfils, Nicolas Paillet, a Perdriau, and a Giraudeau. In 1763, just as Canada was being given up to Great Britain, and the Society of Jesus was being suppressed, a member of the committee wrote, 'We enjoy, thank God, the greatest quiet and we have a score of houses where we gather to hear sermons and chant psalms as publicly as at Amsterdam.'[28] At Bordeaux also, Protestant parish life began to revive during the 1750s: early in 1758, for instance, a Calvinist minister, Jacques Sol, married François Havy of Normandy and Québec to a local Huguenot woman, and recorded the marriage in a parish register that survives to this day.[29] Persecution was renewed in 1758-9 when prison sentences were meted out for 'the crime of religious assembly', but for all that, Bordeaux was safer than most cities because its maritime trade 'acted powerfully', as a French historian writes, 'in favour of tolerance'.[30]

[25] Montesquieu, *De L'Esprit des Lois* (1748), 4th part, bk. xx, 'Du Commerce: le commerce guérit des préjugés destructeurs etc.'; F. G. Pariset *et al.*, *Bordeaux au XVIIIe siècle*, (Bordeaux, 1968), p. 151.

[26] Jean Perier, *Le Prospérité rochelaise au XVIIIe siècle et la bourgeoisie protestante* (Mesnil, Eure, 1899), p. 67.

[27] ADG, Lagénie (Bx.), Oct. 1747.

[28] Perier, op. cit., pp. 59-60; Miot, 'La Révocation', p. 178.

[29] Arch. mun. de Bordeaux, GG 863, no. 22.

[30] Pariset *et al.*, *Bordeaux au XVIIIe siècle*, p. 151.

The uncertain existence of a persecuted minority made the Huguenots so discreet that they are not easy to identify. I have found hardly any memoirs, letters, or tracts written by or about Canada merchants which discuss their identity as Huguenots. Letters were commonly opened by government authorities in that age, as they are in authoritarian countries today, and Huguenots knew this. 'Cadet is in the Bastille by order of the King,' *Paillet et Meynardie* wrote to Madame Guy at Montréal in February 1761.'We shall let you know what follows at the proper time and place [but] you understand that it is not easy for us to write to you at greater length.'[31] It was natural for them to avoid making any waves lest they suffer the fate of their forebears and of other less fortunate Huguenots of their own generation. Besides, they were merchants toiling in their counting-houses early and late. Who was Protestant under the cloak of enforced Catholic conformity, and who was genuinely Roman Catholic? This is a problem for the historian only slightly different from that which faced Bourbon authorities in the eighteenth century.

These authorities were often anxious about the loyalty of Huguenots whose strong family and religious ties with Holland, England, and New England made them suspect in wartime. Certainly there were Huguenots working against the French imperial cause. For gathering intelligence during the Seven Years War, 'the English consul at Rotterdam relied largely on French sources, tapped through the many Huguenot merchants there'.[32] French efforts to draw Dutch neutral shipping into the provision trade to Canada were frustrated by Dutch ministers after reading the correspondence between Versailles and the French representative at the Hague, Count d'Affry. The Dutch could read that correspondence because Pierre Lyonnet (1707-89), the Huguenot cipher-clerk to the States General of Holland, broke D'Affry's cipher in the spring of 1756. Lyonnet, it may be added parenthetically, was a famous Huguenot naturalist, author of *La Traité anatomique de la chenille qui ronge le bois de saules* (1760), who with a Huguenot refugee at Geneva, Charles Bonnet (1720-93), laid the foundations of insect anatomy.[33]

The Canada merchants, meanwhile, were vociferously loyal to the

[31] Université de Montréal, Collection Baby, U 9261.

[32] Alice Clare Carter, *The Dutch Republic in Europe in the Seven Years War* (London, 1971), pp. 57, 124, and 135.

[33] A. Wolf, *A History of Science, Technology and Philosophy in the 18th Century*, rev. ed. (NY, 1961), vol. ii, p. 463; Preserved Smith, *The Enlightenment, 1687–1776* (NY, 1961), p. 101.

French cause in their correspondence with clients at Québec. The French cause was of course their own, on the sea, at any rate. 'That proud nation [i.e. the British] still has the advantage at sea,' Jean-Mathieu Mounier remarked in 1746 when reporting the loss of ships in the Canada trade.[34] 'There is no hope of settlement with England,' *Paillet et Meynardie* wrote from La Rochelle to Augé of Montréal in April 1756. 'They take all the ships they meet and unfortunately we cannot take revenge in the same way.' On 1 August 1759 this Huguenot firm was hoping for the success of the preparations to invade England, and described them in detail; on 28 February 1762 they were hoping that France could recover Canada in the peace negotiations.[35] Seven months earlier, Admyrault *fils* already had grave doubts about this. 'I learned with much feeling the sad fate of the colony,' he wrote to Québec in January 1759, adding that he hoped the Crown would manage to save it.[36] Thus, wartime correspondence is filled with Huguenot anxiety over the safety of French vessels, and shows a patriotic attitude to the war. In this respect, merchants were no different from Huguenot soldiers, many thousands of whom were to be found in the armies of both sides in the imperial wars.

In matters of religion, the authorities of Church and State were usually satisfied with an outward obedience to Roman Catholic practices, chiefly in the sacraments of marriage, infant baptism, and a periodic confession and communion. But they knew, as we know, that many New Converts remained Protestant in their beliefs and loyalties. A calculated hypocrisy can be seen in the behaviour of a few who abjured as required and then reverted to their Protestant religion. The authorities of Church and State sometimes regarded these 'lapses' as sins that could be confessed and expiated like other sins, and sometimes as crimes punishable by law. For instance, when in 1752 Élie Allenet of Tonnay-Charente went to assist Daniel Augier in his trade at Louisbourg,

> he behaved very badly [Governor Prevost wrote later], and committed actions in matters of religion at a little harbour called Laurenbec and at la Baleine sufficient to bring him to trial. He escaped justice only by throwing himself into the arms of the bishop's *grand vicaire* named Monsieur Maillard and by pretending to embrace the Catholic religion. He in fact made an abjuration

[34] Université de Montréal, Collection Baby, U 8922.
[35] Ibid. U 9244, 9259, and 9263.
[36] Ibid. U 21.

some time afterwards in order to marry, and immediately took up his former religion again.[37]

Another example is Jean Grelleau *l'aîné* born on 5 August 1714 to Jean Grelleau and Petronille Bourrillon, who baptized him three days later at the Catholic church of St Abden et Senner, parish of Corbarrieu, eight kilometres south of Montauban.[38] As a young man he worked for Nicolas Beaujon in Bordeaux for 1,000 livres a year as a clerk in the Canada trade until 1746 when Soumbrun of La Rochelle offered him 1,500 livres to serve as his agent at Québec.[39] Whether or not he sailed to Québec that spring on *La Vierge de Grace*, as arranged with Soumbrun, he went to Canada and worked as an independent merchant in the transatlantic trade. We know he was a Protestant because the Intendant at Québec put his name on a list of Protestants sent to Versailles, and because he abjured at La Rochelle on 18 May 1757 in order to marry Catherine de Chaumejan Sorin by a contract of 26 May.[40] When his wife died not many months later, he reverted to Protestantism and married a New Convert like himself, Anne-Elisabeth Manceau, daughter of Étienne Manceau, a merchant, and of Susanne Nezereau.[41] This second wife died some three years later leaving him with two infants, and he himself fell ill and died at his widowed mother's house on 31 March 1764. She buried him where she had baptized him fifty years before, in the Catholic parish of St Abden et Sennen 'after the necessary sacraments', says the parish register.[42]

Two Huguenot brothers from Montauban, the merchants Alexandre and Antoine-Libéral Dumas, abjured at Québec to marry into Catholic families and then returned to the Protestant fold. Alexandre Dumas married Josephte Laroche, widow of a sea-captain, Jean Requiem, on 6 October 1760, but baptized two of his children Protestant and later made a second marriage with a Protestant. His

[37] Bibl. de l'Arsenal (Paris), Bastille ms. 12, 145, fols. 358-60, Prévost de la Croix to Sartine, 4 Sept. 1762.

[38] A. D. Tarn-et-Garonne, Corbarrieu, parish registers, 8 Aug. 1714.

[39] A. D. Ch.Mar., Tardy (LR), 1 June 1746; ADG, Faugas (Bx.), 7 Sept. 1745, see *Contrôle des actes* for that date.

[40] A. D. Ch. Mar., St Barthélemy(LR), 18 May 1757, *abjuration*; Tardy (LR), 26 May 1757, marriage.

[41] A. D. Ch. Mar., Tardy (LR), 16 Sept. 1759, marriage signed by Pierre Boudet and other Huguenot merchants.

[42] A. D. Tarn-et-Garonne, Corbarrieu, parish registers, 31 Mar. 1764.

brother abjured in 17 July 1761 before a Recollet priest, Emmanuel Veyssière, in order to marry Marguerite Cureux on 27 October.[43]

Most others are less easy to identify. Officials evidently had their own methods of testing Huguenot suspects, for they made no bones about calling them Protestants. In 1741 and again in 1754, the Intendant at Québec drew up a *Liste des protestants qui sont en Canada* which coolly identifies nine merchants on the first occasion and thirty (including some children) on the second as Protestants even though they must have had Catholic baptismal certificates (*extraits des registres*) duly signed by parish priests, in order to obtain the passports needed for passage to a colony.[44] We know, indeed, that they did. Antoine-David Thouron, for instance, was baptized at the parish church of St Antonin-en-Rouergue on 16 October 1712, his brother Bernard on 16 September 1714. Jean-Mathieu Mounier was baptized at the church of St Pierre, Jarnac-en-Saintonge, on 2 October 1715; Pierre Glemet at the same church on 26 May 1723; Abraham Dérit at the church of St Jacques, Bergerac, on 1 February 1723; and so on.[45] All these were on the Intendant's list at Québec.

In Admiralty registers at French ports, the clerks described each Huguenot passenger bound for Québec as 'ancien Catholique', thereby identifying him as not being a 'nouveau converti', even though that is what he in fact was. True, some carried the marks of a Protestant background on their baptismal certificates. For example, when Pierre-Tresahar Bonfils applied for (and received) a sea-captain's papers at La Rochelle, his certificate signed by the priest of St Jean-du-Perrot, La Rochelle, recorded that at his baptism on 19 September 1714, 'the father did not want to attend the baptism'.[46] Huguenots usually married in Catholic churches, as Pierre Meynardie, *jeune*, did on 25 August 1764, no other form of marriage being legal, and they lived as Roman Catholics, as he declared twenty-five years later when recording his marriage in the Protestant parish registers that had at last been opened as a result of the famous decree of 1787.[47] Though their status is puzzling, the people on the Canadian Intendant's lists were certainly Huguenots. The historian's problem is that there are

[43] Marcel Trudel, *L'Église canadienne sous le régime militaire, 1759–1764*, vol. i (Québec, 1956), p. 183.

[44] For these lists, see AN, Colonies C^{11A}, vol. 75, fol. 27; D^2 C, vol. 53;D2 D,carton 1.

[45] I found these and other such baptismal entries in the parish registers at the town halls of the towns named, or in some cases at the Arch. départementales.

[46] A. D. Ch. Mar., B 5971, *réception de capitaine de navire*, 18 June 1737.

[47] .Bibl. mun. de Bergerac, Protestant registers, entry for 9 Apr. 1789.

very few such lists, and that some New Converts lived in a state of religious ambiguity, especially after a generation or two of enforced Catholic conformity.

Proof positive exists for the identity of many families at La Rochelle in the Protestant parish records that were revived about 1760: Alaret, Benoît, Bernon, Bonfils, Morin, Mounier, Paillet, Texier, Thouron, and others.[48] Many La Rochelle families, French and foreign, are identified in the alphabetical *Fichier de mariages protestants, 1760–92*, and in the *Grand Livre des protestants*, a manuscript register 'where the records of the deaths of Protestant foreigners are recorded beginning on 21 May 1731 and ending on 17 April 1781'.[49] At Bordeaux, Protestant parish registers were reconstituted starting from 1748 on the basis of declarations made after the law of 1787 which granted a certain limited civil status to Protestants.[50] The families of many Canada merchants appear in them: Allaret, Baour, Bonfils, Boudet, Dommenget, Dumas, Dutilh, Emmerth, Frescarode, Garrisson, Goudal, Massac, Menoire, Meynardie, Paillet, Pecholier, Penettes, Rauly, Rocaute, Texier, Thouron, Vernhès, and others.

Earlier, and throughout the age of New France, corroborating evidence is clear in the patterns of marriages. Marriage between families of New Converts is a sure sign of Protestantism, even if the marriages and baptisms appear in Catholic registers. Thus, for several generations the Augier, Allenet, and Richard families intermarried at Tonnay-Charente and elsewhere in Saintonge.[51] When, therefore, on 19 March 1755, Daniel Augier married Hippolyte Jacau at Louisbourg, where he had sailed in 1750 with Élie Allenet, he may have been marrying as a sincere Roman Catholic, but we are entitled to doubt this because of his Protestant background, and because the ceremony was attended by a Benoit and a Morin, and Allenet was not present only because the governor and Intendant had sent him back to France in disgrace for heresy.[52]

If there is a certain religious confusion in marriages such as this one, many others are plainly alliances of Huguenot families discreetly faithful to their own social and religious community. Genealogical charts are easily drawn showing marriage links between the Aliés,

[48] Protestant registers at municipal libraries at La Rochelle, Marennes, Nieulle, etc.

[49] A. D. Ch. Mar., 2 J 94 and the mun. lib. of La Rochelle.

[50] Arch. de la ville de Bx., alphabetical tables.

[51] Paris registers at the town hall of Tonnay-Charente.

[52] PAC, G[1] 409, *État civil de Louisbourg*; Bosher, 'French Protestant Families in Canadian Trade', p. 193.

Bonfils, Boudet, Dumas, Meynardie, Paillet, and Thouron families; or the Goudal, Massac, Peire (or Lapeyre), and Texier families; or the Admyrault, Giraudeau, and Oualle families, and so on. At Bordeaux, La Rochelle, and Montauban, Huguenot families were nearly all related in some degree, but by the scattering of fugitive families they also had relatives in several towns of the south-west, and even at foreign ports. Huguenot families were seldom confined to one town or even to one country. If they were not all related, this was not because of geographical dispersion but because rich successful clans seldom intermarried with poor struggling clans. They employed them: the Huguenot merchants who came out to Canada were nearly always the younger members of a family or its poor relatives. If they were not related to their richer employers who stayed in France, then they were unlikely to bridge the social gulf separating them, except by becoming rich themselves. Pierre Payes of Montauban was at Québec in the 1730s as an agent for Daniel Rauly; François Havy of Normandy was there as an agent for Robert Dugard of Rouen; and Joseph-Abraham Dérit was there in the 1750s as an agent for Pierre Guiraud and Pierre Fesquet of Bordeaux, who employed his brother, Jacques Dérit, as their clerk.[53]

Marriage alliances between families of New Converts are almost certain signs of Protestantism, whereas alliances with old or official Catholic families betray a weakening of links with Protestant society. In some families, different branches went in different directions, as each couple with children to marry wrestled with the difficulty of remaining faithful to the harried and dispersed Protestant community and with the temptation of opportunities that were open only to Catholics. For example, a little study suffices to discover that some of the Dubergier and Minvielle families of Bordeaux married into Catholic society whereas others remained firmly Protestant. At La Rochelle, the Bultel, Depont, and Seignette families divided in the same way. To illustrate the complexity of the problem it is worth pointing out that John Clark, in *La Rochelle and the Atlantic Economy of the Eighteenth Century*, identifies the Depont and Seignette families as Protestant in the eighteenth century, whereas Robert Forster, in *Merchants, Landlords, Magistrates: the Depont Family in Eighteenth Century France*, declares that 'the Depont family was among the *négociants* who converted' and that 'Already in 1690 a few important Protestant

[53] ANQ, Barolet (Que.), 28 Oct. 1735 and 7 Oct. 1736; ADG, Rauzan (Bx.), 17 Nov. 1754.

notables were converted, including ... Doctor Seignette'.[54] For the Depont family, Forster drew his conclusions from an intensive study of family papers including correspondence showing the firm Catholic views of Paul-François Depont (1700-74). This, at least, seems to be firm ground, until we discover that this Catholic member of the family continually urged his son in Paris to rely on the friendship of François-Abraham-Marie Mouchard (1712-82) from another family of New Converts related to the Depont family in the previous generation, and we find a Protestant, Abraham Mouchard, settled at Amsterdam by 1720 as a merchant and banker.[55] Even the Depont family and their Mouchard relatives melt into a mist of religious ambiguity. Should we describe them as Catholic New Converts to distinguish them from Protestant New Converts? To escape persecution and to win the advantages of royal office, these families had converted–or had they? What prompted Charles-Jean Depont to join the revolutionary Committee of Thirty in 1789 and to strike up an acquaintance with Edmund Burke?[56]

The problem of religious identity was often posed in the eighteenth century, and in various forms, as may be seen in the case of the Aché-Penettes-Rocquier clan of Bordeaux. At some time after the revocation of the Edict of Nantes (1685), part of the Protestant Aché family emigrated to Amsterdam where a certain Pierre Aché was still living as a merchant in the 1740s. His two nieces, daughters of his brother, Jean Aché, who remained at Bordeaux, married merchants in 1713, one a Huguenot, Pierre Penettes, who was trading with Pierre Aché of Amsterdam, and the other a certain Mathieu Rocquier. When Rocquier died in 1750, his widow in 1753 went into partnership with her brother-in-law, Jacques-Armand Penettes *jeune*, whereupon one of her late husband's friends drew up a formal warning that Penettes would have a Protestant influence on the Aché children which was contrary to Rocquier's desire to have them brought up Catholic.[57] This case offers a glimpse of the religious struggle in certain merchant families and the problem of distinguishing Protestants from Catholics.

[54] Clark, *La Rochelle and the Atlantic Economy during the Eighteenth Century*, pp. 45 and 95; Robert Forster, *Merchants, Landlords, Magistrates: The Depont Family in Eighteenth-Century France* (Baltimore, 1980), pp. 19-20.

[55] Forster, *Merchants*, pp. 29 and 71; Price, *France and the Chesapeake*, p. 535; A. D. Ch. Mar., notes Garneau for both names.

[56] As Forster describes, *Merchants*, pp. 185-91.

[57] ADG, Bernard (Bx.), 9 May 1713, marriage contract for Marguerite Aché and Pierre Penettes; Rauzan (Bx.), 1 July 1755; Bernard (Bx.), 22 May 1753; Séjournée *l'ainé* (Bx.), 29 June 1753.

Identifying Huguenot merchants has not interested Canadian historians much. This is partly because only people who lived in Canada are thought to be of any interest in our history. By focusing attention upon the merchants established at Québec, Montréal, or Louisbourg, the Canadian historian has been able to ignore the Huguenots because they were forbidden to settle here in families. They remained a fraction of the *marchands forains*, outsiders or intruders in New France, almost as insignificant as the Jews. Also, most economic and social historians assume a merchant's religion to be irrelevant, in the belief that human behaviour is determined by economic circumstances.[58] Anyone who interprets merchants as part of a bourgeois class engaged in a struggle with the feudal nobility is likely to overlook families and religious groups. He is unlikely to notice that religious groups were also social groups. Most of all, a historian who tries to identify and interpret Huguenots can easily appear to be bigoted.

Marc-André Bédard's efforts, for instance, seem bigoted to Marcel Trudel, who writes: 'In his book, *Les Protestants en Nouvelle-France*, Marc-André Bédard . . . persists in classifying as Huguenots some immigrants who, after recanting, signed Catholic acts [of baptism etc.]. He supposes these converted Huguenots were able to keep their religious principles secretly. The thing is not impossible, but how can the historian prove it in individual cases? The impossibility of seeing into the private conscience in no wise troubles this author, who goes on adding to his lists of names with total unconcern.'[59] As these remarks of Trudel suggest, anyone who wishes to argue that Huguenot merchants were in fact Catholic has only to produce all the proofs of Catholicity which French authorities used to wring from the Huguenots. Identifying Huguenots is certainly difficult for the historian who, like Professor Trudel or Monsieur Bédard, tries to identify individuals in Canada without tracing their kin. But whoever makes a special study of Huguenot families, clans, and communities, following them where they went, tracing the marriages that kept them together generation after generation, will see them quite clearly. Table 11 shows my own list, to be treated with caution for the reasons explained in these pages.

[58] For example, the otherwise excellent works of Lionel La Berge, *Rouen et le commerce du Canada de 1650 à 1670* (L'Ange-Gardien, 1972); Dale Miquelon, *Dugard of Rouen* (Montréal, 1978); and Pierre Dardel, *Navires et marchandises dans les ports de Rouen et du Havre au XVIIe siècle* (Rouen, 1966).

[59] Marcel Trudel, *Histoire de la Nouvelle-France*, vol. iii, tome 2, 'La Société' (Montréal, 1983), p. 31.

Table 11. Some Huguenot Families in the Canada Trade 1715–1760

Name	Town	Years known
Admyrault, Pierre-Gabriel	LR	1748-58
Aliés, Joseph	LR	1752-9
*Allenet, Élie	Tonnay-Charente and Louisbourg	1740s-50s
*Augier, Étienne	Tonnay-Charente and Louisbourg	1740s-50s
Baour, Pierre	Bx.	1750s
Bérard, Joseph	Bx.	1750s
Blanzy, Henri	Bx.	to 1715
*Bonfils, Pierre (and several other members of the family)	LR and Québec	1715 to 1750s
Boudet, Pierre	LR	1736-59
Brevet, Henri	LR	1740s-50s
Courrejolles, La Veuve de Gabriel	Bayonne	1750s
*Courrejolles, Bernard	Québec	1750s
Delacroix, Théodore	LR	from 1749
*Delanne, Pierre	Montauban and Québec	from 1749
Delon, Simon, Jacob, Jean-Pierre, etc.	Montauban	1750s
*Dérit, Joseph-Abraham	Québec	1751
Dérit, Jacques	Bx.	1750s
Desclaux, Pierre	Bx.	1750s
Domenget, Jean and Pierre	Bx.	1750s
Draveman, Théodore	Bx.	1750s
Dugard, Robert	Rouen	1729-48
*Dumas, Alexandre	Québec	from 1751
*Dumas, Libéral	Québec	from 1751
*Dumas de St Martin, Jean	Québec	from 1751
Dutilh	Montauban	1750s
Emmerth, Wilhelm-Christian	LR	1750s

Faneuil	Boston and LR	*c.* 1714
Faure, Élie	Martinique	1727-30
Faure Lacaussade, Jean-Antoine	Bx.	1758
Fesquet, Pierre	Bx.	1730-40
*Fraisse, Jean-Antoine	Québec and Montauban	1749
Frescarode, Dominique and Pierre	Bx.	1740s
Garesché, Isaac and Jacques	Marennes an LR	from 1730
Garrisson, Pierre	Montauban and Bx.	1740s
*Gauthier, Jacques	Québec and Montauban	from 1752
Germé, Sébastien and Noel	Bx.	to 1730s
*Giraudeau, Antoine	Québec and LR	1750s
*Giraudeau, Benjamin	Louisiana and LR	1750s
*Glemet, Pierre	Québec and Jarnac	from 1744
Goudal, Henri	Bx.	1742-54
*Grelleau, Jean, *l'ainé*	Québec and LR	from 1748
*Grelleau, Jean, *jeune*	Québec and LR	from 1753
Guiraud, Pierre, *fils ainé*	Bx.	1751
*Havy, François	Québec, LR and Bx.	from 1730
*Jarnac, Pierre de	Québec and LR	1744-52
Jauge, Simon	Bx.	1740s-50s
Lacaze, Joseph	Bx.	1753-6
*Lacaze, Jean	Québec and Montauban	1740s-50s
*Lacaze, Jean, *jeune*	Québec	from 1754
*Lagrange, Conte	Québec and Bx. (?)	from 1753
Laurens, David	Rouen	1729-48
*La Peyre (or Peire), Pierre	Québec and LR	1709
La Peyre (or Peire), Jean-Pierre, *jeune*	LR	1724
La Peyre (or Peire etc.), Étienne, *l'ainé*	Bx.	1740s
*Lefebvre, Jean	Québec	1732-58
*Leveque, François	Québec	1749-87
Luetkens, Jean-Jérome and Henry	Bx.	1740s
*Malroux, Antoine	Québec	from 1749

Table 11. (Cont.)

Name	Town	Years known
*Marette	Québec and Rouen	1750s
Mariette (many family members)	Montauban	1740s-50s
Massac, Pierre, *père*	Bx. and Tonneins	1740s-50s
Massac, Pierre, *fils ainé*	Rouen	1750s
Massac, Louis (nephew)	Bx.	1750s
*Maurin, François	Québec	1750s
*Meynardie, Pierre-Claude	Québec	1750-5
*Meynardie, Élie	Québec	1755-9
*Morin, Henri	Québec	1754
Morin, Victor	LR	1750s
*Mounier, Jean-Mathieu	Québec and LR	1736-58
*Mounier, François	Québec	1740-60
*Mounier, Jean	Québec	1750
Oualle, Thomas	Bx.	1750s
Paillet, Nicolas	LR	1748-58
*Payes, Simon and Pierre	Québec and Montauban	1730s, 1741
Penettes, Jacques-Arnaud	Bx.	1750s
Penne, Pierre	Bx.	1750s
Perdriault, Pierre-Louis	LR	1748-58
Rasteau, Pierre-Jacques and Pierre-Isaac	LR	from 1748
Rauly, Jean and Arnaud	Montauban	1750s
*Richard, Jacques	Québec and LR	1718-22
Richard, Pierre	LR	1718-22
Rocaute, Jean-Baptiste	LR	1733
Rocaute, David-Pierre	Paris	1753
*Rouffio, Jean	Québec	from 1749

*Rouffio, Joseph	Québec	from 1750
Rouffio, Dominique, François, Pierre	Montauban	1750s
Roullaud, Jacob	Bx.	1703-23
*Schindler	Québec and Bx.	1750s
*Schmidt	Québec and Bx.	1750s
*Senilh, Joseph	Québec	1752-64
Senilh, Jean-Pierre	Montauban	1750s
Serres, Bernard, Jean and Jean-Pierre	Montauban and Bx.	1740s
*Texier (?)	Québec and Bx.	1730s
Texier, Jacques	Bx.	1750s
*Thouron, Antoine-David	Québec	1741-50s
*Thouron, Bernard	Québec	1751-50s
Thouron, Jean-Isaac	LR	1729-60
*Turpin, David	Québec	1741
Vernhès, Abel	Bx.	1744-54
Vincent, Gédéon and Gédéon-Samuel	Rouen	1729-45

* visited Québec or Louisbourg.

7

Huguenot Recovery in the Trade

THE problem of identifying Huguenots in the Canada trade is at its worst for the years when persecution was at its worst; that is, before about 1730. They were largely driven out of the trade in the years 1685 to 1730. Only a few remained in it, and they are comparatively unknown. In the 1730s and 1740s Huguenots began to come back into the trade, and their share of it increased until the British conquest. This increase cannot be reduced to tidy tables because there are no archival sources for compiling complete figures of cargoes, ships, or financial returns. It can be shown in a general way, however, by identifying trading families and clans and gathering the fragmentary evidence of their trade that survives at several ports. This evidence, slowly accumulated from voluminous notarial minutes that bear mainly on other subjects, affords a knowledge of the Canada merchants that can be gained in no other way. In the absence of anything better, the historian has to be grateful for it.

At Bordeaux, the family firm of Pierre and Henry Blanzy, *père et fils*, and Jacob Roulland (husband of Marie Blanzy) were in the trade until their bankruptcy on 27 July 1715, and we find that Jacob Roullaud, who must have recovered, was still in the trade when he died on 8 April 1731.[1] This firm was formed in 1695, and in 1703 Roullaud, then resident at La Rochelle, asked a certain Paul Berthon to collect money due in Canada. In 1714, *Blanzy et Roullaud* sent a shipment of cloth to Catignon at Québec, one shipment of many but the only one to come to our attention.[2] The firm's bankruptcy the next year was apparently precipitated by the suspicions of one of their creditors, a big Catholic merchant, Jean Jung de Saint Laurent, who on 26 July 1715 formally requested all *Blanzy et Roullaud's* debtors to pay him directly until he had been repaid for cargoes of sugar and indigo he had brought for them that year on his ship, *Le Saint Laurent*, which

[1] ANQ, Chambellon (Que.), 13 Nov. 1703; ANG, Bernard (Bx.), 26 July and 23 Sept. 1715 and 30 July 1733, Lamestrie (Bx.), 9 July 1721 and 30 Apr. 1723; 7 B 396; A. D. Ch. Mar., Delavergne (LR), 17 Aug. 1761.

[2] A. D. Ch. Mar., B 4202.

had, as usual, called at Québec.[3] At least three of their creditors who met on 31 July at Jacob Albert's house, rue Neuve, were known in the transatlantic trades: Albert himself, Paul Depont of La Rochelle, and *Pigneguy et Crespin* of Bordeaux.

By 1721, however, Jacob Roullaud was back in the trade, borrowing from a fellow Huguenot, Paul Griffon, for his half interest in *La Suzanne Marguerite* bound for the West Indies that year, and acting for friends at La Rochelle, such as Jacques Leclerc, Sieur Daguesta, who in 1723 sent *La Marie-Joseph* of La Rochelle (Captain Pierre Bonfils) to Québec and Martinique, and who still owed 2,391 livres to Roullaud's widow in 1733.[4] Roullaud also did much business with the Québec-La Rochelle partnership of Estournel and Catignon in the years 1719-25. We lose track of Roullaud's family thereafter, but in the 1760s his daughter was still in a Huguenot shipping firm with the well-known Huguenot families of Nairac and Balguerie. There was no ambiguity in the Huguenot marriage alliances of the Blanzy and Roullaud families. Their marriages took place at Catholic churches, of course, as did their baptisms, but they married into the families of Rocaute, Nairac, and DelaCroix whose Protestant identity was firm beyond any doubt.

Another Huguenot clan active in the Canada trade throughout the worst years of persecution was the Bonfils-Germé clan.[5] The Bonfils family came from the village of Vaux near Royan and the estuary of the Seudre River, characteristically Protestant, whence they sent fishing vessels to Newfoundland in the 1660s and 1670s. During that period, Pierre Bonfils, merchant of Vaux, married into the family of Pierre Chaillé of Chaillevette near by, and their children became merchants and sea-captains in the transatlantic trades of La Rochelle and Bordeaux. They were, for example, part-owners of *Le Saint Jérôme de Canada*, 250 tx. (Captain Jean Dupuy), wrecked on 'l'île du cap de Sable' on the return journey from Canada in 1714, and owners of *La Princesse de La Rochelle*, which went to Québec in 1715. During the chaotic post-war years, following the Treaty of Utrecht (1713), they got into difficulties. A new partnership arrangement formed on 8 March

[3] ADG, Bernard (Bx.), 26 July and 23 Sept. 1715.

[4] ADG, Bernard (Bx.), 30 July 1733; A. D. Ch. Mar., B 4202.

[5] A. D. Ch. Mar., E 5711, 7 May 1715 and 24 Sept. 1715; ADG, 6 B 23, fol. 13 (1 Jan. 1718), 7 B 396 (1715), Bernard (Bx.), 27 Apr. 1714, 1 Aug. 1720, Lamestrie (Bx.), 13 May 1722 (2 minutes); St Michel (Bx.), 16 Aug. 1736, marriage of Pierre Germé and Marie Marcon; ANQ, Dubreuil (Que.), 9 Feb. 1716 (*inv.*: AN Y 11654, *scellés* for Jean Bonfils, Colonies C^{11A} 36, fol. 164, MC Étude CXXI, 23 Mar. 1725. *inv.*

1715 by three of the brothers, Pierre Bonfils of Alvert-en-Saintonge, Hellies Bonfils of Bordeaux, and Jean Bonfils of La Rochelle, failed to save them from the effects of their wartime losses and what they described as 'the insolvency of most of their debtors'.[6] On 1 April 1715, they came to an agreement with their assembled creditors to repay 60 per cent of their debts in eighteen months. To recover what was owing to them, Jean went to Havana, St Domingue, and Jamaica, and Pierre to London and Jamaica 'to pursue the recovery of their frigate, *L'Aymable Marie*'. At Québec, their agent, another Pierre Bonfils who lived 'sous le fort', died on 15 October, soon after receiving news of the bankruptcy, and the Pierre Bonfils *jeune* who came to clear up their affairs had difficulty in realizing their assets, including a small vessel, a bark of 20 tx. worth 2,500 livres, a half share in a ketch, *La Sainte Anne* worth 5,000 livres, and some wheat kept at Batiscan by Charles de Bled, worth 1,680 livres. By 1 August 1720, the Bonfils brothers were asking their creditors to accept the 7 per cent they had managed to collect. Five years later they were still trying to recover what was owing to them. Jean Bonfils of La Rochelle died alone in Paris on 8 February 1725 in a fourth-floor furnished room in the rue St Honoré, leaving a leather trunk full of claims on his family's debtors for 50,000 livres from the estate of the big Canada merchant, Pierre Plassan, and large sums from de Neuville, from Desroches, from the naval treasurers, and others.

In the 1740s, a later generation of Bonfils merchants, still staunchly Protestant, were back in the Canada trade, and a Charles Bonfils was trading in St Domingue. By then, too, they had intermarried with the DelaCroix and Admyrault families, both in the trade during the mid-eighteenth century.[7] Pierre-Tresahar Bonfils and Theodore DelaCroix sent *La Couronne* of La Rochelle (300 tx.) to Québec in March 1748 and she returned on 28 June 1749. In 1757, they both bought shares in a snow, *Le Chonaguen* (125 tx.), Bonfils five-twelfths and DelaCroix one-twelfth, the remaining half share being owned by Abraham Dérit of Québec (one-sixth) and three other Huguenots; together they dispatched her immediately to Canada with a cargo from Marseille.[8]

Meanwhile, since the 1690s two of the Bonfils sisters, daughters of

[6] ADG, 7 B 396 (1715); Bernard (Bx.), 1 Aug. 1720.

[7] J. F. Bosher, 'A Quebec Merchant's Trading Circles in France and Canada: Jean-André Lamalétie before 1763', *Histoire sociale* (Ottawa), vol. ix (1977), p. 29.

[8] A. D. Ch. Mar., B 5747; Université de Montréal, Collection Baby, U 9252.

Pierre Bonfils and Marie Chaillé of Vaux, wives of two brothers from a Huguenot family of Brittany, too, had been active in the transatlantic trades. The two husbands, Sébastien and Noel Germé, traded with Irish and Breton ports, with Louisbourg during its earliest years, and in the Newfoundland fishing trade, all in association with their Bonfils relatives. In 1718, one of their sons had qualified at Bordeaux as an ocean pilot, having served on voyages to Newfoundland, the West Indies, Spain, Portugal, England, and the Canary Islands. In 1722, they borrowed 7,000 livres from Raymond Dubergier for Élie Bonfils *jeune*, a merchant of La Tremblade-en-Saintonge, who was sending his ships, *La Catherine de la Tremblade*, 80 tx., to Cape Breton Island and Martinique, and *Le Gédéon Galère*, 80 tx., to the Newfoundland fishing banks. After *Germé frères* went bankrupt on 10 January 1725, and Sébastien died three years later, there remained enough wealth and prestige in the family for a son of Noel Germé and Esther Bonfils to marry into the respectable Huguenot family of Élie Marcon, related to the Balguerie, Goudal, and Peire families.

There are certainly other Huguenot firms still to be identified in the trade during the early eighteenth century, but so difficult to find that our clues and speculations may be worth reporting. Jean-Pierre Lapeyre (sometimes 'Peire') of La Rochelle, trading in Canada as early as 1701 and in partnership at Québec from 1724 with Jean-Pascal Taché, was probably from the same family as Étienne Lapeyre *l'aîné* of Bordeaux, and so related to the Bérard, Texier, and Goudal families of Huguenot merchants, all in the Canada trade at one time or another.[9] Taché himself was probably not a Protestant, though he traded a great deal with the Huguenot, Abel Vernhès of Bordeaux, and later employed a Protestant clerk, Antoine Malroux, at Québec. Yet another Huguenot merchant in the Newfoundland cod trade and general transatlantic shipping in this period was Jacques Fesquet, the son of a Nîmes merchant, in partnership with his brother, Pierre Fesquet, resident at Marseille, from sometime before 1720.[10] After Jacques Fesquet's death on 22 February 1730, his widow and sons carried on the business and in the 1750s employed a Protestant from Bergerac, Jacques Dérit, who had a brother trading at Québec. This was Joseph-Abraham Dérit who went to Québec in 1751 and died in the British Isles on his return journey to France in December 1759.

[9] A. D. Ch. Mar., *Rivière et Soullard* (LR), 14 Feb. and 20 July 1709.

[10] ADG, Bernard (Bx.), 25 May 1710, marriage of Jacques Fesquet and Jeanne Guiraud, 5 July 1720, 2 June 1722, 28 Sept. 1724.

Other names will certainly be discovered to add to these few, but there were not many in the early eighteenth century.

Huguenot merchants had only a small share of the Canada trade in the twenty years after the Treaty of Utrecht. Decimated and demoralized by persecution, they had little chance of trading successfully in a Catholic outpost such as Québec until times had changed. And, from the 1720s, times did begin to change for at least four reasons: the Crown's anti-Protestant crusade began to die down after the death of Louis XIV in 1715, at La Rochelle from about 1725, as Louis Pérouas has explained;[11] after a period of economic recession in the later years of Louis XIV's reign, French trade and industry began to revive; the Canada trade expanded with all the colonial trades and with the growth of the Canadian population; and the commercial and naval power of the rising Protestant countries aided and stimulated the Huguenots. For these reasons, from approximately 1730 Huguenot firms showed new enterprise. Canada was not as big a market as the Levant for woollens, but as its population grew it attracted more and more of the trade in woollens from Montauban, in cotton and linen goods from Rouen, wine and brandy from Bordeaux and La Rochelle, and in a wide range of hardware and houseware. Huguenot firms of manufacturers and traders were prominent in these trades.

The best-known is the *Compagnie du Canada* founded at Rouen in 1729 by Robert Dugard with several partners, of whom Laurens and Vincent may have been Huguenot, D'Haristoy may have been, and France was almost certainly descended from a branch of the Portuguese Jewish family of Francia that still flourished at Bordeaux under its original name.[12] This company sent at least thirty-three vessels to Canada in the years 1730 to 1749, mostly with cargoes from La Rochelle or Bordeaux, and created a considerable network of business relations. All or nearly all were Protestant: Havy, Lefebvre, and Levèque who were their agents at Québec, Luetkens and then Goudal at Bordeaux, Aliés at La Rochelle, Feray at Le Havre, Rocaute and Desfiguières at Marseille, and most (though not all) of their other correspondents. There were other Huguenot Canada merchants at Rouen, notably Le Vieux in partnership with David

[11] Louis Pérouas, *Le Diocèse de La Rochelle de 1648 à 1724: sociologie et pastorale* (Paris, 1964).

[12] For the history of this firm's trade and shipping, Dale Miquelon, *Dugard of Rouen: French Trade to Canada and the West Indies, 1729–1770* (Montréal, 1978).

Turpin at Québec, to whom he sent *La Minerve* (150 tx., Captain Michel Petrimoux) from Le Havre in 1737 and 1739.[13]

From Montauban, Huguenot merchants went out to the Atlantic ports and on to Canada in the course of a revival of the woollen industry.[14] Abel Vernhès, one of the earliest, was apprenticed for two years in 1701 to a Huguenot merchant at Bordeaux, Charles Raymond. In the 1730s and 1740s, until his death on 14 August 1754, Vernhès was sending mixed cargoes from the rue de la Rousselle in Bordeaux to various Québec customers, notably to Taché and to fellow-Huguenots such as Havy, Lefebvre, and Pierre Payes.[15] Vernhès never went to Canada, as far as I know, nor did some of the other Montauban merchants in the Canada trade at Bordeaux: Pierre Garrisson and various members of the Dutilh, Rauly, and Serres families.

Pierre Garrisson, son of Isaac Garrisson of Montauban, first appears in records of the Canada trade at Bordeaux in 1747 when he and a Huguenot of La Rochelle, Joseph Aliés, each bought a five-twenty-fourths share in *Le St Esprit* (100 tx.) of Québec with Pierre Payes, a Montauban Huguenot at Québec, who kept the remaining seven-twelfths. They then renamed her *Le Dragon* of Bordeaux and Nicolas Beaujon fitted her out for a voyage to Québec where she arrived early in July.[16] The next year, Garrisson bought a two-sixths interest in a Dutch dogger, a prize offered at an auction at Brest. The other owners were Jean Mur and 'Giraudeau dit filleau', each for one-quarter, and Jean Fraichinet, a Huguenot merchant of Montpellier, for a sixth. They then sailed her as *La Paix de l'Europe* of Bordeaux. In 1754, Garrisson signed the admiralty registers at Bordeaux for *L'Heureuse* of Québec (120 tx., Captain François Courval) and *Le Saint Firmain* of St Valéry (101 tx., Captain Jean Bremon), bound for Québec.[17] Like all Canada merchants, Garrisson sent consignments of goods on various other men's vessels; for example, to a dozen Canadian customers, including Havy and Lefebvre, in 1748 on *Le St Francois* and *Le St Victor* of Bordeaux owned by *Doumerc et Rozier*.

[13] AN, Colonies, F[2B] 11; Pierre Dardel, *Navires et marchandises dans les ports de Rouen et du Havre au XVIIIe siècle* (Paris, 1963), p. 422.

[14] T. J. Markovitch, *Les Industries lainières de Colbert àla Révolution* (Geneva, 1976), p. 317.

[15] ADG, Guimard (Bx.), 18 May 1701,fols. 547, 590-1; PRO, HCA 32: notably on *L'Aimable Gracieuse* (1744), *La Légère* (1746), and *Le St François* (1748). The apprenticeship was arranged by Abel Petit, merchant, on behalf of the father, David Vernhès, merchant of Montauban.

[16] ADG, 6 B 98*, fol. 97; 6 B 1358 (29 Mar. 1747).

[17] ADG, 6 B 101*, fol. 43.

These vessels were both captured on the way to Canada, as it happened, but Garrisson prospered sufficiently to marry Marie Lafon, in 1749 daughter of Daniel Lafon *l'aîné* and Jeanne Nairac, who brought him a dowry of 20,000 livres in cash.[18]

The Garrisson family were successful enough not to need to go to Canada, but could employ poorer relatives there. Others in this case were the Mariette, Rauly, and Serres families. When Bernard Serres, established as a merchant at Bordeaux, married Marie Roborit in July 1740, they brought the huge total of 123,000 livres to their marriage.[19] When in 1743 Arnauld Rauly, son of Daniel Rauly, a merchant established in the parish of St Seurin, Bordeaux, and of Jeanne Mariette, married Marie Serres, daughter of Paul Serres and Madeleine D'Hollier, the Rauly family brought 30,000 livres to the marriage and the Serres family 22,000 livres.[20] Like an echo, the marriage of their son, Daniel Rauly, at Bordeaux in 1773 was to Suzanne Serres 'living for the last nine years at Bordeaux at the house of Demoiselle Lambert'. When Dominique Delon of Montauban married Susanne-Marie Serres in January 1745, his father promised him 30,000 livres before the marriage, another 20,000 after his own death, and the family house in Montauban.[21] Such families as these might fit out vessels for Canada, as the firm *Serres et Jean Bizet* did in the Seven Years War, but they would not travel there themselves. They had poorer relatives ready to go out to the colonies, families whose dowries ranged as a rule from 3,000 livres to 6,000.

The Rauly family, from Castres, were related to the Dumas, Malroux, Serres, Mariette, and other merchant families of Montauban, of south-west France, and indeed of Atlantic trading society in general.[22] One of the earliest Rauly relatives in Canada was Pierre Payes, son of Paul Payes and Anne Malpela of Villeneuve, a suburb of Montauban, who came to Québec in 1734 to trade in partnership with his Montauban relatives, Arnauld and Estienne Rauly. Another, who came out to Québec later, was Jean-Jacques Gautier. He and his brother Pierre, who stayed in Montauban, both married daughters of

[18] ADG, Lagénie (Bx.), 25 Nov. 1749; Derey (Montauban), 2 July 1748; PRO, HCA 32: 111 pt. 1, and 157.

[19] ADG, Bolle (Bx.), 30 July 1740 registered in the *Contrôle des actes* on 18 Aug. 1740.

[20] ADG, Guy (Bx.), 3 June 1743; A. D. Tarn-et-Garonne, Delmas Montauban), 2 May 1741.

[21] Arch. mun. de Bordeaux, GC 863, no. 285; SSP of 9 Jan. 1745 at Duras registered (*insinué*) 15 Apr. 1746 and deposited with the notary Navarre.

[22] ADG, Guy (Bx.), 3 June 1743; Chaussinand-Nogaret, *Les Financiers de Languedoc*, pp. 137-8.

Marc Dumas and of Marie de Rauly of Montauban.[23] From 1752 to 1759, the firm of *Pierre Delannes & Jean-Jacques Gauthier* at Québec (Delannes had gone out in 1749) were receiving goods from Daniel Mariette *l'aîné*, Dumas and Rauly *frères* of Montauban, and were in partnership with them. They employed a certain Pierre Fraisse (or Fresse) of Montauban as a clerk at Québec, where Jean-Antoine Fraisse had traded since his arrival in 1749. The latter had somehow succeeded in taking his wife, Catherine Delon, in 1750, and they had several children in Canada. I know of no other Huguenot merchant who managed to do this.

Among the Mariette kin at Québec was Joseph Senilh from Caussade-en-Quercy, near Montauban, who went to Québec in 1752 on *Le César* of Bordeaux (Captain Étienne Dassié) at the age of twenty-three and was buried there on 13 August 1764, the first Huguenot to be buried in a Roman Catholic cemetary at Québec.[24] In 1725, the merchant Étienne Mariette had married Jeanne Malroux, daughter of a merchant dyer, and here was another related family ready to go to Canada. Antoine Malroux went to Québec in 1749 at the age of twenty-four to work as a clerk for Taché. Six years later, he returned from a visit home on *La Vièrge de Grace* of St Valéry (Captain Louis Lambert) and remained at Québec until the conquest. In 1757 he bought a five-twelfths share in *Le Monplaisir* (130 tx.), of which the other owners were Élie Vivier (a quarter) and Emmanuel Weis (a third).[25] More prominent in trade at Québec were the three Dumas brothers, Alexandre and Jean Dumas de St Martin from 1751, and Antoine-Libéral from 1752, related of course to the leading merchant families of Montauban.

Working closely with this clan were the Rouffio and Lacaze families of Montauban. Members of the Lacaze family in the trade were scattered about in a useful way. Jean Lacaze *l'aîné* remained in the woollens business at Montauban; at least one member of the family went to St Domingue; Jean Lacaze *jeune* went out to Québec in 1754 to work as a clerk for Jean and Joseph Rouffio, who had gone there in 1749 and 1753. Joseph Lacaze settled at Bordeaux near other Canada

[23] A. D. Tarn-et-Garonne, Hucafol (Montauban), 23 July 1746, marriage; 1 Nov. 1756, will.

[24] ADG, 6 B 51* (14 Apr. 1752); 6 B 403; Trudel, *L'Église canadienne sous le régime militaire*, vol. i, p. 180.

[25] A. D. Tarn-et-Garonne, Vignarte (Montauban), 5 Aug. 1725; ADG, 6 B 52* (20 Mar. 1755); AN, Colonies D^2 C, vol. 53, carton 1, undated letter of the intendant; A. D. CH. Mar., B 5747.

merchants in the rue de la Rousselle. We find him investing in a voyage of *Le St Esprit* (Captain Maubourguet) and in a consignment on *L'Amitié* of Bordeaux (Captain Canonier), both sent to Claparède at Louisbourg in spring 1751. Both these investments were in enterprises of Bernard Douezan who went bankrupt before Lacaze was paid for his goods, worth about 3,000 livres. In February 1756, Joseph Lacaze was arranging for Captain Joseph Rozier of *Le Robuste* of Bordeaux to collect 3,065 livres from Alexandre Dumas at Québec.[26]

The Montauban interest in the Canada trade, entirely Huguenot, was large enough for the loss of Canada in 1759-63 to deal a severe blow to the town. Yet Montauban merchants had no larger a share in the trade than the great Huguenot families of the south-western ports. Some of these, too, went to Québec, or sent their sons or brothers, but most remained at home in their counting-houses, warehouses, and country houses. Theirs was the life that every Huguenot merchant strove to win, for he could aspire to nothing greater, except the life of a merchant and banker in Paris, London, Amsterdam, Geneva, or Hamburg. For most merchants from humble families, or bankrupt families, Canada offered hopes of profitable business, and of business and marrige links with more successful Huguenot families in the transatlantic trades.

At La Rochelle, Pierre Boudet (1705-85) took up the Canada trade in 1733 or thereabouts. In his post-mortem inventory was an item, 'accounts, letters and invoices of Sieur Boudet for Canada, 1733', and similar items for the following years.[27] He sent goods to Canada in 1735 on *La Renommée*, Captain La Fargue, and lost several bales of Canadian furs when *La Vièrge de Grace*, Captain Troplong, was wrecked at 9.30 p.m. on 6 December 1735 at La Prée aux Bœufs on the Marsilly coast near La Rochelle.[28] From 1736, if not earlier, he was in a partnership with his Huguenot cousin, Isaac Thouron, who managed their business at Québec. In 1736 and 1737 they fitted out *La Marie Anne* (180 tx., Captain Charles Macarty), which they named after Boudet's wife, Marie-Anne Dumas, daughter of Moise Dumas of La Rochelle, and in 1738 *Le Orry* (200 tx.). They were selling furs to the Huguenot firm of Sollicoffre at Marseille, to Valentin Schober and Jerome-Frederick Silber of Nuremberg, and many others. In 1741 Boudet bought *Le Saint Pierre* at Québec, and fitted out *Le Saint*

[26] ADG, Lavau (Bx.), 19 June 1753, 30 Apr. 1754, and 27 Feb. 1756.
[27] A. D. Ch. Mar., Delavergne (LR), 8 Feb. 1766.
[28] A. D. Ch. Mar., *Rivière et Soullard, liasses*, 12 Dec. 1735.

THE BOUDET—THOURON CLAN

(Huguenot)

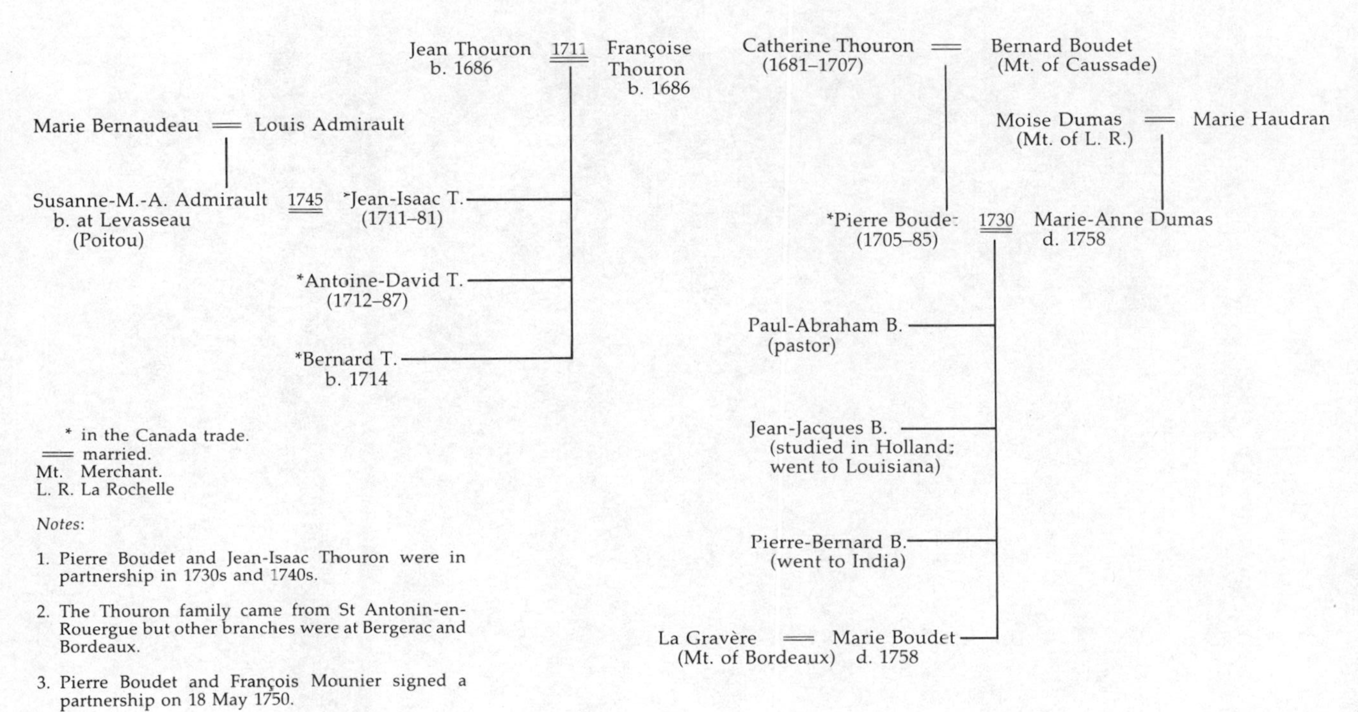

* in the Canada trade.
═ married.
Mt. Merchant.
L. R. La Rochelle

Notes:

1. Pierre Boudet and Jean-Isaac Thouron were in partnership in 1730s and 1740s.

2. The Thouron family came from St Antonin-en-Rouergue but other branches were at Bergerac and Bordeaux.

3. Pierre Boudet and François Mounier signed a partnership on 18 May 1750.

The Port of La Rochelle. *Engraving from a painting by Joseph Vernet.*

Francois (217 tx.) as commission agent for Jean Martel of Québec. In 1743, he and Thouron hired *Le Mars* of Dieppe (90 tx., Captain Jean Élie) for Québec, and in 1746 and later years, these two cousins fitted out *Les Deux Cousins* (200 tx., Captain Jacques Fourneau), also for Québec. On 18 May 1750 Boudet signed a partnership in twenty-six articles with François Mounier, a Huguenot merchant living at Québec, and he also worked closely with Jean Grelleau there in the early 1750s.[29] Without detailing all the evidence of ships and cargoes, it is plain in Boudet's post-mortem inventory and in the files of his principal notaries at La Rochelle that he became a major Canada merchant in the 1750s corresponding with other merchants throughout the Atlantic trading community.

Boudet's cousin, Jean-Isaac Thouron (1711-81), was the son of a goldsmith of St Antonin-en-Rouergue and grandson of a tailor there. He and two of his younger brothers, Antoine-David and Bernard, came early to La Rochelle where they all went into the Canada trade as a family firm. They all went to Québec at various times, Antoine-David, indeed, from 1741 to the middle 1750s, and Bernard from 1751 as his clerk. Other branches of the Thouron family were established at Bordeaux and Bergerac (Dordogne) where they, too, were tradesmen, shopkeepers, and sometimes merchants. In 1745, Jean-Isaac married a first cousin of another big Canada merchant at La Rochelle, Pierre-Gabriel Admyrault (1723-81).[30] The Thouron cargoes on various vessels were many and large, but in 1755, 1756, and 1757 the Thouron brothers fitted out a ship of their own, *Le Beauharnais* (260-300 tx.). When she was seized on 26 May 1757 and sold as a prize at Portsmouth, her captain, Pierre Sicard (a Huguenot mariner from La Tremblade), carried certificates showing her to be carrying flour from Nérac and Moissac and other food worth 44,126 livres, military equipment, and consignments of goods for *Thouron frères*, Admyrault, and others at La Rochelle worth 28,560 livres, freight charges included.[31]

An even larger clan in the Canada trade at La Rochelle formed around Isaac Garesché (1700-69), established at St Sornin near Nieulle and Marennes-en-Saintonge, not many miles from La Rochelle. His was one of the grand Huguenot families with relatives

[29] A. D. Ch. Mar., B 248 (29 May 1738); B 250, *soumission* (14 Apr. 1741); ANQ, J. C. Panet (Que.), 29 Oct. 1753.

[30] A. D. Ch. Mar., Guillemot (LR), 27 July and 3 Aug. 1745.

[31] PRO, HCA 32: 169; A. D. Ch. Mar., Chameau (LR), 20 June 1757.

all over the Atlantic world and links with other merchants in the transatlantic trades.[32] His second wife, Marie-Anne Monbeuille, born in 1710, had been imprisoned as a girl for three months in the convent of Sainte Claire at Saintes in 1730 and there can be no doubt about the Protestant faith of this family. Their children married into three other Huguenot families in the Canada trade: Bonfils, Paillet, and Meynardie. Nicolas Paillet, born to Elisée Paillet and Thérèse Faneuil at Marennes-en-Saintonge on 13 August 1721, was likewise from a substantial but scattered Huguenot family: an André Paillet had emigrated to New York as a Huguenot refugee about 1690; a Jean Paillet at Marseille in 1729 had been commission agent for the Huguenot firm of *Henri Goudal et Renac frères.*[33]

On 11 February 1756, one of Isaac Garesché's daughters married the Canada merchant Pierre-Claude Meynardie *l'aîné* born at Bergerac on 12 September 1719, who at the same time formed a trading partnership with her sister's husband, Nicolas Paillet. Meynardie, who had himself spent some years in Canada, brought 35,000 livres to the capital of the firm.[34] A brother at Québec, Pierre Meynardie *jeune*, cheerfully announced this 'advantageous' arrangement to clients at Montréal.[35] Here was certainly one of the biggest clans of Canada merchants, all firmly Huguenot. They were related, too, to families trading with Canada in a minor way, such as Bonneau (Nicolas Paillet's second wife was a Bonneau), Vivier, Frescarode (of Bergerac, related to Meynardie), and Valette. The Couzard family of Bordeaux was related to a Bordeaux branch of the Meynardie family.[36] Of course these were not all members of the same firm, but for the study of the growing Huguenot share of the Canada trade it is appropriate to group them.

The great family of Rasteau at La Rochelle appear to have been part of this clan, for their Canada trade at least. There were several Rasteau-Paillet marriages, notably of Pierre-Jacques Rasteau (1712-69)

[32] See above, ch. 6; 'Pierre-Isaac Garesché', *Revue de Saintonge et d'Aunis, Bulletin de la Société des Archives historiques*, tome xvi, 4e livraison (July 1896), pp. 288-98; Dorothy Garesché Holland, *The Garesché, de Bauduy and des Chapelles Families: History and Genealogy*, privately printed, (St Louis, USA, 1963), 295 pp.

[33] Lucien J. Fosdick, *The French Blood in America* (1906; Baltimore, 1973), p. 222; ADG, Bernard (Bx.), 17 Oct. 1729.

[34] A. D. Ch. Mar., Chameau (LR), 15 June 1759.

[35] Université du Montréal, Collection Baby, U 8483, Meynardie *jeune* (Que.) to Étienne Augé (Mtl.), 27 June 1756.

[36] For example, Mansset (Bx.), 12 Mar. 1750, Marie Meynardie's will; Perrens (Bx.), 5 Feb. 1750, *cession.*

THE ALIÉS—GARESCHÉ—MEYNARDIE—PAILLET CLAN

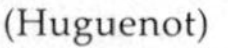

(Huguenot)

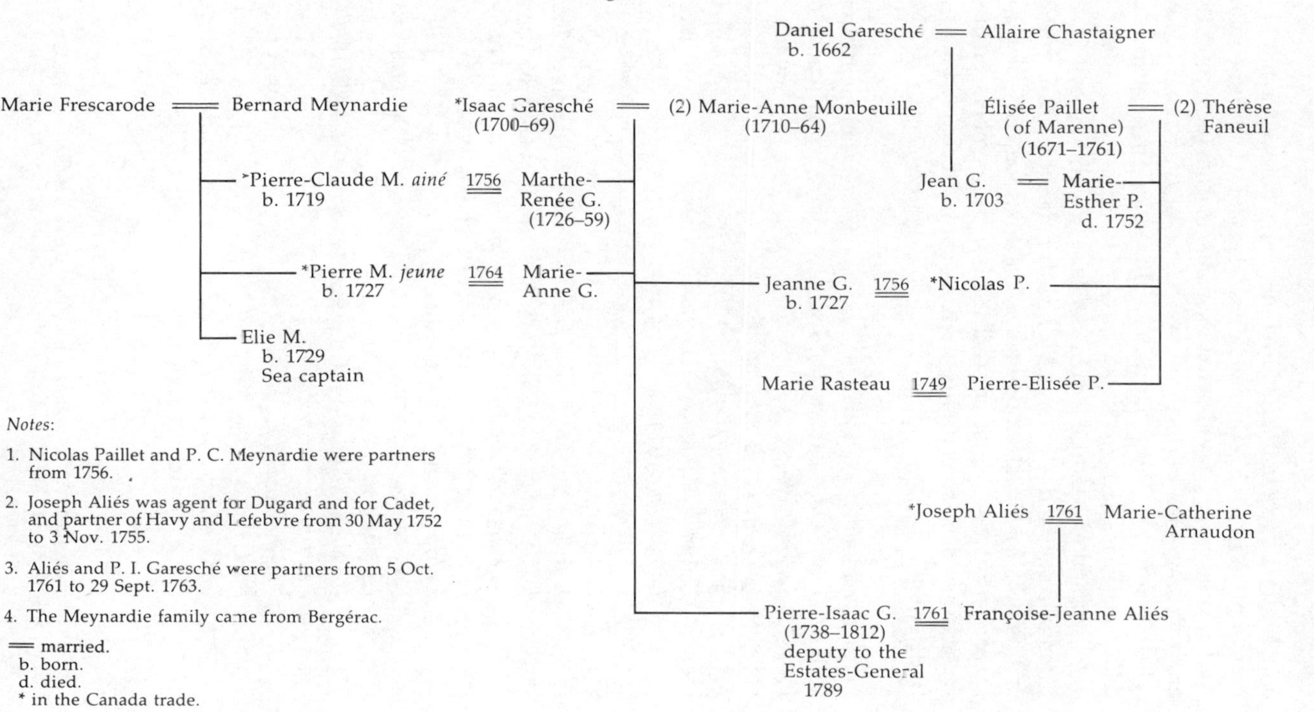

Notes:

1. Nicolas Paillet and P. C. Meynardie were partners from 1756.
2. Joseph Aliés was agent for Dugard and for Cadet, and partner of Havy and Lefebvre from 30 May 1752 to 3 Nov. 1755.
3. Aliés and P. I. Garesché were partners from 5 Oct. 1761 to 29 Sept. 1763.
4. The Meynardie family came from Bergérac.

= married.
b. born.
d. died.
* in the Canada trade.

and Marie-Elisabeth Paillet in June 1748. He was a big shipping merchant and with his brother, Pierre-Isaac, he had some interest in the Canada trade. They claimed 28,464 livres from the Crown for flour and other supplies shipped to Louisbourg on *L'Elisabeth* in May 1754. Their relative, Jacques Carayon, had a share in the expedition of *L'Impératrice* in the 1750s.[37]

Paillet and Meynardie traded extensively with François Chevalier, Étienne Augé, and others at Montréal, and Pierre Meynardie *jeune* at Québec. In the absence of sources for total lists of ships and cargoes, a partial list of ships fitted out by members of this clan, reconstructed from scattered sources, shows their growing Canada trade:

1737	*L'Amitié* (250-300 tx.) of LR	(by) Henri Bonneau
1738	*La Providence* (60 tx.) of LR	Michel Couzard
1747	*La Dorade* (90 tx.)	Nicolas Paillet
1748	*Le Dauphin* (120 tx.) of LR	Nicolas Paillet
1750	*Le Vainqueur* (90 tx.) of St Valéry	N. Paillet
1751	*L'Aimable Marguerite* (120 tx.) of Calais	N. Paillet
	Le Voltigeur (95 tx.) of St Valéry	É. Vivier
1752	*Le Vainqueur*	N. Paillet
1753	*Le Vainqueur*	N. Paillet
1754	*L'Achille*	Jacques Garesché
1756	*La Saintonge* (360 tx.)	Paillet & Meynardie
	Le Dauphin (120 tx.)	Jacques Garesché de Nieulle
1757	*La Jeanette* (170 tx.), a quarter share	*Paillet & Meynardie*
1757	*Le Monplaisir* (130 tx.), a quarter share	Élie Vivier
	La Gracieuse (100 tx.)	Jacques Garesché
	Le Maréchal de Saxe (160 tx.)	Rasteau *frères*
	La Touraine (200 tx.)	Charles Valette
1758	*Le Prince de Condé* (260 tx.)	Paillet & Meynardie
	La Gracieuse	Jacques Garesché
	La Touraine	Charles Valette
	La Canadien (formerly *La Sirène*)	Paillet & Meynardie owned 6/16ths; Valette 5/16ths; Chevalier Lambert, a Paris Banker, 3/16ths.

[37] AN, MC, Étude LXVIII, 8 June 1748, marriage of Rasteau and Paillet; A. D. Ch. Mar., Tardy (LR), 19 May 1755; Arch. de l'État, Geneva, F 31 *bis*, Eynard (Geneva) to Carrayon (LR), 5 Jan. 1759.

In 1758, at the height of their trade, Paillet and Meynardie sent at least 25,816 livres worth of goods to Québec in consignments on ten ships as follows:[38]

La Friponne Capt. Cordier	4,484 livres
Le Prince de Condé, Capt. Bigrel	9,821
La Fille Unique, Capt. Coindet	4,435
Le Grand Gédéon, Capt. Mitau	3,951
L'Orignal, Capt. Dassier	273
L'Astrée, Capt. Sussau (?)	435
La Molly, Capt. Gramont	288
La Légère, Capt. Pascaud	99
L'Aigle, vaisseau du roi	2,030
Le St Dominique, Capt. Darmore	?
	Total 25,816 livres

Among their assets in June 1759 they counted at least 73,000 livres owing at Québec as follows:[39]

A three-sixteenth interest in *La Bonne Amie* and *La Légère* of LR sold at Québec	42,575 livres
A one-eighth interest in *L'Amitié* of LR now *en route* to Québec for the Crown	5,738
A one-quarter interest in *Le Canadien* now at LR	8,000
A nine-sixteenths interest in 15,000 livres due at Québec 'for the effects on *Le Prince de Conde*'	8,000
Due from various clients in Canada	15,000

Another clan in the Canada trade came from Jarnac on the Charente River, where their births are recorded in parish registers and a *Liste des protestants* at the town hall. Their relatives are to be found at Cognac near by, at St Maixent-les-Écoles, and at La Rochelle; among them was Jean-André Mounier, born at Cognac on 7 April 1726 to Jean-Adam Mounier and Jeanne-Françoise Mounier, and 'mort à Québec'.[40] The first of this clan to go to Canada, Jean-Mathieu Mounier (1715-*c.* 1774), arrived in 1736 and stayed for more than twenty years, in partnership with Jean Veyssière of Limoges for much of that time. A nephew, François Mounier (*c.* 1721-69), joined him at Québec in 1740 and traded in partnership with Pierre Boudet and Jean

[38] Université de Montréal, Collection Baby, U 9254, *Paillet et Meynardie*, 10 June 1758.
[39] A. D. Ch. Mar., Chameau (LR), 15 June 1759, inv.
[40] Cognac, Bibl. mun. MM 24.

Grelleau; a cousin, Pierre Glemet (1723-*c.* 1771), came out in 1744, and two more nephews, Henri and Jean, in 1750 and 1751. At some time in the later years, another cousin from Jarnac arrived: the notorious François Maurin, assistant to Joseph Cadet the Purveyor General during the Seven Years War. The archives have much scattered evidence of this clan's transatlantic trade, and Jean-Mathieu Mounier returned to France at the conquest with a fortune of more than 300,000 livres.[41]

At Bordeaux, a large clan of Canada merchants formed around two prominent Huguenot merchants, Henri Goudal from Tournon-en-Agenais, and Pierre Massac *l'aîné* from Tonneins near by, both active in the trade during the 1740s and 1750s. In 1714 Goudal married Marianne Marcon who was related to the Baour, Bonfils, and Texier families. Their daughter Anne married the Canada merchant Étienne Peire *l'aîné* in 1734, and their daughter Henriette married the wine merchant Georges Draveman. In the 1720s Henri Goudal formed a partnership with *Renac frères* whose sister, Marie, had married Mathieu Risteau, Montesquieu's friend, in 1718.[42] The link with the Massac family came on 2 March 1750 when Henri Goudal and Pierre Massac each married a nephew to one of the daughters of Jean Benoist and Jeanne Durfoirt. This brought both families into kinship with Faneuil DelaCroix, born in 1691, of La Rochelle who had married a Benoist cousin, daughter of Noe Benoist and Ester Bussereau, in 1739.

Pierre Massac was related to the Canada merchant Jean Beaujon, whose mother was Ester Massac, but he traded with Canada principally in partnership with the above-mentioned nephew, Louis Massac, and with his own son, Pierre Massac *l'aîné*, who established himself at Rouen. A link with the port of Marseille was established when Massac's daughter Françoise married Charles Raymond, a Huguenot merchant there, son of the Charles Raymond of Bordeaux who had engaged Vernhès in 1701 as an apprentice.[43] Their first involvement in the Canada trade was probably when Robert Dugard of Rouen engaged Henri Goudal as his Bordeaux agent. Goudal's signature is to be found on the admiralty registers for departing ships, such as *Les Trois Maries* of Rouen on 18 May 1742 and 5 April 1743.[44]

[41] A. D. Ch. Mar., B 1459, B 1757 (18 Nov. 1773); Fleury (LR), 14 Jan. 1774, inv.; PRO, HCA 32: 253, *Le Vainqueur*, a few family letters.

[42] ADG, Bernard (Bx.), 7 Aug. 1718; Guy (Bx.), 2 Mar. 1750.

[43] ADG, Guy (Bx.), 2 Mar. 1750, two marriages; Roberdeau (Bx.), 23 Mar. 1724, *partage*; 3 B Présidial, 12 Feb. and 23 Mar. 1767.

[44] ADG, 6 B 97*, fols. 122, 185.

THE GOUDAL—MASSAC CLAN OF BORDEAUX

(Huguenot)

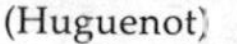

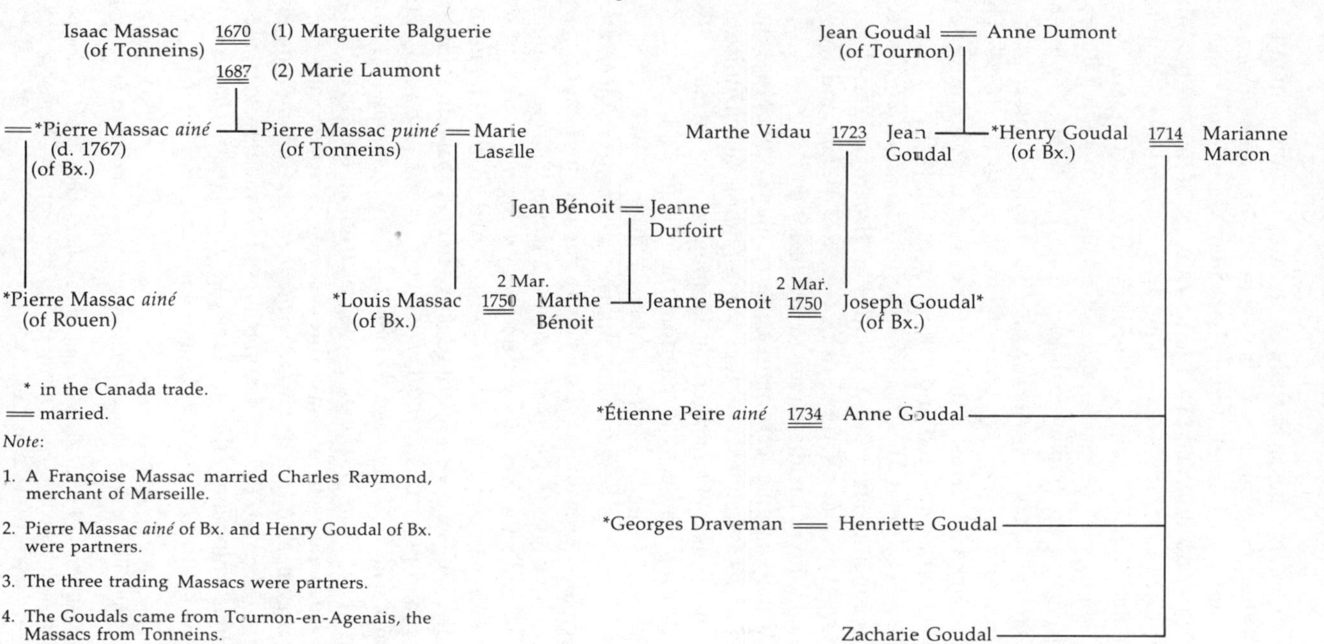

* in the Canada trade.

═ married.

Note:

1. A Françoise Massac married Charles Raymond, merchant of Marseille.
2. Pierre Massac *aîné* of Bx. and Henry Goudal of Bx. were partners.
3. The three trading Massacs were partners.
4. The Goudals came from Tournon-en-Agenais, the Massacs from Tonneins.
5. Henry Goudal was Robert Dugard's agent at Bordeaux.

Goudal then began to trade on his own account, and in 1752 his son and Draveman, his son-in-law, sent *Le Marquis de Malauze* (280 tx., Captain Élie Lortie) to Québec and Martinique. She sailed on 14 April and returned on 21 January 1753, in time to be refitted and sent to Canada again on 29 June. In 1754 a relative, Paul Raymond, dispatched *La Concorde* of Bordeaux (150 tx., Captain Pierre Hirogoyen). By then the firm of *Goudal & Massac* (including Pierre Massac of Rouen) were trading with Havy and Lefebvre of Québec, and in 1753, 1754, and 1755 they sailed *L'Aimable Marthe* (115 tx.) and *L'Aimable Rose* (130 tx.), both of Honfleur, to Québec.[45] They were both seized by British forces on the return voyage in October 1755, loaded with dried cod and timber from Gaspé being sent by Pierre Jehanne to Joseph Aliés at La Rochelle. *L'Aimable Rose* also carried all the belongings of the Naval Controller, Bréard, in seven large packing cases.[46] This was a severe loss to *Goudal & Massac*, and seems to have brought their Canadian trade to an abrupt end.

By these middle years of the century, many other Huguenots whose affiliations are not easy to trace were sending merchandise and fitting out ships. Jean Domenget (or Dominget), for instance, dispatched goods from Bordeaux throughout these years and sent *Le Bien Aimé* (*c.* 200 tx., Captain Pierre Amblard) in 1748. We know he was a Protestant from Bergerac and married a daughter of Jean Dumas and of Jeanne Donnadieu Pelissier at Bordeaux in October 1742, but we know little else. *J. Thouron frères* of La Rochelle were helping to settle the Canadian affairs of a François Domenget in 1766.[47] For another instance, *Arnaud Penne père et fils*, related to the Huguenot Testas family, sent *Le Scipion* of Bordeaux (160 tx., Captain Paul Fradin) in 1752; and two ships in 1758, *L'Aimable Lilique* (400 tx., Captain Jean Reau) and *La Charmante Manon* (400 tx., Captain Henri de Saint Père).[48] Thomas Oualle of Bordeaux, from an old Huguenot family of La Rochelle, sent at least three ships: *L'Achille* (380 tx., Captain Dharaneder) in June 1751, *L'Hercule* (180 tx., Captain Laurent Domé) in 1752, *Le Mars* (250 tx., Captain Joseph Nadau) in 1755. He also sent various shipments, for instance on *Le Marquis Duquesne* (Captain Pisanes), owned by the Huguenot, Fraisse Delon, in 1754.[49] At

[45] ADG, 6 B 1439; 6 B 100*, fols. 147, 150.

[46] PRO, HCA 32: 162, 166.

[47] Arch. mun. de Bordeaux, fonds Delpit, no. 81, Thouron *frères* to Domenget, 1 June 1766.

[48] Paul Butel, 'La Croissance commerciale bordelaise dans la seconde moitié du XVIIIe siècle', thesis, 2 vols. (Univ. of Paris, Lille, 1973), vol. II, p. 687.

[49] ADG, Guy (Bx.), 7 May 1754.

Bayonne, the Courrejolles family, originally merchant hatters of the little town of Damazan, near Agen, sent goods and ships to Bernard Courrejolles at Québec in the 1750s.

To sum up without adding any more details, our shipping lists and other evidence for these years show an abundant and increasing Huguenot share of the trade. In 1757, a busy year in shipments to Canada, Huguenots sent out at least twenty-five vessels, or roughly half of the total. These are listed in Table 12. Already in 1755 the Minister of Marine and Colonies at Versailles had said, in a letter to the Bishop of New France, that the Huguenot firms with representatives in Canada amounted to 'fourteen firms which do three-quarters of the trade of the country, and if we chase them out this would do great harm to the colony, the Canadian merchants not being numerous or rich enough to furnish everything that is needed'.[50] The fourteen firms he referred to were those established in the trade for some years. By then, some of the big families in the West India trade with strong international connections were also shipping to Canada, no doubt in response to appeals and contracts from the Crown.

[50] Minister to Bishop, 15 July 1755, quoted in Abbé Auguste Gosselin, *L'Église du Canada*, 3e partie (Québec, 1914), p. 236.

Table 12. Huguenot Shipping to Québec in 1757

Name	Tonneaux	Owners or Managers
Beauharnois	300	Jean Thouron *frères* (LR). Cargo: food worth 44 125 liv., goods 28 560 liv.
Caducée	300	Izaac Couturier (Bx.), 22 Apr.
Cerès	72	Joseph Aliés (LR, agent for Cadet).
Chonaguen	125	Trés. Bonfils (LR), Abraham Dérit (Que.), Ant. Jacquelin (the capt.), Jean Péry Couillandeau (LR), Th. DelaCroix. A snow, sailed from Marseilles in spring.
Coquette	230	Serres & Bizet (Bx.), 15 Apr.
Diamant	200	Pierre Rocaute de Bussac (Bx.), 11 Mar.
Fortuné	200	Risteau *père & fils* (Bx.), 27 Apr.
Gracieuse	50 or 100 (?)	Jacques Garesché (LR), 12 Mar.
Jeannette	150	André Bernon (LR) P. I. Rasteau (LR), Jacques Carrayon (LR) Paillet & Meynardie (LR) Risteau (Bx.), 2 May.
Liberté	400	Pierre Rocaute de Bussac (Bx.), 25 Apr.
Magdeleine	80	Joseph Aliés (LR, agent for Cadet).
Maréchale de Saxe	160	Pierre-Élie Rasteau (LR) 12 Mar.
Marquise de Galifet	350	Th. DelaCroix, Trésahar Bonfils (LR), Simon Jauge (Bx.), 16 Apr.
Minerve	140	*Veuve* Rocquier & Penettes (Bx.).
Monplaisir	130	Owners: Weis & Co. (LR), J. Malroux (Que.), Élie Vivier (LR), 29 Jan.
Nouvelle Constante	240	*Courtez & Foussat* (Bx.).
Nouvelle Victoire		Pierre Desclaux (Bx., owner and manager). This is not Pascaud's snow of same name and date.
Petite Suzanne	75	Antoine Giraudeau (LR), 12 May.
Rameau	130	*Serres & Bizet* (Bx.).
Saint Antoine	300	Pierre Baour (Bx.), 24 Mar.
Saint Domingue		Mounier (Que., owner), Jean Lagrange (LR, Mounier's agent), Pierre Veyssière, signed.
Surprise	110	Pierre-Gabriel Admyrault (LR, owner). Manager: Jacques Rodrigue (Rochefort).
Touraine	200	Charles Valette (LR), 30 Mar.
Trois Amis	200	Jean Béatrix (Martinique, owner). Manager: Pierre Texier (Bx.), 25 Apr. Québec agent: Dérit.
Turbot	230	*Serres & Bizet* (Bx.).

Note

The dates are of signatures on admiralty registers.

8

The Protestant Refuge

DESCRIBING Huguenots in relation to the French Roman Catholic majority shows them as a shadowy, persecuted minority. They appear in quite a different light when studied in relation to the cosmopolitan world of Huguenot refugees abroad. Huguenots in the Canada trade belonged, in a sense, to those expatriate communities as much as did their friends and relatives who had fled to them. After all, several Canada merchants were to remain in Canada after the British conquest, serving naturally in courts of law, councils, and other institutions of British public life. There was, of course, the obvious religious link by which a Huguenot might find a welcome at one of the thirty-five Huguenot churches in eighteenth-century London, or at churches in Amsterdam, Rotterdam, Hamburg, Berlin, Stockholm, Norwich, New York, and other Protestant cities.[1] But the issues were not merely religious.

In that age, religious differences were inseparable from other differences. A common Protestantism carried with it a political and social tradition of independence, of resistance to oppression, of self-government, which Huguenots shared with the Dutch, English, American, Swiss, German, and Scandinavian cities where refugees had settled. A common struggle for survival against Roman Catholic imperial forces, Habsburg or Bourbon, Spanish or French, gave all these peoples a common historical experience and a common tradition that was very much alive in the eighteenth century. In addition, foreign trade brought together merchants from all the trading nations, but particularly those of the great and growing Protestant seaports. They already formed a cosmopolitan society of their own which we may call, for convenience, Atlantic trading society. It was fundamentally different from Bourbon official society, and a study of that difference is essential to an understanding of the merchants in the Canada trade.

[1] Samuel Smiles, *The Huguenots, Their Settlements, Churches and Industries in England and Ireland* (1868), 6th ed. (London, 1889), pp. 162-3.

The merchants in the Protestant countries were politically much stronger and the clergy much weaker. In the Estates of Holland, merchants and commercial interests had a decisive influence, and these Estates virtually ruled the entire United Provinces through the Grand Pensionary for long periods. From 1651 to 1672 and from 1702 to 1747, the stadtholder of the princely house of Orange was eclipsed by the Holland Estates. Even William III (1672-1702), William IV (1747-51), and his widow, Queen Anna of Hanover (1751-9), daughter of the king of England, governed in accordance with trading interests and the republican institutions that expressed them. In Hamburg meanwhile, noblemen could acquire neither citizenship nor real estate, and the constitution of 1712 had confirmed the governing power of the merchants.[2]

In England, Parliament never lost the fundamental powers it had won against the House of Stuart in the interregnum (1641-60) and even during the last years of Stuart rule maintained an independence 'based on the position of the gentry and provincial merchants in local government. The extent of social, political and judicial power in their hands was formidable, and behind this power lay the sanction of arms, for in the last resort they controlled the militia.'[3] When Parliament came to power in the Glorious Revolution of 1688-9, all those institutions that were to survive in France until 1789–divine right monarchy; 'absolute', authoritarian, paternal government; the authoritarian Catholic Church–were doomed in England, and merchants had a strong voice in the Parliaments of Dutch William III and his successors. Among the members of Parliament in 1720 were more than three score merchants and bankers, including eight directors of the Bank of England, nine East India directors, four South Sea directors, and some distinguished Huguenot refugees.[4] There were never less than fifty merchants and bankers in Parliament during the eighteenth century.[5] In general, the great merchants were already part of the British ruling class. 'About 1760,' writes Sir Lewis Namier, 'trade was

[2] Hajo Holborn, *A History of Modern Germany, 1648–1840* (NY, 1964), vol. 1, p. 31.

[3] J. H. Plumb, *The Growth of Political Stability in England, 1675–1725* (London, 1967), p. 33.

[4] J. R. Jones, *The Revolution of 1688 in England* (London, 1972), p. 330; P. G. M. Dickson, *The Financial Revolution in England* (London, 1967), p. 106.

[5] Romney Sedgewick, *The House of Commons 1715–1754* (London, 1970), vol. i, p. 155; Sir Lewis Namier and John Brooke, *The House of Commons, 1754–1790* (NY, 1964), vol. i, p. 131.

considered the foundation and purpose of the Empire.'[6] This could not be said of France in that period, when imperial strategy and military power appear to have been ends in themselves.[7]

Merchants were even more powerful in the English colonies of North America. In those colonies closest to New France, merchants struggled against religious and landed interests in the colonial councils of the seventeenth century, and emerged in the eighteenth century as 'the ruling aristocracy of New England'.[8] Among the great clans of that aristocracy were Huguenot families such as Faneuil and Baudouin in Massachusetts and Bernon and Ayrault on Rhode Island, to which we might add the Jay and Delancey families of New York and the Manigault, Godin, and Huger families of South Carolina.[9] From 1717, the council of New Hampshire was 'completely dominated by merchants' from Portsmouth and Newcastle, and in Maryland a merchant-planter class with various enterprises became similarly powerful.[10] By the middle of the eighteenth century 'the largest proportion of Philadelphia's wealth as well as social prestige and political power was concentrated in the hands of Quaker merchants of whom a few were of Huguenot origin'.[11] Even Virginia, ruled by tobacco planters, was represented in London by a strong group of merchants who, from the Virginia Coffee House and the Virginia Club on Virginia Walk, were putting pressure on the House of Commons as early as 1670.[12]

Merchants in the Protestant 'republics' had all the more power and prestige because they were not overshadowed by a class of financiers

[6] Sir Lewis Namier, *The Structure of Politics at the Accession of George III*, 2nd ed. (London, 1957), p. 250 and *passim*; Nicolas Rodgers, 'Money, land and lineage: the big bourgeoisie of Hanoverian London', *Social History* (Hull), vol. 4 (1979), pp. 437-54.

[7] W. J. Eccles, 'The Social, Economic, and Political Significance of the Military Establishment in New France', *Canadian Historical Review*, vol. lii (1971), pp. 1-22; 'A Belated Review of Harold Adams Innis, *The Fur Trade in Canada*', *Canadian Historical Review*, vol. lx (1979), pp. 422-3; and 'The Fur Trade and Eighteenth-Century Imperialism', *William and Mary Quarterly*, 3rd series, vol. xl (1983), pp. 342 ff.

[8] Bernard Bailyn, *The New England Merchants in the 17th Century* (1955); NY, 1964), p. 197.

[9] Jon Butler, *The Huguenots in America: A Refugee People in New World Society* (Cambridge, Mass., 1984), chs. 4 and 5.

[10] David E. Van Deventer, *The Emergence of Provincial New Hampshire 1623–1741* (Baltimore, 1976), pp. 219, 224; Paul G. E. Clemens, *The Atlantic Economy and Colonial Maryland's Eastern Shore* (Ithaca, 1980), pp. 134-5.

[11] Frederick B. Tolles, *Meeting House and Counting House: The Quaker Merchants of Colonial Philadelphia, 1682–1763* (1948; NY, 1963), pp. 32, 117.

[12] Alison G. Olson, 'The Virginia Merchants of London: A Study in Eighteenth-Century Interests-Group Politics', *William and Mary Quarterly*, vol. xl (1983), pp. 363-88.

as French merchants were. Business and government in England and Holland were not dominated by financiers such as those looming over the Canada trade, collecting duties, managing the financing of the colony and the navy, issuing the bills of exchange on which merchants depended, dabbling in trade, and dominating the business life of Paris, including the big marine insurance companies. What? exclaims the British historian! What about 'the fifty-odd County Receivers . . . notoriously sluggish in transmitting the money to the Exchequer'?[13] The 'nearly two hundred government *placemen* present in Parliament'? The 'medieval supercargo of redundant officials and expensive sinecurists' in the Customs, Excise, and Salt Tax services, and the Post Office? The Receiver General of the Post Office who 'enjoyed the interest on a part of the quarterly revenue, his regular balance being £15,000 in mid-century'?[14] All the financiers listed in John Carswell's excellent 'South Sea Directory, 1711-21'?[15] The 'jobbers', 'underwriters of loans', the 'government financiers' of whom Namier counts twenty-two in Parliament, the 'monied interest' who made 'the biggest fortunes in the City . . . out of this business of supplying money to the Government'?[16] The Accountant-General of Chancery, the Paymaster of the Forces Abroad, the Treasurers of the Navy and the Navy Board, and all the other paymasters and treasurers? Were not these and their kind equivalent to the financiers of Bourbon France?

No, as anyone who compares the two societies will see, they were not. The Marquis d'Argenson, who compared them in the 1740s, saw the difference clearly: 'The Order of financiers is in France what the Order of merchants (*commerçants*) is in England, and these scoundrels (*maltôtiers*) are only leeches of the people. It is not thus in England, or very little.'[17] He went on to complain of the powerful financier, Paris Duverney, whom he accused of being an absolute ruler 'of three departments of the kingdom, finance, war, and foreign affairs'. He might have added that financiers permeated the business life of Paris

[13] Henry Roseveare, *The Treasury* (London, 1969), p. 95.

[14] Ibid., pp. 87 and 95; Kenneth Ellis, *The Post Office in the Eighteenth Century* (Oxford, 1958), p. 28; E. E. Hoon, *The Organization of the English Customs System, 1696–1786*, new ed. (Newton Abbot, 1968), ch. 1.

[15] J. Carswell, *The South Sea Bubble* (London, 1960), pp. 273-85.

[16] Charles Wilson, *England's Apprenticeship, 1603–1673* (London, 1965), pp. 321-8; Namier, *The Structure of Politics*, pp. 53-6; Roseveare, *The Treasury*, pp. 112-13; D. A. Baugh, *British Naval Administration in the Age of Walpole* (Princeton, 1965).

[17] Voyer d'Argenson, *Journal et mémoires*, 9 vols. (Paris, 1859-1867 vol. 5, pp. 89-90, 100.

and had a stronger voice than merchants in the French government. They and other members of Bourbon official society dominated all the big Paris companies such as the Company of New France in the seventeenth century, the Indies Companies in the age of New France, and the marine insurance companies founded on 29 January 1750 and 27 September 1753, to mention only a few. The comparable English and Dutch companies–the East India, Newfoundland, Hudson's Bay, and Dutch West India, Royal Exchange, and London Assurance Companies–were dominated by merchants.

To understand the difference d'Argenson was discussing, one must begin with the term 'financier' which, like many cognates, is misleading, for it does not mean the same thing in English as it does in French. In eighteenth-century French, a *financier* was defined as 'A man who handles the finances, that is to say the King's funds. In general, this name is given to every person known to have interests in the tax farms, *régies*, enterprises or businesses that concern the King's revenues.'[18] That is, a *financier* was a Farmer General of Taxes, a Receiver or Receiver General, a Treasurer or Treasurer General, or a Payer or Payer General, who had bought his place or office and owned it for the express purpose of managing government funds for profit. He was not merely a *rentier* or investor.

He was not a banker (*banquier*) either, nor had he, in most cases, ever been one. He was even, in a sense, the opposite of a banker, who by definition was a merchant trading in private money as an adjunct to trading in commodities. 'A banker', says P. J. Masson's *Instruction des négociants* (Blois, 1758, p. 6), 'is, properly speaking, a man who trades in money at various places in the world, according to the extent of his (commercial) correspondence; everyone may be a banker; there is no guild (*il n'y a pas de maîtrise*).' Herbert Lüthy uses these terms in the eighteenth-century French sense when he contrasts Protestant merchant bankers with Catholic official financiers.[19] Historians of eighteenth-century England, however, do not see much difference between a banker and a financier, and usually describe a banker who lends money to the Crown as a financier. P. G. M. Dickson, for instance, refers to a group of members of Parliament in 1720 as 'merchants or financiers', though they were certainly bankers in the French sense of the term, and not financiers at all.[20] Dame Lucy

[18] *Encyclopédie méthodique: partie Finance* (Paris, Panckoucke, 1785), vol. ii, p. 203.
[19] Lüthy, *La Banque protestante*, pp. 446, 774, etc.
[20] Dickson, *The Financial Revolution*, pp. 106, 321-8.

Sutherland's 'monied interest' turns out to be, in her own words, 'the rich merchants who might act as contractors or subscribe to government loans and the great corporations on which national credit depended'; and Sir Lewis Namier's 'leading City men in close touch with the Treasury and deeply engaged in Government finance' were, in French terms, *marchands banquiers* rather than financiers, especially as he deliberately omits two who best fit the French term *financier*.[21] The English use of these terms reflects a difference in English institutions and society.

Irrespective of the words used, men in England who acquired wealth and prestige equivalent to those of a French Farmer General or Receiver General were usually either landed noblemen or successful merchants or bankers. Most wealth came from land or trade, not from the manipulation of public revenues. This was because the Bank of England, the Public Debt, and the system of short-term borrowing by Exchequer tallies and bills, departmental credit, and short-term securities, made *les finances* of the French type both unnecessary and impossible.[22] Yet it is doubtful whether there was a class of *financiers* in England even before the administrative changes of the financial revolution. In 1697, only three years after the founding of the Bank of England, Gregory King reckoned that English 'persons in office' were roughly equal in wealth to 'merchants and traders by land' and only half as wealthy as 'merchants and traders by sea'.[23] In no other category but 'persons in office' could he have meant to put the *financiers*, who seemed to him to be neither a major élite nor even a separate social element at all. Merchants were a large, wealthy, prominent class in England, and they eclipsed such *financiers* as there were.

In accordance with the power and prominence of merchants in the seaports of Protestant Europe, society was freer than the society of Bourbon France. As Montesquieu put it in 1748, 'the northern peoples have and will always have a spirit of independence and of liberty, which the southern peoples do not have'.[24] In general, the reporting of news and the discussion of political and religious matters was free,

[21] Namier, *The Structure of Politics*, p. 55; Lucy S. Sutherland, *The East India Company in Eighteenth-Century Politics* (Oxford, 1952), pp. 21-2.

[22] The history of those institutions is partly in Dickson, *The Financial Revolution*, in Roseveare, *The Treasury*, and in Sir John Clapham, *The Bank of England* (Cambridge, 1945), 2 vols.

[23] Wilson, *England's Apprenticeship*, p. 239.

[24] Montesquieu, *De L'Esprit des lois*, 5th part, bk. xxiv. 5.

fearless, and public in the big Protestant ports, but not in the French Catholic ports. Until the late eighteenth century France had nothing equivalent to the many Dutch and English journals founded over a century before. The first daily newspaper appeared in Paris in 1777, but London's first dated from 1702 and by 1760 there were dozens of London dailies and weeklies. Even provincial towns had newspapers, beginning with *The Norwich Post* (1701) and *The Bristol Postboy* (1702), and by 1760 weekly papers were reporting news of foreign and national affairs and transatlantic traffic in at least twenty-nine towns. 'The great mass of news from the Continent was read with a consuming interest week after week by people all over England. . . .'[25] In English North America the history of newspapers is, of course similar. It goes back to 1704 in Boston, and all the colonial cities had newspapers before John Bushell started the first one in what had been a part of New France, *The Halifax Gazette* founded in 1752. The first *Québec Gazette* was not founded until 1764, after the British conquest.[26] In France meanwhile, *La Gazette de France* (1631), *Le Courier Français* (1649), *Le Mercure de France* (1672), and their imitators were quite different, more interested in the royal court, diplomacy, and literature than in politics, maritime trade, and banking. This was true of *La Gazette* published at La Rochelle by Michel Salvin from 1730.

The principal reason for the difference is that the Bourbon government maintained a firm grip on publishing, and censored books and journals with great strictness until the middle of the eighteenth century. This was normal practice in an 'absolute' monarchy, indeed part of the meaning of that term. Heresy, which is to say liberal or republican views on politics and Protestant views on religion, was what French authorities feared, and why they employed 102 Royal Censors (in 1753), at least a quarter of them clergymen, to read and judge everything printed in France or imported: nine for theology, fifteen for jurisprudence, sixteen for 'natural history, medicine and

[25] E. S. de Beer, 'The English Newspaper from 1695 to 1702', in Ragnhild and J. S. Bromley, *William III and Louis XIV: Essays 1680–1720 by and for Mark A. Thomas* (Toronto, 1968), pp. 117 ff.; R. M. Wiles, *Freshest Advices: Early Provincial Newspapers in Englnd* (Ohio State UP, 1965), pp. vii, 193, 198, 218; Joseph Frank, *The Beginnings of the English Newspaper, 1620–1660* (Cambridge, Mass., 1961); J.-P. Poussou *et al., Études sur les villes en Europe occidentale* (Paris, 1983), vol. 2, pp. 168–9.

[26] Isaiah Thomas, *The History of Printing in America*, 2 vols. (Albany, 1874); The Colonial Society of Massachusetts Publications, *A Checklist of Boston Newspapers, 1704–1780* (Boston, 1907); the *Québec Gazette* was a bilingual journal irregularly but frequently published beginning on 21 June 1764. *La Gazette* Michel Salvin, 1730 to 1751, is at the La Rochelle public library (Pér. 398).

chemistry', three for surgery, ten for mathematics, one for 'geography, navigation and voyages', and the rest for 'belles-lettres, history, etc.'.[27] From an Atlantic merchant's point of view, the few journals published in France were dull and false, like Russian journals in our time. They gave no news, for example, about events such as the surrender of Louisbourg to British-American forces on 26 July 1758, and late in September the Paris lawyer, Barbier, was complaining that 'nothing whatever has been said in *La Gazette* about Louisbourg or Cape Breton'.[28]

Consequently, French readers preferred the journals published abroad in French by Huguenot refugees, such as *La Gazette de Leyde*, the best-informed in Europe, edited from 1678 by a graduate of the Calvinist academy at Saumur and from 1738 by the son of a Bergerac merchant.[29] Other favourites were *La Gazette d'Amsterdam* (1663), reprinted at Liège and Geneva from 1728, and *La Gazette d'Utrecht* (1710). These were largely free from censorship or harassment, like all journals in the Dutch Republic and, from 1695, in England. If certain ministers of the Crown, such as Robert Walpole, were able to make vigorous use of the libel laws to silence their political opponents, the swelling volume of news and commentary that appeared in English and other Protestant ports seemed all the greater in contrast with the authoritarian silence that prevailed at French and other Catholic ports. Some of the French Intendants carried on a lively correspondence with the Chancellor at Versailles in an effort to stem the flow of books and newspapers continually arriving in Dutch ships or from the Channel Islands.[30] Even that liberal director of the censorship service (*la librairie*), Lamoignon de Malesherbes, who served from 1750 to 1762, was hostile to foreign gazettes.[31] But he could not keep out all the 'bad' books, including commercial gazettes, that came in from the Protestant countries.

In the half century 1713-63, then, merchants enjoyed much more freedom and political representation in Protestant countries than in France. Merchants in those countries, better able to arrange

[27] *Almanach royal*, Paris, 1753, pp. 366-9.

[28] Edmond-Jean-François Barbier, *Chronique de la Régence et du règne de Louis XV (1718–1763)* (1866), vol. 7, p. 94.

[29] Claude Bellanger *et al.*, *Histoire générale de la Presse française* (Paris, 1969), vol. i, pp. 77-330 (by Louis Trenard).

[30] F. G. Pariset, *Bordeaux au XVIII siècle* (Bordeaux, 1968), pp. 74-5; André Lespagnol *et al.*, *Histoire de Saint Malo*, p. 210; ADG, C 3308, a reference I owe to Miss Jane McLeod.

[31] Pierre Grosclaude, *Malesherbes, Témoin et Interprète de son Temps* (Paris, 1961), p. 73.

institutions to favour international trade, had prospered throughout the age of New France. At the time Québec was founded in 1608, Amsterdam was the commercial and financial capital of Europe, and when Québec was conquered in 1759 London had succeeded to that position. The story of Anglo-Dutch success in maritime trade and international banking has often been told.[32] Geneva, too, became a great banking centre, and so did Hamburg, notable for its exchange bank founded in 1619, and for 'the readiness of Hamburg merchants to give long credit to their customers'.[33] In the course of their activities the merchants of these countries had slowly formed a cosmopolitan society of their own.

This mixed society, which I call Atlantic trading society, was characteristically Protestant because it had formed in the course of those religious conflicts which played such a large part in seventeenth-century affairs. British trade with continental Protestant countries had been encouraged by the reigns of a Dutch king, from 1688 to 1702, and Hanoverian kings from 1714, and by the union with Scotland in 1707. As Charles Wilson and Herbert Lüthy have shown, Dutch and English enterprise had merged by the eighteenth century and formed family networks throughout the Protestant realms.[34] Such English families as the Cliffords, the Barings, and the Hopes, of whom an elder brother, Henry Hope, emigrated to Boston about 1730, became established bankers in Holland, and Dutch bankers such as the van Necks, the van Hemerts, and the Crayesteyns settled in London. It was two merchants from London who formed the Rotterdam marine insurance company in 1720.[35] Prominent in trading and banking circles at all the capitals of the Protestant trading world were French Huguenot refugees. In London and Amsterdam, Geneva and Hamburg, they formed marriage alliances with other Protestant banking families. For example, in London in 1732, the famous Dutch banker Joshua van Neck married Marianne Daubuz, daughter of a Huguenot merchant of London, and in 1734 Gerard van

[32] In many books and articles by C. H. Wilson, J. H. Parry, C. R. Boxer, and especially in Ralph Davis, *The Rise of the Atlantic Economies* (London, 1973), chs. 11 to 18.

[33] Kristoff Glamann, 'European Trade 1500-1750', *The Fontana Economic History of Europe* (London, 1974), vol. 2, p. 512.

[34] C. H. Wilson, *Anglo-Dutch Commerce and Finance in the Eighteenth Century* (Cambridge, 1941); Lüthy, *La Banque protestante.*

[35] Marten G. Buist, *At Spes Non Fracta: Hope & Co. 1770–1815: Merchant Bankers and Diplomats at Work* (The Hague, 1974), ch. 1; Price, *France and the Chesapeake, passim*; Patrick Crowhurst,'Marine Insurance and the Trade of Rotterdam, 1755-63', *Maritime History*, vol. 2 (1972), p. 140.

Neck married the daughter of Hilaire Reneu, a refugee merchant from Bordeaux, widow of Sir Denis Dutrey, another Huguenot refugee in London. International partnerships were formed, such as Tourton (Huguenot) and Guiguer (Swiss), Muilman (Huguenot-Dutch) and Thellusson (Swiss-French).

Huguenots were very much at home in Atlantic trading society, and remarkably successful. Sir Theodore Janssen, a Flemish Huguenot, became one of the founders of the Bank of England and its first director (1694-7), while Sir John Houblon, a descendant of sixteenth-century Huguenot refugees, was serving as the Bank's first governor.[36] Later, other Huguenots served as directors and governors of the Bank, and they came from a rich refugee community that bought about one-tenth of the stock of the various public funds in England, those of the East India Company, the South Sea Company, and the Bank of England, in the period 1694-1714, and over one-fifth of the 3 per cent stock issue of 1726.[37] In addition, according to the names that were registered, most of the early German accounts at the Bank of England were taken out by Huguenots, who also comprised fourteen of the nineteen Dutch subscribers to the earliest Bank stock, while 'of the hundred Irish-domiciled owners of South Sea stock (eighty-three of whom lived in Dublin), no less than eighty-five had Huguenot names'.[38] The biggest of the first three North American holders of British government securities was a Huguenot, André Faneuil of Boston, who held £3,800, and by 1750 there were four Huguenots on the list of fifteen American owners of Bank stock. By then, some 14 per cent of the East India stock was owned by Huguenots living in or around London, and if these are counted together with Dutch-domiciled Huguenots the figure rises to 17 per cent.[39]

Huguenot merchants and bankers also invested in marine insurance in London. In the Royal Exchange Assurance founded there in 1720, at least a score of the 158 governors and directors of the eighteenth century were Huguenots. Some families, such as Bosanquet and Fonnereau, became veritable dynasties of insurance men. When the London Assurance Company was founded in 1720, Huguenots bought about 15 per cent of the first stock issue and

[36] Dickson, *The Financial Revolution*, p. 259 note.

[37] Ibid., p. 321; A. C. Carter, 'Financial Activities of the Huguenots in London and Amsterdam in the Mid-Eighteenth Century', *PHSL*, vol. xix (1956), p. 319.

[38] Dickson, *The Financial Revolution*, pp. 306, 314-17.

[39] Ibid., pp. 321, 330.

comprised about 15 per cent of the total list of investors.[40] They held just under 25 per cent of it by the year 1743, though this figure fell to under 18 per cent during the Seven Years War.

Many of the London stockbrokers and agents were Huguenot. Among them were Pierre Reneu from a Bordeaux merchant family. Alexandre Mariette certainly from Montauban or Orléans, Pierre La Vallette from La Rochelle, and Robert Le Plastrier from Rouen, 'a biggish buyer of skins from the Hudsons Bay Company'.[41] Most Huguenot investors, including the fairly large contingent of women investors, preferred to attend to their own business rather than entrust it to agents, but even they were soon dependent, like investors in general, upon a list of stock prices published annually from the 1690s by a Huguenot refugee, Jean Castaing. His *The Course of the Exchange and Other Things* became a standard manual in the eighteenth century.[42]

The refugees were in touch with their New Convert relatives and friends in France who must be counted as belonging, in some sense, to cosmopolitan Protestant society, even though they were watched and their movements controlled. Refugee families commonly left an abjuring member in France to care for family interests there. Even some of the banking families that served Louis XIV belong on this list. In the English business community could be found the widow, son, daughter, and granddaughter of Barthelemy Herwart (1606-76); several relatives of the fabulously wealthy Samuel Bernard (1651-1739), the famous abjuring member of the family; several members of the rich timber and banking family of Girardot; and members of the Formont family.

A similar case is that of Philip Bureau's daughter from La Rochelle who settled at Ipswich with her husband, Claude Fonnereau, a Huguenot linen merchant, who had spent some years in Hamburg.[43] Their two sons, Thomas Fonnereau (1699-1779) and Zachary Fonnereau (1706-78), became London merchants and bankers and members of Parliament in the same generation as many other Anglo-

[40] Barry Supple, *The Royal Exchange Assurance: A History of British Insurance 1720–1970* (Cambridge, 1970), pp. 76-8; Carter, 'Financial Activities of the Huguenots', pp. 325 ff.

[41] A. C. Carter, 'The Huguenot Contribution to the Early Years of the Funded Debt, 1694-1714', *PHSL*, vol. xix (1956), pp. 34-7; and her 'Financial Activities', p. 319.

[42] Dickson, *The Financial Revolution*, p. 488.

[43] Sedgewick, *The House of Commons, 1715–1754*, vol. ii, p. 41; Carter, 'The Huguenot Contribution', pp. 27-9, 38; Claude-Frédéric Lévy, *Capitalistes et pouvoir au siècle des lumières, des origines à 1715* (The Hague, 1969), *passim.*

French families of Huguenots. Among these were Nicolas Tourton, related to Louis Tourton of Paris, who was a London agent for Continental investors early in the century; Sir John Lambert from the Île de Ré; and a Sellon from Languedoc. Nearly a dozen London bankers were agents or members of Languedoc families: *Elisée et Pierre Auriol, Jean Boissier, Gaspard Sellon et Claude Aubert, Sellon fils et compagnie, Romilly*, and *François Gaussen.*[44] The Gaussen family and their Bosanquet relatives both produced directors of the Bank of England, and members of Parliament. Henry-Charles Raguenneau de la Chesnay, brother of a Paris banker, was reported to be living at 'Beverley, comté de Yorck en Angleterre'.[45] Meanwhile, Huguenot refugees at Hamburg, such as His, Boué, and Godeffroy, had similarly become rich merchants and bankers with many enterprises.[46]

For generations, some Huguenots had been rising to positions of wealth or influence in England, where they lived as attractive examples to the Huguenots still in France. Two members of Parliament from families of sixteenth-century French refugees, John Dubois (1622-84) and Thomas Papillon (1623-1702), both elders of the Huguenot church in Threadneedle Street, were active in the general Protestant cause during the later seventeenth century.[47] Charles Delafaye (1677-1762), served at the British embassy to The Hague (and was present when the Treaty of Ryswick was signed in 1697) and at the High Commission in Dublin, before rising to the eminence of an under-secretaryship in 1717. At his death he left £100 each to the Society for Propagating Christian Knowledge in the Highlands and Islands of Scotland and the Society for Promoting English Protestant Schools in Ireland.[48] He had been elected to the Royal Society in 1725 for his scientific collection and learning, as had the famous Huguenot traveller from Lorraine, Jean Chardin (Sir John Chardin), before him.[49] At least four Huguenots in addition to Delafaye rose to influential positions in the offices of the British secretaries of state.[50]

[44] Price, *France and the Chesapeake*, p. 519; Chaussinand-Nogaret, *Les Financiers de Languedoc*, pp. 182-9.

[45] AN, MC, Étude LXXXIII 536, 7 June 1769, *partage.*

[46] Edouard Mourgue-Molines, 'Les Huguenots refugiés à Hambourg', *Bulletin de l'Académie des Sciences et Lettres de Montpellier*, tome 9 (1978), pp. 62-73.

[47] B. D. Henning, *The Commons, 1660–1690* (London, 1983), vol. iii, pp. 202, 237.

[48] J. C. Sainty, 'A Huguenot Civil Servant: the Career of Charles Delafaye, 1677-1762'., *PHSL*, vol. xxii (1971-6), p. 412.

[49] Laleh Labib-Rahman, 'Sir Jean Chardin, the Great Traveller, 1643-1712/13', *PHSL*, vol. xxiii (1981), pp. 309-18.

[50] These were Claudius Amyand, Antoine Chamier, Benjamin Langlois, and Pierre-Michel Morin (Sainty, 'A Huguenot Civil Servant', p. 399).

Pierre Delmé, to take another example, became Lord Mayor of London in 1724, by which time he owned nearly £300,000 in shares of the Bank of England, the East India Company, and the South Sea Company.[51] He had been a member of Parliament, like Sir Samuel Romilly (1757-1818) and Peter Romilly, sons of a successful merchant jeweller of London who had fled from Montpellier. Still other Huguenot members of Parliament during the early eighteenth century were Richard Du Cane (Du Quesne, 1681-1744), Thomas Fonnereau (1699-1779), John Laroche (*c.* 1700-52), and Isaac Le Heup (*c.* 1686-1747).[52] A Huguenot refugee from Auch in Gascony became one of the official artists of the British navy, known for such pictures as *The Battle of Quiberon Bay* celebrating the destruction of the French fleet on 20 November 1759 while it was preparing a flotilla for the invasion of England. This was Dominique Serres (1722-93), who was appointed to the Royal Academy in 1768 and showed a total of 108 paintings there over thirty years, during which time he was named to the post of marine painter to King George III.[53]

Large, successful communities of Huguenots in Protestant countries were natural magnets for their fellows in the Canada trade. Huguenot merchants marginal in France and Canada were tempted to join one of the communities at Protestant seaports. Why did they not? The principal reason was that their Huguenot connections gave them commercial advantages in France and the French empire. Certain maritime trades, even major ones, were dominated by Dutchmen, Englishmen, Germans, and others in the cosmopolitan trading society of the Atlantic wherein Huguenots had a place. French wine, West Indian sugar and indigo, textiles, salt, and other products were shipped in growing quantities to northern Europe from French ports, but largely in Dutch, German, British, or Scandinavian ships. French vessels comprised only 2.2 per cent of the ships taking French cargoes to Danzig, the biggest Baltic port in the eighteenth century, and only 3.7 per cent of the ships taking cargoes from Danzig to French ports.[54]

[51] J.-P. Poussou *et al.*, *Études sur les villes*, vol. 2, p. 132.

[52] Sedgewick, *The House of Commons, 1715–1754*.

[53] David Cordingly, *Marine Painting in England 1700–1900* (NY, 1974), p. 83. Serres was by no means the first Huguenot artist to succeed in England. More than a century earlier, in the Elizabethan years 1583-1616, Isaac Olivier from Rouen had become one of the famous miniature painters in the kingdom (Carl Winters, *Elizabethan Miniatures* (London, 1943, pp. 12-13).

[54] Edmund Cieslak, 'Sea-borne Trade Between France and Poland in the XVIIIth Century', *Journal of European Economic History*, vol. 6 (1977), pp. 52-3; W. S. Unger,

In 1743 Dutch and German vessels accounted for well over a quarter of the total shipping that arrived at Nantes.[55] Nearly two-thirds of the Bordeaux wine exported during the last years of Louis XIV was taken off in Dutch ships for re-export, and thereafter the Hanseatic towns became the greatest clients, taking more than one-third of the wine exports.[56] Trade in the brandies of Cognac and Jarnac, near La Rochelle, had long been a Dutch enterprise. Holland and northern Europe took well over half of the brandy exported through La Rochelle throughout the half-century from 1713 to 1763; in some years as much as three-quarters of it, and seldom less than 15 or 20 per cent of the total.[57] In all these trades, Huguenot merchants at French seaports were the natural commission agents for Dutch, German, and British firms. Relations and friends abroad provided the same services for Huguenots trading on their own account.

In the enormous and growing tobacco trade, France became almost wholly dependent on British firms. The French Farmers General of Taxes were the biggest customer of English and Scottish firms throughout the eighteenth century. This was because French and French colonial tobacco could not compete on the French market with tobacco from Virginia and Maryland. In 1713 'the purchasing agents of the French tobacco monopoly in Holland were the great banking house of André Pels & Son, the Amsterdam correspondents of Samuel Bernard. In London, his and their correspondents were the Huguenot firm of Tourton & Guiguer, an offshoot of the Paris house of the same name, though with different partners.'[58]

In 1719 the tobacco monopoly in France was entrusted to a consortium of business men which included a number of New Converts, notably François Mouchard, Deputy of Commerce for La Rochelle, and Elizée Gilly de Montaud, a Paris merchant. Others in the wings were Demeuves and Bertrand. A Simon Gilly was still active in the 1750s as a director of the Indies Company in association with

'Trade Through the Sound in the Seventeenth and Eighteenth Centuries', *Economic History Review*, 2nd series, vol. xii (1959), pp. 206-21.

[55] Butel, 'La Croissance commerciale bordelaise', vol. i, pp. 244-345; Jean Mayer, *L'Armement nantais dans la deuxième moitié du XVIIIe siècle* (Paris, 1969), pp. 75, 171-4; André Lespagnol *et al.*, *Histoire de Saint Malo*, p. 153.

[56] Christian Huetz de Lemps, *Géographie du commerce de Bordeaux à la fin du règne de Louis XIV* (The Hague, 1975), pp. 101, 105; Butel, 'La Croissance commerciale bordelaise', vol. i, pp. 244-345; Roger Dion, *Histoire de la vigne et du vin en France* (Paris, 1959), ch. 13.

[57] Clark, *La Rochelle and the Atlantic Economy*, pp. 173-4.

[58] Price, *France and the Chesapeake*, vol. i, pp. 186, 253, 531.

another New Convert, Gabriel-Julien Bouffé. In fact, as Jacob M. Price tells the history of British tobacco sales to France, a very large part in it was played by such prominent Huguenot merchants as Sir John Lambert; Daniel Hays (1659-1732) from Calais; Pierre Simond and his partner, Jacques Benezet, of London, whose brother, Jean-Étienne Benezet, had become a Quaker merchant in Philadelphia; Pierre and Caesar Le Maistre from Paris; a Peloquin at Bristol; a Daltera at Liverpool; Louis Guillemin in London; the William Alexander at Edinburgh whose wife was first cousin to Théodore DelaCroix of La Rochelle and therefore related to *Girardot et Cottin* of Paris; and Georges Grand of Amsterdam, brother of the Huguenot Paris banker, Ferdinand Grand.[59]

An understanding of seaborne trades like these is a necessary step in the study of the Canada trade as it fell further and further into Huguenot hands. And an understanding of the refugee communities at the great Protestant seaports is a necessary step in the study of the Huguenot merchants who took an increasing share of the Canada trade. By remaining in France, families like Bonfils, Dugard, Garesché, Massac, Meynardie, and Mounier were able to use their connections abroad in developing the foreign and colonial trades in French products. It might even be said that they reaped commercial advantages from the religious and political policies that separated the French empire from the cosmopolitan Atlantic world. With such competition as this, could Bourbon official society keep control of the Canada trade?

The Canada trade was being lost to Atlantic trading society for many years before it was formally lost near the end of the Seven Years War. And when Canada was formally ceded to the British empire, and so became another refuge for Huguenots, it did so under the eyes of refugees who had joined the British army and of Huguenot merchants who met them at Québec in 1759. Huguenot officers were obviously useful in new French-speaking parts of the British empire. When Acadia and Newfoundland were occupied in 1710, a Huguenot officer was posted to Acadia and soon became a member of the colonial council, a lieutenant-colonel from 1742, and a full colonel from 1750. This was Paul Mascarene (*c.* 1684-1760), who had been smuggled from Languedoc to Geneva in childhood and educated there. He had moved to England where in 1706 he had joined one of the many

[59] Ibid., p. 722, and the index for names.

regiments raised among the Huguenot immigrants.[60] in 1709 he was posted to Boston, Massachusetts, where he married, raised a family, and eventually died. Meanwhile, from the beginning his duties took him to the newly won colonies of Newfoundland and Nova Scotia where he served under Samuel Vetch (1668-1732), a Scot who had studied at Utrecht whence he had joined the forces of William of Orange bound for England in 1688 and eventually been posted to New York and then Nova Scotia as governor.

Vetch and Mascarene, two Calvinists with command over a former colony in New France, were only the first of several such imperial representatives. After them came others such as Henry Bouquet (1719-65), Thomas Desbrisay (*c.* 1732-1819), Hector Theophilus Cramahé (1720-88), Francis Maserès (1731-1824), Jean Bruyères, and also Huguenots like Josué Mauger (1725-88) from Jersey, the biggest shipowner at Halifax from 1749 to 1760, elected MP for the English port of Poole in 1768; and Mauger's associate, Isaac Deschamps (*c.* 1722-1801), a judge and politician in Acadia.[61] Many of these were posted out to the new colonies under the orders of Jean-Louis Ligonnier (1680-1770), a Huguenot from a refugee family of Castres, Languedoc, and a frequent adviser to Pitt, first Earl Ligonnier, Master-General of the Ordnance, member of Parliament, commander-in-chief of the British Army during the Seven Years War.

When Canada followed Newfoundland and Acadia into the British empire, several Huguenot merchants decided to remain at Québec. Among these were François Levêque (1732-87) from Normandy, Joseph Senilh, Alexandre Dumas, Antoine-Libéral Dumas, and Jean Dumas Saint-Martin (1733-94), all from Montauban, and Pierre Du Calvet (1735-86), son of Pierre Calvet and Anne Boudet of Caussade near Montauban. François Chevalier was still at Montréal in June 1764 asking the London firm of *Mavit & Cazenave* to collect what was due to him from his old employers, *Paillet et Meynardie* of La Rochelle.[62] These and other Huguenots who remained at Québec did so, partly at least, for reasons expressed by one of their number, François Havy, who decided to return to France and there wrote, in July 1759: 'I regard the surrender terms for Guadeloupe as the model

[60] J. B. Brebner, 'Paul Mascarene of Annapolis Royal', in G. A. Rawlyk, ed., *Historical Essays on the Atlantic Provinces* (Toronto, 1967), pp. 17-32.

[61] *DCB* vols. iii to v, *passim*; Frégault, *La Guerre de la conquête*, p. 272.

[62] Bibl. mun. of La Rochelle, ms. 1954, copy of a notarial act of Mézière (Mtl.), 8 June 1764.

of the ones that will be made for Canada. Those terms are most attractive for the *habitants.* Only people whose hearts are truly French will be able to complain of them.'[63] As Havy foresaw, Canada was on the verge of becoming a part of the British empire, a part of Atlantic trading society, and a Protestant refuge.

[63] AN, 62 AQ 31, Havy (LR) to Robert Dugard (Rouen), 7 July 1759.

9
The Cosmopolitan Canada Trade (1743-1763)

THE growing Huguenot share of the Canada trade brought with it a cosmopolitan character unknown in the reign of Louis XIV. The religious and imperial policies of Louis XIII and Louis XIV had been directed against the many Dutch, English, Swiss, and German business interests that were in league with the Huguenots. The Sephardic Jews who had settled at Bordeaux were also a target for the Roman Catholic imperial policy: in November 1684 the government expelled ninety-three Jewish families from south-western France, and in June 1749 another seventy-eight families.[1] The revival of Huguenot interests in the Canada trade meant much more, in fact, than merely a relaxing of religious persecution. It signified the gradual opening of the trade to that mixed Atlantic trading society which inhabited Amsterdam, London, Hamburg, Boston, and other ports in Protestant countries. Canada remained a closed, authoritarian theocracy, what Lionel Groulx described as 'a sociological milieu of rare moral hygiene', but its Atlantic trade became cosmopolitan again, even more, indeed, than it had been before the reign of Louis XIV.[2]

The Huguenot families in the Canada trade were cosmopolitan. Their connections with the maritime Protestant countries were more often personal ones than the connections of Catholic merchants were. Catholic firms were certainly closer to Dutch, English, or northern German firms than to Muslim Turks, or to Indian traders at Pondicherry, but even so there was a social barrier between them that was fundamentally a religious barrier. On the other hand, the Huguenot family of Texier at Bordeaux and Bayonne were in touch with Jean Texier of Amsterdam, the London firm of *Baril et Texier*, and *Bernard Texier et fils* of Hamburg. Bernard Texier visited Bordeaux in

[1] Gérard Nahon, ed., *Les Nations Juives portugaises du sud-ouest de la France (1684–1791): Documents* (Paris, 1981), p. 3-35; A. de Boislisle, ed., *Correspondance des Contrôleurs généraux des Finances*, Paris, 3 vol., 1874-1897 vol. i, p. 148.

[2] Lionel Groulx, *Histoire du Canada français depuis la découverte* (1950), 4th ed. (Montréal, 1960), p. 366.

February 1727.[3] 'Monsieur et Cher Cousin' began the letters of the firm of *Jean Cossart et fils et Bouwer* of Amsterdam addressed to the Huguenot, Robert Dugard of Rouen.[4] Pierre Boudet of La Rochelle had a current account, signed on 8 March 1754, with Jean Boudet of Rotterdam.[5] In 1720, Jacques Thouron of La Rochelle and Bergerac was trading with his brother, Jean Thouron, 'merchant of Amsterdam'.[6] In 1718-24, the Courrejolles family of Bayonne and Damazan (Lot-et-Garonne) was in contact with Jacques Courrejolles of Rotterdam; in 1738, Dutilh of Montauban was in touch with Jacques Dutilh, also of Rotterdam.[7] Théodore DelaCroix of La Rochelle was first cousin to Marianne-Louise DelaCroix who married the Scottish merchant, William Alexander, in Paris in February 1720 at the British embassy church. This couple settled in London where they baptized their first son at the Huguenot church in Threadneedle Street. There in London they were related to the Huguenot merchant, Daniel Hays, son of Claude Hays of Calais and Marie DelaCroix.[8] Vernhès of Bordeaux was in the wine and liqueur trade with Vernhès of Amsterdam, and in 1721 his relative, Marianne Vernhès, married a Huguenot pastor at Voorbourg in Holland, Jean-Louis Claparède. The Rauly family of Montauban and Bordeaux, originally from Castres, 'was related to all the [Huguenot] Castre families distributed among the big cities of Europe: the Malecares (London, Lisbon, and Carolina), the Auriol (London, Geneva, and Lisbon), the Ligonnier (London, where they were related to William Pitt)'.[9] *Bethmann et Imbert* of Bordeaux traded with *Bethmann frères* of Hamburg; Penettes of Bordeaux with a Penettes of Dublin; and Pierre Garrisson of Bordeaux with *Étienne Garrisson et fils* of Amsterdam–the list goes on and on.

Many such family links–more than we know of–were formed or renewed in the course of the eighteenth century. Pierre Frescarode, a merchant of Bordeaux, married the daughter of Henry Lenhoff and Catherine Diers de Ras from the Netherlands in 1721 and went on to deal in wine sales to northern Europe, surviving a bankruptcy in

[3] ADG, Bernard (Bx.), 12 Feb. 1727; Butel, 'La Croissance commerciale bordelaise', pp. 144, 161 note 93, 349, 585, 590, and 1027.

[4] AN, 62 AQ 41, e.g. a letter of 27 Mar. 1749.

[5] A. D. Ch. Mar., Delavergne (LR), 8 Feb. 1766, inv.

[6] ADG, Parrans (Bx.), 29 Mar. 1721, with an appended copy of an act of Marolles (Amsterdam), 10 Oct. 1720.

[7] ADG, Faugas (Bx.), 7 May 1749, inv. for Pierre Doumerc.

[8] Price, *France and the Chesapeake*, pp. 606, 1016 note 48, and 1043 note 90.

[9] Chaussinand-Nogaret, *Les Financiers de Languedoc*, pp. 137-8, 175.

1726.[10] Jean-Pierre-Antoine Giraudeau was sent from La Rochelle to Holland as a young man to learn trade and the Dutch language before qualifying as a sea-captain at La Rochelle on 18 March 1750, and he later married a Dutch merchant's daughter, Ann-Esther Krafft.[11] Robert Dugard of Rouen started his business career in Amsterdam at the age of seventeen and kept many business friends there.[12] Later on, the agent he chose at Bordeaux for his *Société du Canada* was the Protestant firm of Jean-Jérôme and Henry Luetkens and Jacob Drewson, who had various relations in Germany, some through the marriage of Marie-Marguerite Luetkens with Wilhelm-Jehan Emmerth, a German merchant settled at La Rochelle. Pierre Boudet of La Rochelle sent his son, Jean-Jacques Boudet, to learn trade in Holland with a certain A. Hallog.[13] A relative of the Québec Huguenot merchant Pierre Glemet remained at home in Jarnac where she eventually married an English farmer's son from Romford, Essex.[14] Jean DelaCroix, whose ancestors had come to La Rochelle in the middle of the seventeenth century, married off the two daughters he had by his Huguenot Flemish wife, one to a Scot and the other to a Dutchman.[15] During the Seven Years War, the Huguenot firm *Thouron frères* of La Rochelle were in touch with a relative in London, Daniel Vialars, a merchant and banker with whom several Canada merchants did business after Canada fell into British hands: 'He is in touch with several of our merchants and more intimately with Messieurs Thouron *frères*, being a relative of theirs,' Denis Goguet wrote from La Rochelle to Pierre Guy of Montréal. 'I don't doubt he will fill any orders you give him to your satisfaction, as he passes here for a most honest man. . . .'[16]

Other Huguenot ties in Protestant countries are visible in indirect ways. For instance, the Meynardie family were sufficiently at home in England to make two wartime visits. The first occurred when on

[10] ADG, Dugrillon (Bx.), 29 Aug. 1721, marriage; St Rémy (Bx.), 26 Nov. 1721; and 7 B 401, *bilan de Frescarode*, 7 Mar. 1726.

[11] Émile Garnault, *Le Livre d'or de la Chambre de commerce de La Rochelle*, pp. 64-6.

[12] Miquelon, *Dugard of Rouen*, p. 19.

[13] A. D. Ch. Mar., 4 J 5, notes Garnault.

[14] Jarnac, Protestant registers at the town hall, 26 Nov. 1770.

[15] Claude Epaud, Le Commerce maritime de la Rochelle en 1720, maitrise d'histoire (Poitiers, 1975), p. 38; Marcel Delafosse, 'Les Origines géographiques et sociales des marchands rochelais au XVIIe siècle', *Actes du 87e Congrès national des sociétés savantes*, Poitiers, 1962 (Paris, 1963), p. 662.

[16] Université de Montréal, Collection Baby, U 4662, Goguet (LR) to Guy (Mtl.), 12 Apr. 1763.

20 May 1756 a British ship seized *Le Saintonge* on its way to Québec for the La Rochelle firm of *Paillet et Meynardie.* Pierre Meynardie *l'aîné* went to England sometime later that year and stayed until March 1757, bought back the vessel and her cargo, and had her sailed under Dutch colours to Dunkirk whence she set out for Québec again under the new name of *L'Actif*. His younger brother, Bernard Meynardie, who was serving the firm at Québec, announced on 12 September 1760, soon after the British invasion of Canada, 'I am leaving soon for old England [i.e. not New England] and Holland where I shall make several visits (*quelques séjours*) before going to Bordeaux, where it seems I am to settle.'[17] The family firm of *Paillet et Meynardie* was already engaged in international trade, and when they went bankrupt in 1766 Denis Goguet assured Madame Guy of Montréal that 'their failure weighs more on foreigners than on our citizens'.[18]

The Perdriau family of La Rochelle had strong ties in Geneva, as Voltaire showed in his amusing fashion in a letter to the Intendant at La Rochelle:

Monsieur,

If you still remember me, allow me to commend to your kindness a citizen of La Rochelle who, in truth has the misfortune to be a minister of the Holy Gospel at Geneva, but who is the most gentle, honest and tolerant of men. He goes to his birthplace for a while only in the interests of his family, and intends to leave as soon as he has settled his affairs. There is no question here of the word of God, which he preaches as infrequently as he can at Geneva, and which he will certainly not preach at La Rochelle. He was pastor of a church where I had a pew, and we used to call him the sheep rather than the shepherd. *C'est le meilleur diable qui soit parmit les hérétiques.* I beg you to grant him your patronage (etc., etc.),

(signed) Voltaire,
Chateau de Ferney, by Lyon
and Versoy (May 1770).[19]

The Perdriau family, like the others mentioned above, sent goods and ships to Canada. In spring 1756 Pierre-Louis Perdriault was trying to recover what was due to him from 'Sieurs Arnou et Boullard' of

[17] Ibid. U 8487, Pierre Meynardie *jeune* (Que.) to Étienne Augé (Mtl.), 20 June 1757; U 8519, Meynardie *jeune* (Que.) to Augé (Mtl.) 12 Sept. 1760; PRO, HCA 32: 246, *Le Saintonge.*

[18] Collection Baby, U 4670, Goguet (LR) to Guy (Mtl), 25 Mar. 1766.

[19] Bibliothèque de Genève, Archives Tronchin,177, no. 32.

Québec, and in 1758 he sent *La Bonne Aventure* (250 tx.) to Québec.[20] He was also trading with Louisiana where he was claiming 13,000 livres from 'Sieur Grevemberg surnommé Flamand' in 1761. How many more of the Huguenot trading connections that we glimpse in the records were based on family relationships?

As we might infer from all these foreign relations, Huguenot merchants in the Canada trade were natural commission agents for foreign merchant houses, and were often engaged in foreign trade themselves. The Germé brothers of Bordeaux were associated with the English wine exporters, William Johnston.[21] Étienne Augier of Tonnay-Charente near Rochefort sent large cargoes of brandy to Hamburg, Bremen, Amsterdam, London, and Lisbon. He served as commission agent for such Dutch merchants as 'Simon Bejrmand', 'Cornelis Kneppelhon', and others of Rotterdam. In November 1745, acting as commission agent for 'Gédéon L'Eglize' of London, he dispatched 205 tx. of wheat on a Dutch vessel to 'Meyendie et Nicholls' of Lisbon.[22]

The Chauvin family at Bordeaux, trading extensively with Irish ports, employed an Irish clerk because their trade 'is of a nature and an extent which requires infinite writing in the English idiom'.[23] In 1756, Isaac and Marc Chauvin bought a prize at Greenwich from the Huguenot firm of Thomas Dobrée of London. They paid for her mainly through the Amsterdam bankers, *André Pels & Son*, to whom they had already sent provision for the necessary 8,872 florins 'at various times in bills of exchange on Amsterdam, Rotterdam, and London.'[24] Pels in turn paid 'Amiand & Rucker' on Dobrée's behalf. The ship was *Le Printemps* of Nantes (450 tx.), and to bring her to Bordeaux in wartime, the Chauvins arranged to have her sold ostensibly to Don Juan Ignacio Y Banez de Zavola of St Sébastien, in northern Spain, who sent a Spanish captain and crew to fetch her from Greenwich. She arrived at Bordeaux on 19 September 1757 under the name *La Notra Dame de Avanzaret* (*sic*) and was soon renamed *Le Rostan* (after Henri Rostan, the naval commissioner at Bordeaux) and

[20] A. D. Ch. Mar., Chameau (LR), 20 Mar. 1756, *procuration* by Pierre-Louis Perdriault for a correspondent at Québec to receive what is owing there.

[21] Butel, 'La Croissance commerciale bordelaise', p. 556.

[22] A. D. Ch. Mar., Cherpentier (Tonnay-Charente), 20 Nov. 1745, 14 Jan. 1747.

[23] Butel, 'La Croissance commerciale bordelaise', pp. 553, 556.

[24] ADG, 6 B 1452 (6 June 1757) and 1455 (21 Oct. 1757); PRO, HCA 32: 241, *Le Rostan.* Were these merchants related to Étienne Chauvin of Nîmes who took refuge at Rotterdam with Pierre Bayle and then at Berlin, where he published the *Nouveau Journal des Savants* (Chaussinand-Nogaret, *Les Financiers de Languedoc*, p. 173)?

fitted out for a voyage to Québec under Captain Martial Cadusseau. This is an example of the kind of foreign commerce many Huguenot families carried on.

The Huguenot merchants were in touch with English and Dutch insurance companies. These were increasingly strong in the years 1713-63, and more and more used by French merchants. For example, when in 1745 Jean Beaujon imported 240 barrels of fish oil from Canada on *Le Saint Antoine* of Cherbourg, he insured them for 7,000 livres in London through the Huguenot Jacob Albert, and in Amsterdam through the Huguenot Pierre de Labat.[25] In 1756, Jean-David Thouron of Bordeaux insured *Le Fidèle* of Bordeaux in London through Knox, Craghead and Company,for 5,000 pounds sterling at a premium of 36¾ per cent, for a voyage home from Martinique.[26] 'I am told',Robert Dugard's Paris agent wrote to him in May 1756, 'that we could insure (*Le Centaure*'s return voyage from Martinique) more cheaply in London.'[27] This can have been no surprise to Dugard who for twenty years had been a partner in a Rouen insurance company founded on 1 March 1736. His agent at Bordeaux, the Huguenot Henry Goudal, had long ago arranged with a partner, Étienne Peyre *l'aîné*, to buy insurance in London on a regular basis through a Huguenot firm there, *Paul Griffon et fils*, originally from Bordeaux.

The gazettes published in French, sought by all merchants for reliable news of trade and international events, came from Holland, England, Germany, and Switzerland where Huguenot refugees had founded most of them in the reign of Louis XIV. They were, of course, illegal in France, and French authorities in the ports tried to keep them out.[28] It is therefore interesting to find several dozen copies of *Le Nouvelles d'Amsterdam*, in tiny print and format for easy concealment, among the papers of *Les Deux Soeurs* of Québec, Captain Martin Dacier, captured in 1757 *en route* from Bayonne to Québec.[29] There are numbers for every third or fourth day from January until the vessel sailed in April, and they contain news of ships, ports, and politics. These and other Dutch journals procured by Huguenots were sent to Canada on many vessels. 'I am sending you twenty-four Gazettes on

[25] ADG, Parran (Bx.), 23 Jan. 1745.

[26] ADG, Guy (Bx.), 5 Dec. 1756.

[27] AN, 62 AQ 35, France to Dugard, 16 May 1756; ADG, Lagénie (Bx.), 30 June 1749.

[28] F. G. Pariset, *Bordeaux au XVIIIe siècle* (Bordeaux, 1968), pp. 74-5; André Lespagnol *et al., Histoire de Saint Malo*, p. 210; Pierre Grosclaude, *Malesherbes, Témoin et Inerprète de son temps* (Paris, 1961), p. 73; ADG, C 3308, a reference I owe to Miss Jane McLeod.

[29] PRO, HCA, 32: 181, *Les Deux Sœurs* of Québec, seized on 9 Apr. 1757.

Le Superbe, Captain Darragory,' a Québec merchant wrote from Bordeaux in 1757 to a friend of lower-town Québec. 'I am sending you eighty-two gazettes on *L'Aimable Marie*, Captain Simon,' wrote a Bordeaux merchant to his Québec correspondent in 1758.[30] This was not a recent development. Lamalétie at Québec was promising to send gazettes to Pierre Guy at Montréal as early as 1745, and Guy expected them every year from his correspondents at La Rochelle.[31]

Many of the Huguenots in the Canada trade were small men, shopkeepers' sons, whose links with international Huguenot bankers were remote. But richer men with stronger banking connections came into the trade during the 1740s with government contracts to ship soldiers and supplies to New France. A good example is the famous Beaujon family established at Bordeaux in the eighteenth century, so well established, indeed, that they are usually identified as a Catholic family.[32] Biographers do not seem to have discovered the Huguenot parentage of the Canada merchant Jean Beaujon, father of the Court Banker Nicolas Beaujon. After his father's death in 1745 Nicolas continued sending ships to Canada. The father's parents were in fact Jean Beaujon (of the same name) and Esther de Massac, daughter of the Protestant Massac family of Tonneins and its environs.[33] Esther de Massac's sister, Anne de Massac, had married a Pierre Desclaux of Tonneins, and so the Beaujon family of the eighteenth century were close relatives of the Protestant Desclaux and Massac families, both in the Canada trade at Bordeaux.

Lest these Huguenot relations be too summarily dismissed as insignificant in the business lives of Jean Beaujon and his son Nicolas, it is worth remarking that in the 1740s they employed a Huguenot, Jean Grelleau, a future Canada merchant, as a clerk at their house in Bordeaux; that in the years 1753 to 1759 Nicolas Beaujon wrote no less than 341 letters from Paris to Pierre Boudet, a Huguenot Canada

[30] PRO, HCA 32: 253, *Le Vainqueur*, 120 tx., letter from Pierre Audriette (Bx.) to Pépin Baronet (Que.), 19 Mar. 1757, 3 pp.; 169, *Le Berger*, letter from Iroix Chauvin (Bx.) to Bernard Cardenau (Que.), 7 Mar. 1758.

[31] Université de Montréal, Collection Baby, U 5113, 5118, 6620.

[32] A. D. Lot-et-Garonne (Agen), les travaux de F. de Lagrange-Ferregue, tomes ix and xxi. I am grateful to Mr and Mrs Gregory Hanlon for this reference to the Beaujon and Massac genealogies.

[33] ADG, Lemoine (Bx.), 27 June 1713, fol. 511, marriage contract of Jean Beaujon, native of 'la juridiction de la Gruère en Condomois', son of Jean Beaujon, 'bourgeois et marchand de la Gruère', and of Ester Massac, and Thérèse Delmestre, daughter of Izaac Delmestre, 'bourgeois et marchand de Bordeaux', and of Raimonde Faget. She brought a dowry of 8,000 livres.

merchant at La Rochelle with whom he had a current account; that such Huguenots as Simon Jauge and Jacques Ribes were partners in the big wheat companies Nicolas Beaujon led in 1748-50; and that when Nicolas Beaujon moved to Paris in 1751 he soon formed a company with Pierre-François Goossens (1701-), a Netherlander in French and Spanish trade, and other Huguenots.[34]

Pierre-François Goossens was born into a Netherlands family settled at Bilbao, and after moving to Paris about 1741 and becoming a naturalized Frenchman in 1743 he kept in touch with his brother, Jean-Henry Goossens, who remained in trade at Bilbao until his death on 17 December 1777.[35] This brother became the Bilbao agent for a big marine insurance company of Paris of which Goossens was one of the founding members in 1750.[36] The same year Goossens formed another company with a Louisbourg merchant recently settled at La Rochelle, Michel Rodrigue (1710-77), for the purpose of fishing and trading for cod and other fish products in French North America and selling them in France and the West Indies.[37] The company had three other shareholders, all anonymous, one an associate of Goossens, probably Nicolas Beaujon, who still had interests in Canadian shipping, and the other two associates of Rodrigue, almost certainly his brothers living at Louisbourg. Rodrigue and his two partners were to put up three-quarters of the firm's capital and to manage the ships, shipbuilding, crews, cargoes, and so on. Goossens and his partner were to manage the banking, financing, and selling in France and the West Indies, business they were well equipped to do because they were deeply engaged in supplying timber to the French navy.

Supplying the navy was the main part of Goossens' business: in 1750 he described himself as 'intéressé dans les fournitures de la Marine'. His name is mentioned in connection with the supply trades even in the early 1740s, and on 5 June 1750, before his formal association with Beaujon, he joined a company with two other naval supply merchants, one of whom, Pierre Babaud de la Chaussade, was a Huguenot who

[34] A. D. Ch. Mar., Delavergne (LR), 8 Feb. 1766, Boudet's inv.; André Masson, *Un Mécène bordelais, Nicolas Beaujon, 1718–86* (Bordeaux, 1937), 218 pp; A. Communay, *Les Grands Négociants bordelais au XVIIIe siècle* (Bordeaux, 1888), pp. 79-80; Butel, 'La Croissance commerciale bordelaise', p. 483.

[35] A. D. de la Seine (Paris), DC⁶ 11, fol. 21vo.

[36] J. F. Bosher, 'The Paris Business World and the Seaports under Louis XV: Speculators in Marine Insurance, Naval Finances and Trade', *Histoire sociale* (Ottawa), vol. xii (1979), pp. 281-97.

[37] AN, MC, Étude LXXXIII 415, Me Gervais (Paris), 22 July 1750.

had been supplying anchors and other ironware since 1736.[38] On the same day, this company signed a contract with the Secretary of State for the Navy, Antoine-Louis Rouillé, to supply masts, timber, pitch, lead, copper, hemp, and other naval commodities to Brest, Rochefort, Le Havre, and Toulon until 31 December 1754. The scale of this business may be judged by a clause binding the navy to pay the company 100,000 livres each month on account.[39] This contract was renewed in some form when it expired, but in 1757 and 1758 Goossens signed several other contracts with the navy to send supplies to the colonies. He acted as a general manager of these shipping enterprises, employing his brother at Bilbao to send Spanish ships and local firms at French ports to send out French ships.[40] By this time, Goossens was associated with Nicolas Beaujon, and on 26 December 1757 the Secretary of State, now Peyrenc de Moras, wrote to ask him whether he and Beaujon would undertake to buy 400 tons of wheat, 400 tons of rice, and 800 or 900 barrels of pork to ship with some passengers to Canada from Dunkirk, where Michel Bégon, son of a former Intendant at Québec, was naval Intendant.[41]

On 8 January 1758, Goossens signed a contract with de Moras undertaking to fit out three vessels, *Le Saint Pierre, La Baleine*, and *L'Annack*, with a total of 880 tons capacity, and to dispatch them to Québec that spring for the price of 350 livres per ton. They were addressed to a prominent Huguenot merchant at Québec, Jean-Mathieu Mounier (1715-*c.* 1774). Beaujon and Goossens used the services of a Dunkirk firm, *Perville, Salles et Compagnie*, and so discreetly that their own name did not appear when the three ships were captured and disposed of as prizes in a British admiralty court. All the captain of *La Baleine*, Pierre Varin, knew or would say was that his ship was 'laden on the French king's account and bound from Dunkirk to Canada'.[42]

[38] AN, MC, Étude XLVIII 114 (18 Aug. 1761, *transaction.*

[39] AN, MC, Étude CXV 585 (5 June 1750); and the full text is printed in Arch. de la Marine, Rochefort, 5 E^2 18-20.

[40] Some of these are listed in AN, F^1 A, vol. 42, accounts etc. with dates of 18 Apr. 1758, 23 Mar. 1758, 27 Mar., 1 and 11 Apr. 1758, 8 Jan. 1758, and 27 Dec. 1757; AN, Colonies B 108, fol. 94, Peyrenc de Moras to Goossens, 17 Mar. 1758. Among the Spanish ships the Goossens brothers fitted out for Canada were *Le Saint Thomas, Le Grand Saint Louis* (180 tx.), *La Ville de Bilbao*, and *Le Jésus-Marie-Joseph* (150 tx.).

[41] AN, Marine C^7 123, dossier Goossens, I am grateful to Monsieur Étienne Taillemite for drawing my attention to these documents and allowing me to publish them in *Histoire sociale* (Ottawa), vol. v (1972), pp. 79-85.

[42] PRO, HCA 32: 172 pt. 1; the contract and letters concerning these shipments, from AN, Marine C^7, dossier Goossens.

The three vessels sent to Canada were only one of the many enterprises of *Beaujon, Goossens & Compagnie*. A full study of their business would fill this book; suffice it to sketch some of its cosmopolitan aspects. Between 1749 and 1757, Goossens alone and then with Beaujon endeavoured to develop trade with St Petersburg with a view to breaking the Anglo-Dutch monopoly in the Russia trade and to importing Russian tobacco as an alternative to American tobacco from England.[43] Then, in February 1757, Goossens sent the ministry a memorandum proposing a scheme for 'a loan of 20 millions for the navy by selling shares (*actions*) in the prizes taken by the King's vessels'.[44] Some version of this scheme was evidently put into effect, for *Beaujon, Goossens & Compagnie* formed a company on 30 December 1758 which invited private investments in French naval frigates.[45] Meanwhile, in March 1758 they had signed a contract to lend the navy 1,500,000 livres, and on 27 December 1758 they undertook to advance the navy three million livres a month throughout 1759, and another half a million a month to the fortification and engineering services which served naval ports in various ways. Then, on 7 February 1759 they undertook to advance another two million directly to the royal treasury, making a total of 44 million of which 36 million was earmarked for the navy and colonies.[46] The firm was to advance these sums in the form of commercial bills of exchange drawn on their agents in the ports to order of one of the Treasurers General, and it was to recover its funds by receiving and negotiating *rescriptions* of the Receivers General of Finance and notes of the General Farm of Taxes. It appears that the Secretary of State for Marine and Colonies was counting on *Beaujon, Goossens & Compagnie* for about half of the funds his department needed in 1759. Where did all this money come from?

Goossens himself obtained part of it from Dutch merchants and bankers whose capital and services appear to lie behind his many enterprises. From 1 September 1756 he was in formal partnership with a Dutch banker in Paris, Jean-Baptiste Vandenyver, first as an equal

[43] Price, *France and the Chesapeake*, pp. 393-7.

[44] AN, Paris, Marine G 132.

[45] The contract is mentioned in AN, MC, Étude LX, 24 Oct. 1759, de Selle's post-mortem inventory.

[46] These contracts are explained in part in a printed *Arret du Conseil d'État du Roi concernant les lettres de change et billets des sieurs Beaujon, Goossens et Compagnie*, dated 14 Nov. 1759, which I read at La Rochelle in the archives of the chamber of commerce, bound volume 4. See also Barthélemy-F.-J. Moufle d'Angerville, *Vie privée de Louis XV ou principaux évènements, particularités et anecdotes de son règne* (London, 1781), vol. iii, p. 184.

partner and then, from 1 January 1760, as a silent partner with Vandenyver as the company's director.[47] They each held a three-sevenths share in the first company and the remaining seventh was held by Vandenyver's younger brother. It may be, as another merchant banker of the time alleged, that Dutch loans to *Beaujon, Goossens & Compagnie* were small and brief, but during the Seven Years War, as before it, Goossens worked as the commission agent of a great many merchants of Amsterdam, Rotterdam, and elsewhere in the Netherlands, managing their investments in French *rentes*, tax farms, and other government enterprises. For instance, in February 1756, while Goossens was on a business trip to Amsterdam, Vandenyver received 10,000 livres on his behalf as a reimbursement from the French postal farm to a Rotterdam merchant, Hermann van Yzendoorn, whom Goossens had served since 1754 or earlier.[48] During the 1750s, Goossens was a prosperous merchant and banker specializing in the northern trades, and from 1749 his name was listed in the *Almanach royal* among the *Banquiers pour les traites et remises de place en place.*

Three more partners joined Beaujon and Goossens in these financial enterprises to form *Beaujon, Goossens & Compagnie*. Two of them were Roman Catholics without extensive Atlantic connections, but one had a Huguenot background like themselves.[49] This was Jean Le Maitre de la Martinière born in 1715, a New Convert who had been able to buy high financial offices in this period, but nevertheless maintained family links abroad. His two brothers, Pierre and Caesar Le Maître, were in fact Huguenot merchants who had settled in London as naturalized British subjects, and had purchased British tobacco for the French Farmers General during the 1730s and 1740s. They were both dead before *Beaujon, Goossens and Compagnie* were in full stride as a banking firm, although one, Caesar Le Maître, was alive until 1758. In any event, they had had business relations with Étienne de Silhouette in their tobacco purchasing, and he was Controller General of Finance from 4 March to 21 November 1759, the very

[47] AN, MC, Étude XLVIII 108, declaration of 6 Mar. 1760; and Lüthy, *La Banque protestante*, pp. 321-3.

[48] Laborde's memoirs, ed. Yves Durand, in *Annuaire-Bulletin de la Société de l'Histoire de France, années 1968–69* (Paris, 1971), pp. 149-50; AN, MC, Étude LXXXIV 455, *procuration*, 4 Dec. 1755, lists Vandenyver as Goossens' bookkeeper. For Goossens' clients in Holland, MC, Étude LXXXIV 456 (6 Feb. 1756); CXV 714 (30 Apr. 1758) and 721 (23 Jan. 1759);L (14 Oct. 1754, 11 Apr. 1752, 13 Apr. 1752, 8 Apr. 1758, and 15 Jan. 1750) and the *répertoire of* maître Patu's minutes. Patu's minutes are missing from 1752 to 1760.

[49] The Catholics were Gabriel Michel (1702-65), a Nantes merchant, Joseph Micault d'Harvelay (1723-86), a financier.

period in which *Beaujon, Goossens & Compagnie* were financing the French navy and colonies.[50] As this brief résumé of an involved subject shows, the French government was endeavouring in 1758-9 to draw upon the vast financial resources of the cosmopolitan Huguenot bankers and their Protestant friends abroad. The ministry of Marine and Colonies needed these funds partly to pay merchants for shipments to Canada on government contract.

It was under the same wartime pressures that the official Purveyor-General for Canada, Joseph Cadet, signed shipping contracts with other Huguenot merchants and bankers. Among the most active was Pierre Desclaux de Latané of Bordeaux, born in 1688, one of the rare Huguenots to hold an office of *secrétaire du Roi* in these years. Desclaux engaged two friends in this service, Pierre Baour and Simon Jauge (1709-82), both Huguenot merchants and bankers, and the three of them assembled dozens of cargoes and fitted out dozens of vessels for Canada. Desclaux even procured a Spanish ship, *La Pastorizza* of Corunna, Captain Augustin Dios Rosalia, for whom the minister provided a false passport for the Terceres Islands to mislead British captors.[51] They were not entirely new to the Canada trade, however, for Jauge had bought 15,000 livres worth of marine insurance for the schooner *La Légère* in December 1754 for a voyage from Québec to Martinique. In 1755, the Québec Huguenot merchant, Revol, owed him money, and he held a one-quarter interest in *Le Grand Saint Ursin* of La Rochelle, Captain Pierre Rodrigue, sailing from Québec to La Rochelle. Jauge also engaged three apprentice bakers for Cadet and shipped them to Québec on one of Desclaux's vessels, *La Nouvelle Victoire* in 1757. Jauge used the services of the Huguenot Paris banker, Jean-Louis Cottin, and many years later, in April 1781, he gave his son, Theodore Jauge, 100,000 livres to establish himself in partnership with Cottin in Paris and to marry Cottin's daughter.[52]

These three were well connected in Huguenot circles. Simon Jauge, originally from Sainte-Foy (Dordogne), had married Judith Rocaute, daughter of Pierre Rocaute, a member of a successful Huguenot

[50] AN, V[1] 361 (1749) and V[1] 407 (1760), filed under name; MC, Étude XCI 861 (5 Feb. 1750), marriage contract for Perrinet de Jars and Martinière's sister' *Almanach royal*, 1753, p. 315; Durand, *Les Fermiers généraux*, p. 82; *France and the Chesapeake*, pp. 576, 1033 notes 67, 68, and 1035 note 97.

[51] Bordeaux, Arch. de la Ville, fonds Beaumartin, Jean de Navarre papers, draft of a letter, 1758.

[52] ADG, Guy (Bx.), 5 Aug., 16, 20 Dec. 1755, 1 Apr. 1757; Bordeaux, Arch. de la Ville, fonds Delpit.

merchant family at Bordeaux, and of Marie Delacroix, who brought 15,000 livres in cash to their marriage in 1740.[53] These two families, Rocaute and Delacroix, had widespread family connections in the principal Atlantic ports. It is not surprising to find Rocaute de Bussac sending two vessels to Québec in 1757, *La Liberté* (400 tx., Captain François Castaing) and *Le Diamant* (200 tx., Captain François Courval). Pierre Baour, son of a merchant dyer of Castres, was wealthy enough by 1746 to put up 25,000 livres for a marriage with Toinette Balguerie of a well-known Huguenot family of Bordeaux who put up the same sum for their daughter's dowry.[54] As for Desclaux, in 1724 he had married Elizabeth Griffon, the daughter of Paul Griffon, formerly a captain in the grenadier regiment of Marsilly, and of Elisabeth Sigal. This wife had brought him not only a dowry of 15,000 livres but also relations with the Huguenot firm of Griffon and Son in London. At least four of their children married into prominent Huguenot merchant families at Bordeaux: Bethmann, Lafon de Ladebat, Sigal, and Desclaux de la Coste (a cousin).[55]

It was in the same spirit and under the same wartime pressures that the Minister of Marine and Colonies arranged shipping contracts with David Gradis, a big Portuguese Jewish merchant of Bordeaux. Two contracts were signed at Rochefort on 25 April and 12 May 1746, the first of many signed over the next twelve years, including one of 10 July 1748 with the Intendant of New France, François Bigot. These swelled the Canada trade not only by the ships and connections of the wealthy Gradis family, but also by the services of their Portuguese Jewish friends and relations. One son-in-law, Samuel Alexandre of Bayonne, owned several of the ships Gradis sent to Québec, and another, Abraham Peixotto, owned at least one other vessel, *La Thésée* of Bordeaux, dispatched in 1747. Like the Desclaux circle, the Gradis circle sent out many hundreds of soldiers, many tons of food and munitions, and dozens of indentured servants. Their contracts for Canadian supplies totalled 527,000 livres in 1755, 1,046,395 livres in 1756, 1,433,147 livres in 1757, and no less than 2,369,216 livres in 1758.[56]

[53] ADG, Bolle (Bx.), 21 Jan. 1740.

[54] ADG, 6 B 1398 (7 Jan. 1751); Q B 121, *Contrôle des actes*, 4 May 1747 for Lagénie (Bx.), 28 Aug. 1746.

[55] ADG, Lamestrie (Bx.), 5 Feb. 1724; Guy (Bx.), 19 May 1760, will; A. D. Lot-et-Garonne (Agen), fonds Lagrange-Ferregues, vol. ii.

[56] ADG, Perrens (Bx.), *passim* in the 1740s and 1750s; Parrans (Bx.), *passim* in 1753-4, and Mansset (Bx.), *passim*, 1745-7; Butel, 'La Croissance commerciale de Bordeaux', pp. 665-8.

Their correspondents in France and abroad were many and influential, including the Paris firm of *Chabbert et Banquet*, who tried to collect the huge sums the Crown owed Gradis for his shipments to Canada; the firms Charles and Antoine Masson and *Verduc, Vincent et Compagnie* of Cadiz; Benjamin Mendès Dacosta of London, who insured *Le Fort Louis* for 1,000 pounds sterling for her voyage to Québec in 1747;[57] Thomas and Adrian Hope, and 'Guillaume Nérac' of Amsterdam; and André France of the Rouen family that had joined Robert Dugard's *Société du Canada* earlier, who was Gradis' Paris agent for many years until his death on 25 November 1757 and 'entrusted by them with making the purchases in Paris of goods which they ordered and then sent to the colonies'.[58] Gradis paid France by endorsing to him bills of exchange drawn in Amsterdam, London, and all the major Atlantic ports.

Several German and Swiss fur buyers took part in the Canada trade in the 1740s and 1750s, and they too show the cosmopolitan trend of the trade at that time, though in a humbler way. Christian Caspar from Prussia and Christian Schindler from Saxony sailed to Québec from Bordeaux in 1749 on *La Providence* with a load of linens, cottons, and other goods to sell for Georges Sacher, a merchant skinner from Silesia who had been living at Bordeaux for twenty years and dealing with André Portes at Québec. Sacher had bought these goods for 8,152 livres from Mariette *frères*, Huguenots of Montauban, and from *Zorn, Messiers et Valet* of Bordeaux, in order to exchange them at Québec for furs and skins which he could sell to various correspondents abroad, such as Jean-Frédéric Schmidt of Frankfurt; F. Cuny, a merchant furrier of Strasbourg (who fled to Holland in 1739 abandoning wife, family, and debts); Hans and Jean-Pierre Hembrock *père et fils*, Jean-Mathieu Sivers, and Jean-Frédéric Bernt of Hamburg; Wegelin of Stockholm, and others. When Sacher died later that year leaving unfinished business in Canada, his widow turned to a Swiss fur merchant of Bordeaux, then at Québec, Jean-Jacques Zorn, who was still there in 1754 but turned up at Bordeaux in 1755.[59] In 1749 a certain *marchand pelletier* from Geneva, Lehemid Mayerd (*sic*), was

[57] ADG, Mansset (Bx.), 18 May 1747.

[58] AN, Y 14677, *scellé* of 25 Nov. 1757; AN, étude XCIX (7 Dec. 1757), post-mortem inv.

[59] A. D. Charente (Angoulême), 3 E 7059, Ouvrard (Barbézieux), 5 Jan. 1739, marriage contract of Georges Sacher and Madeleine Dupuy, her dowry 4,000 livres; ADG, Barbaret (Bx.), 5 Apr. and 16 June 1755; Zorn was staying with *Veuve Sacher & Cie* and about to sail to Québec.

buying furs at La Rochelle. No doubt other foreign connections might be discovered in the business accounts of such fur merchants as Abraham Bernard and Jean Missonet of La Rochelle.[60]

In New France, the temptation to trade with New York and New England was particularly strong in the eighteenth century. Certainly huge profits were made earlier, smuggling furs from Montréal to Albany: during the War of the Spanish Succession (1701-13) New York managed to maintain an unofficial neutrality, and French authorities then reckoned that from one-half to two-thirds of the beaver brought to Montréal found its way to Albany.[61] This illicit trade does not seem to have declined after the war. In the years 1727 to 1752 the Caughnawaga allies of the French and the Desauniers sisters carried furs from Sault St Louis, often over the ice in winter. 'The smuggling here is beyond words', wrote the Intendant Dupuy in 1728, complaining that dozens of Englishmen were walking about Montréal and Québec bent on trading.[62] Even with frequent seizures, merchants in the smuggling business reckoned to lose only about 10 per cent on their furs and could easily bear that rate of loss. In the 1720s, the Huguenot Stephen Delancey, who owned ships for exporting furs to Britain and Holland, was the first-ranking or second-ranking trader in New York, and he was thought to procure most of his furs from Canada through Albany merchants, especially Cornelius Cuyler and Philip Livingstone. During the 1750s, Robert Sanders, merchant mayor of Albany, also had most of his furs from Montréal. His letterbook for 1752-8 shows that he concealed the identity of his Montréal correspondents by referring to them with Roman numerals and corresponding with them in a private code. By then, the Canada traders were almost a party in New York with several seats in the Legislative Assembly.[63]

International trade in New France was much encouraged by the founding of Louisbourg on Cape Breton Island as a substitute for the port of Plaisance, lost with Newfoundland by the treaty of 1713. 'The

[60] ADG, Barbaret (Bx.), 29 July 1749 and 29 Oct. 1754, inv. dated 29 July 1749; P. G. Roy, ed. *Ordonnances de l'Intendant* (Québec, 1919), vol. iii, 20 Aug. 1754.

[61] Cyrille Gélinas, *The Role of Fort Chambly in the Development of New France, 1665–1760* (Ottawa, 1983), pp. 32-7; T. E. Norton, *The Fur Trade in Colonial New York 1686–1776* (Madison, Wisc., 1974), p. 56; Yves Zoltvany, *Philippe de Rigaud de Vaudreuil* (Toronto, 1974), p. 75.

[62] Jean Lunn, 'The Illegal Fur Trade out of New France 1713-60', *Report of the Canadian Historical Ass.* (1939), pp. 61-76; Guy Frégault, *La Guerre de la conquête* (Montréal, 1975), pp. 44-7; J. C. Dubé, *Claude-Thomas Dupuy* (Montréal, 1969), p. 288.

[63] Norton, *The Fur Trade*, pp. 86 ff., 123 ff.

British colonies', writes Christopher Moore, 'sent fresh food, large quantities of lumber and brick, and several vessels annually, to be exchanged for rum and molasses.'[64] Throughout the 1720s, Britain and France being then at peace, thirty or more New England ships visited Louisbourg each year, and at least eighty-six of them were sold there between 1733 and 1743. Naval authorities there complained that La Rochelle merchants trading with Louisbourg were often related to Huguenot merchants in New England, and there is evidence of trade among these families, such as that between Pierre Faneuil of Boston and Abraham Tabois of Louisbourg in 1732.[65] During the mid-century wars, Île Royale came to rely so heavily on New England and the West Indies that 'these two regions far outweighed France in Île Royale's total trade'.[66] Links with New England were, of course, further strengthened between 1745 and 1748 when British forces occupied Louisbourg during the War of the Austrian Succession; in 1758 this part of New France was brought permanently into the British Empire.

The war years put a strain on the Canada merchants. For the established Roman Catholic families with members on both sides of the Atlantic, the strain was double because of the growing competition from Huguenots and Jews with cosmopolitan connections. Some Catholic families were rich enough to return to France, buy royal offices, form marriage alliances with noble families, and begin to move into government financing or landowning: Pascaud and Goguet at La Rochelle, Trottier Désauniers, Lamalétie and Estèbe at Bordeaux.[67] But a remarkable number of others went bankrupt in these years. Of course Huguenots, too, went bankrupt, but most of the big Catholic failures occurred in the 1740s and 1750s before Canada was lost, whereas most of the big Huguenot failures came in 1759 or later. This order of events shows yet another aspect of the decline of Bourbon official society in the Canada trade.

Bourgine's was the first big Catholic bankruptcy. In difficulties for some years, he turned his balance sheet over to the *juridiction consulaire* on 20 May 1745 and awaited the decision of his many creditors.[68] Their deliberations ended on 1 July with a proposal that his *rentes* and

[64] C. Moore, 'The Other Louisbourg: Trade and Merchant Enterprise in Île Royale 1713-58', *Histoire sociale* (Ottawa), vol. xii (1979), p. 80.

[65] C. Moore, 'Merchant Trade in Louisbourg', MA thesis (Univ. of Ottawa, 1977), pp. 67, 72, 97-8.

[66] Moore, 'The Other Louisbourg', p. 93.

[67] See above, ch. 3.

[68] A. D. Ch. Mar., Guillemot (LR), 1 July 1745, *abandon de biens.*

moveable property should not be sold up yet, and he should carry on gathering whatever he could from his debtors. Sums recovered were to be kept by one of the creditors, Jean-Gilbert Bourgine, a relative who had lent him 14,000 livres the previous year as a bottomry loan on the voyage of *La Reine des Anges*, and when 20,000 livres had accumulated it was to be distributed among the creditors.[69] The biggest debts were 46,376 livres to Denis Hersan of Paris, some 40,000 livres to the representative of the Jesuit North American missions, 12,683 livres to a certain Louis Pierre, and sums of over 11,000 each to Maurice Pechaud of Paris and Chotard, a merchant of Tours. Bourgine's wife had a prior claim of 26,000 livres, the sum of her dowry, but she waived it in favour of two widows who had entrusted their fortunes to Bourgine, and their own son-in-law, Pierre Blavoust, to whom they still owed 8,472 livres of their daughter's 40,000-livre dowry. Blavoust claimed an additional sum of 3,400 livres but was soon in debt himself for much larger sums.

In a family firm of that period, a bankruptcy tended to drag down relatives and trading partners far and near. The Blavoust fortune was evidently frail and inflated with much credit: in less than five years he also failed in a mighty crash due, he told his creditors, 'to the delay of the considerable funds he was expecting from the colonies in America and Africa, the scarcity of specie, the general discredit at all maritime centres, trading difficulties, and the losses he has suffered'.[70] He listed a total of 1,375,188 livres in losses, including enormous sums due to war. Among these were 60,000 livres lost on *Le Grand Conti*; many other ships in the Canada, Louisiana, and West India trades 'seized by the English'; a great deal in insurance, such as 25,000 livres lost in 'insurance taken out for Messieurs Mahet, Denin, Neau, Audouin and Quenet on brandy loaded in Dutch ships confiscated in England'; and about 50,000 livres lost on 'sugar, coffee and indigo sent abroad on my account'. Also lost shortly after the bankruptcy was a load of 3,000 Canadian deerskins and other pelts on *Le Lys*, wrecked on the island of Oléron.[71] He reckoned that 143,513 livres were due to him for what he had sent in 1750 'to the address of Nicolas Massot [of Québec] on the ships, *Le Lys, l'Auguste, Le St Sébastien*, and *L'Espérance*';some 52,000 livres 'in Canada under Monsieur de Voizy, which Monsieur Porte left him'; and several hundred thousand livres for ships and

[69] A. D. Ch. Mar., Chameau (LR), 14 Apr. 1744 SSP.
[70] A. D. Ch. Mar., Tardy (LR), 5 Jan. 1746; B 1795.
[71] A. D. Ch. Mar., Tardy (LR), 21 Jan. 1751.

goods he had sent to Louisiana and the West Indies. Nicolas Noordingh of Amsterdam owed him about 35,000 livres for cargoes of indigo, and several London houses owed him relatively small sums: Pierre Simon (11,800 livres), *J. Tessier & Co.* and *Blake & Guin* (each 6,000 livres), and Jacob Albert (3,974 livres). He claimed only 8,000 livres from the Crown.

His biggest debts were 209,378 livres to his aunt and uncle, 'Messieurs Marchand et Veuve Marie Blavoust', 178,885 livres to *de Brus & Co.* of Paris, 106,172 livres to Jean Veyssière, 59,433 livres to *Veuve Tassin & Fils* of Paris, and 50,000 to Pierre Vanrobais of Paris. He owed money to nearly everyone in La Rochelle, Protestant and Catholic, and also 29,224 livres to Pierre Mousnier *fils* of Amsterdam, 17,694 livres to Jean Phillips of Rotterdam, 7,098 livres to Dacosta of Rennes, and 1,100 livres to Jean-Étienne Jayat of Québec. Blavoust's affairs took more than a decade to clear up. Not until 18 April 1759 did he and Jayat of Québec settle their differences over 35 barrels of olive oil and a case of china destined for Québec on Blavoust's ship *Le Depleure* in 1748, but left at La Rochelle when the ship's destination was changed at the last moment.[72]

Only three weeks after Bourgine's failure, a Bordeaux merchant from another Catholic Franco-Canadian family went bankrupt, on 10 June 1745. This was Amand Nadau whose agent at Québec was the same Jayat who served Bourgine and Blavoust. Nadau had sent several ships to Québec, starting with *Le Saint Amand* on which a cousin, Joseph Nadau from Blaye, began his career as a mariner in 1740 and 1741. This cousin was to qualify as an ocean pilot at Québec on 14 August 1750 and as a ship's captain at Bordeaux on 22 March 1755.[73] Amand Nadau must have been in trouble from the beginning of the war in 1744, for in April that year he found himself unable to sign for the premium needed to insure his ship *Le Jean Joseph* bound for Guadeloupe, and had to make arrangements for Guillaume-Joseph Saige to sign in his place.[74] When he went bankrupt his creditors granted him a fresh start by agreeing to settle for 15 per cent of what he owed them, but a new series of losses caused him to suspend his payments again on 15 January 1749. He had suffered 'cruel losses' which he reckoned at 137,569 livres up to 10 June 1745 and

[72] A. D. Ch. Mar., Fredureaux-Dumas (LR), 12 Feb. 1760 (SSP of 18 Apr. 1759).

[73] ADG, 6 B 1445 (22 Mar. 1755), son of Amand Nadau, *bourgeois* of Blaye and of Jeanne Sotteau.

[74] ADG, Roberdeau (Bx.), 16 Apr. 1744.

145,000 livres since then, mostly in ships and cargoes lost to the sea and the enemy. One of his losses was on *Le Saint Yves de Tréguier* (130 tx.) which he freighted to Québec in 1748 but found so unseaworthy that she could not sail. All those who had put consignments of goods in her claimed compensation. The minutes of *maîtres* Guy and Parran fairly hum with the case in July and August 1748.[75]

Nadau's was a relatively modest affair, but May 1753 saw the collapse of two more merchants of Bordeaux, both from Catholic families well established in Canada and France. One was Guillaume Pascaud (1692-1762), a nephew of the Widow Pascaud of La Rochelle and busy with the family's Canada trade at Bordeaux since about 1720. From 1725 he had also been a commission agent for Bourgine, preparing cargoes for Canada and Louisiana, buying and recovering insurance, and taking steps to recover other debts due. Among the bad debts in his balance sheet in 1753 was a sum of 13,374 livres due from Bourgine. Pascaud's business was closely linked with that of his neighbour in the rue Neuve (parish of St Michel), Jean Jung, and indeed he rented rooms in Jung's house during the 1730s, 'a store-house, cellar beneath, and nine rooms, including bedrooms, anti-chamber and offices (*cabinets*)' for 600 livres a year.[76] When either of them travelled, he left power of attorney with the other, but I find no evidence of formal partnership. When Pascaud went bankrupt on 8 May 1753 Jung died, by his own hand, I suspect, leaving many debts and only 35,000 livres in goods and chattels (*meubles et effets*), an inheritance his heirs promptly repudiated.[77] I could not find full figures for these two bankruptcies, but they marked the failures of two Catholic families established in the Canada trade since early in the century. Their losses in ships and cargoes seized in the War of the Austrian Succession had been substantial.[78]

Earlier that year, on 7 February, another Catholic merchant in the trade, Gabriel Grateloup, failed at Bordeaux. He was originally from Dax (Landes) and had strong business connections in Bayonne and Spanish ports. His Canada trade was not uppermost in his balance

[75] ADG, Guy (Bx.) and Parrans (Bx.), *passim*; 6 B 1379, 1380, 1391; 7 B 415 (30 Aug. 1749).

[76] ADG, Lagénie (Bx.), 22 Sept. 1738; Bernard (Bx.), 15 Sept. and 14 Oct. 1721, 4 July 1723, etc.

[77] ADG, 6 B 653* (19 Aug. 1754), 15 pp.; QB 158, vol. 140, *contrôle des actes*, fol. 46 (22 June 1753); Charrou (Bx.), 18 June 1753 (lost).

[78] *L'Aimable Gracieuse* (1744), *La Légère* (1746), *Le Bien Aimé*, *Le Saint François*, and *Le Saint Victor* (all in 1748).

sheet, but in partnership with a merchant of Madrid, Pierre Casamayor (*sic*), he had sent 14,071 livres worth of goods to Estèbe of Québec, and various consignments to Trottier Desauniers (who owed him 9,435 livres), Pierre Chaboisseau and Godefroy de Tonnancourt, all in Canada.[79] In 1742 he was part-owner of *La Gracieuse* of Bayonne (130 tx., Captain Martin Dacier) which was at Québec on 3 September, and in 1748 he was part-owner of *Les Trois Cousins* (Captain Marsan Hirigoyen) which took indentured servants to Québec and left on 9 November with a cargo of furs.

A few months after the Pascaud-Jung débâcle, Bernard Douezan of Bordeaux went bankrupt on 22 January 1754. Douezan had married the daughter of an Acadian merchant, Louis Lachaume, and worked in the Louisbourg trade in association with Beaubassin, Dupleix, Silvain, Claparède, and others there. His agents at Québec were *Morin et Pennisseault* who owed him 2,995 livres.

A much bigger Catholic merchant, Jean-Baptiste Soumbrun, got into difficulties in December 1755. He struggled along with the indulgence of his creditors until 28 June 1757 and then, after a second arrangement, until autumn 1758, by which time his debts totalled 181,686 livres. By 7 February 1759 they had risen to 330,478 livres.[80] Soumbrun, son-in-law of the Canadian merchant Simon Lapointe, had gone into the Canada trade on a large scale, beginning in 1746, sending goods to Detcheverry, Bernard Soumbrun, a younger brother posted at Québec, and then to Jean-Baptiste Amiot. In the early 1750s he sent at least two ships a year to Québec. These were soon lost, *La Légère* (100 tx., Captain Lambert Cohornen) wrecked on the Madeleine Islands on 5 May 1755 *en route* to Québec from Martinique, and *Le Grand St Ursin* (250 tx., Captain Nicolas Brossard) seized on 26 April 1756 *en route* to Québec, carrying Soumbrun's brother, 120 soldiers, and a mixed cargo, and taken to Plymouth.[81] Soumbrun's claims for insurance bogged down in litigation. He lost on the sales of his Canadian furs, and also by the failures of several debtors. He blamed his brother at Québec for incompetence. The sixty pages of his accounts with Amiot for the three years 1753-5 show Amiot owing him 12,000 livres, but these claims took years to settle.[82]

This bankruptcy and that of André Chabot in 1753 put a strain on

[79] ADG, 7 B 418 (7 Feb. 1753).
[80] A. D. Ch. Mar., Fredureaux-Dumas (LR), 7 Feb. 1759.
[81] PRO, HCA 32: 195; ADG, Guy (Bx.), 5 Aug. 1755.
[82] A. D. Ch. Mar., Fredureaux-Dumas (LR), 8 Feb. 1759 and 4 Dec. 1760; Des Barres (LR), 11 Mar. 1754; Guillemot (LR), 13 Apr. 1756, inv.

the Widow Lapointe's affairs, already affected by war and strong competition. She sent no ships herself after 1752, however, and so lost none in the Seven Years War. Her trade survived until after the loss of Canada, when she failed in March 1764.[83] Thus ended a transatlantic trading business that had begun more than forty years before. When she and her husband began, the Canada trade had been almost a Roman Catholic monopoly, but during the last twenty years it had grown into a branch of that cosmopolitan trade characteristic of the Atlantic in the eighteenth century.[84]

These failures of Roman Catholic firms trading with Canada occurred in the same circumstances as the failure of another Catholic enterprise, that of Antoine de la Valette, *supérieur général et préfet apostolique* of the Jesuit missions in the American colonies. Valette, who managed a considerable transatlantic trade for the Society of Jesus at St Pierre, Martinique, was in difficulties as early as June 1754, when he journeyed to Bordeaux and put up at the Jesuit professed house there to settle his current account with David Gradis. It turned out he owed Gradis 86,846 livres, and he arranged to pay this sum over the next three years.[85] It is possible Valette's affairs had suffered by Bourgine's bankruptcy in 1745, for Bourgine recorded a debt of some 40,000 livres owing, he said, to Jean-Pierre-François Dominique de Sacy, *procureur général* for the Jesuit missions in North America. It is certain that the Jesuit trade suffered from war and new competition, like other Catholic firms accustomed to a near monopoly in the French empire. In any event, de la Valette was the principal debtor of the firm *Jean Lioncy et Gouffre* of Marseille which went bankrupt in February 1756. The Society of Jesus was eventually ordered to pay *Lioncy et Gouffre* more than one and a half million livres.[86] This affair soon led to the denunciation and expulsion of the Society from France, and that political result grew out of a commercial failure very much like the failure of the old established firms in the Canada trade. Under the onslaught of two maritime wars French colonial trade had ceased to be a French Roman Catholic monopoly.

[83] A. D. Ch. Mar., Tardy (LR), 9 Mar. 1764, *abandon de biens.*

[84] A. D. Ch. Mar., Fleury (LR), 22 Sept. 1722, marriage.

[85] ADG, Perrens (Bx.), 18 June 1754, *obligation.*

[86] Dale Van Kley, *The Jansenists and the Expulsion of the Jesuits from France, 1757–1765* (New Haven, 1975), pp. 92, 134.

IV

A French Crisis (1756-1763)

10

Merchants at the Conquest

FOR most merchants in the Canada trade, the conquest of Canada by Great Britain in 1759-60 was a catastrophe. But this platitude does not do justice to the complexity of the crisis brought on by the War of the Austrian Succession (1743-8) and the Seven Years War (1756-63). The naval and military defeats were partly the result of weaknesses in a financial system dependent on the credit of government financiers. Unable to pay its debts and defeated in battle, the government suspended the Canada bills on 15 October 1759 and soon went bankrupt altogether.

These catastrophic events led to three more crises. First, the Crown blamed the events in Canada, financial and military, on its own officials, and put about fifty of them on trial in the noisy *affaire du Canada*, which gave the Crown an excuse to reduce its Canadian debts, but publicized the essential corruption of Bourbon official society. Secondly, most Canada merchants who had not gone bankrupt earlier, notably the big Huguenot merchants, now collapsed one after the other. Thirdly, the Society of Jesus, one of the pillars of the Counter-Reformation, was dragged into the bankruptcy of its Martinique trading firm and assaulted by the Jansenist Parlements. Having abandoned the cause of the Counter-Reformation in the 1750s, the Crown was persuaded to outlaw the Society in 1762-4 at the same time that it was turning its back on that other pillar of the Counter-Reformation, the colony of New France. These events marked a profound change in religious policy that matched the changes wrought by the British government in New France. The Crown began to set itself against the persecution of Huguenots, and to give way to the Atlantic trading society that had grown so powerful in the eighty-five years since the revocation of the Edict of Nantes. Bourbon official society was doomed in old France as well as in New France. So brief a summary of such startling events leaves much to be explained.

Louis XV's government, dogged throughout the mid-century wars by a shortage of funds, was soon unable to pay sailors and their families, or merchants for goods and services, and went bankrupt in October and November 1759.[1] This bankruptcy was not merely a result of momentary weakness owing to unfortunate circumstances or to mistakes in judgement. Nor was it a result, as so many historians have thought, of fighting on too many fronts at once. The French financial system was fundamentally and inherently weaker than those of Great Britain, the Dutch Republic, and even perhaps of Brandenburg-Prussia. Its weaknesses, as I have explained elsewhere, were to bring it before long to the brink of the French Revolution.[2] Already in the 1750s and 1760s the Crown was hampered in its war effort and discredited among its own people, especially its merchants, because it could not pay its way as well as its British, Dutch, and Prussian enemies could.

Merchants in the Canada trade suffered directly from their government's inability to pay. As early as March 1748, a partner in Dugard's *Société du Canada* reported from Paris that Maurepas, the Secretary of State, and Mouffle de Géorville, the naval Treasurer General, kept putting him off with promises. 'It seems that we have to have ourselves listed on the *État de distribution*' he wrote. 'Furthermore, *chez* Monsieur de Maurepas I saw a list of more than twenty merchants in the same case as we are in . . . C'est le diable pour tirer de l'argent du Roy.'[3] Ten years later, on 18 October 1758, the Crown appointed five magistrates, the famous 'Fontanieu Commission', to examine and settle the debts of the Ministry of Marine and Colonies totalling some forty-two million livres of which twelve million were for the War of the Austrian Succession (1743-8), three million for the inter-war years (1748-55), and twenty-seven million for the years 1755 to 1758. Some officials put the debt much higher than that.[4]

Among the ministry's creditors were most of the shipping merchants in the Canada and Louisbourg trades. These had engaged their

[1] These financial difficulties of the French government I have discussed in various articles such as 'Les Trésoriers de la Marine et des Colonies sous Louis XV:Rochefort et La Rochelle', *Revue de la Saintonge et de l'Aunis*, tome v (1979), pp. 95-108, 'The French Government's Motives in the *affaire du Canada*, 1761-63', *English Historical Review*, vol. xvci (1981), pp. 59-78; and 'Financing the French navy in the Seven Years War: *Beaujon, Goossens et Compagnie*', *Social History* (London), vol. 28 (July 1986), pp. 115–33.

[2] J. F. Bosher, *French Finances 1770–1795: From Business to Bureaucracy* (Cambridge, 1970), 370 pp.

[3] AN, 62 AQ 35, France (Paris) to Dugard (Rouen), 14 Mar. 1748 and 28 Apr. 1748.

[4] Henri Legohérel, 'Une Commission extraordinaire du Conseil d'État du Roi: La Commission de Liquidation des Dettes de la Marine et Colonies (1758-68)', *Faculté de Droit et Sciences économiques de Dakar* (Paris, 1968), 32 pp., and AN, Colonies E 45, 'Précis concernant la dette du Roy pour le Canada (29 June 1764)'; BN, ms. fr. 11340, Le Normand de Mézy.

ships at one time or another to transport soldiers, munitions, supplies, or food to Canada. When the Crown had engaged certain vessels, such as *La Complaisante, Le Pacquet de Londres, Le Cytoen, La Maréchale de Broglie*, and *La Badine*, for transport to Canada in 1758, and then delayed and sent the ships to the West Indies, the merchant owners naturally claimed compensation. Not only had the Crown deferred its debt to them, but the Commission set up to deal with these debts now proceeded to reduce many of them on the grounds that the Crown had been a victim of wartime profiteering when it had signed the original contracts. By the end of 1759, the Commission had received creditors' claims to a total of 4,338,734 livres, and had cut them down to 3,368,137 livres.[5]

This was excessively arbitrary considering that there were two sides to the question of wartime contracts. We know from much scattered evidence that wartime freight rates to Québec and other transatlantic destinations rose steeply as a result of British naval supremacy. *Paillet et Meynardie* wrote to François Chevalier of Montréal on 26 April 1758, 'our enemies are ready to come out with immense forces, with which they threaten to blockade our ports of France, which is very easy for them ... our warships think only of saving themselves ...', etc.[6] Marine insurance premiums rose from about 5 per cent in peacetime to 40 per cent in the early years of both mid-century wars, and by the later years insurance was practically unobtainable in France. 'Insurance is eating up profits,' Pierre Guy wrote from from Montréal as early as 1747.[7] French losses in shipping were extremely heavy, especially in the Seven Years War. Crews and ships became scarce. Return cargoes could seldom be found, as merchants often complained. As any merchant could see, the wartime shipping market had naturally imposed high freight rates: 240 livres and then 400 livres per ton soon became normal for Canadian cargoes, this without any profiteering. 'Freight rates at Bordeaux amount to 400 livres a ton, and it is impossible to buy insurance,' Meynardie *jeune* wrote on 19 May 1758.[8] Early the next year, *Paillet et Meynardie* reported from La Rochelle, 'We wanted to freight an entire ship for 550 livres a ton, but we were refused.'[9] Even while the Fontanieu Commission was at work

[5] BN, ms. fr. 11337, Berryer to Fontanieu, 18 May 1759; BN, ms. fr 11338, Fontanieu to Berryer, 31 Dec. 1759.

[6] Bibl. mun. de La Rochelle, ms. 1954.

[7] Université de Montréal, Collection Baby, U 5113.

[8] Ibid. U 8503; AN, Colonies, B 108, Minister to the Marseille Chamber of Commerce, 18 Feb. 1758.

[9] Collection Baby, U 9256 (1 Feb. 1759).

in spring 1760, the Minister approved freight rates to Canada of 400 livres per ton.[10]

On receiving objections, argued along these lines, to the Crown's refusal to honour its contracts, the Commission showed a typical eighteenth-century misunderstanding of the inflationary process. Fontanieu himself remarked that merchants who complained were merely piqued at losing their ill-gotten profits. 'It seems that the avarice of a considerable number of the merchants at our ports led them to form a sort of conspiracy among themselves to profit from the urgent needs of the Kingdom, and to make immense gains by extorting exorbitant prices for ships which the *ordonnateur* and the Ministers of Marine had to hire (*affrêter*) to take defenders and munitions of all kinds to the colonies, and goods which these same merchants supplied for prices just as exorbitant.'[11] In this belief the Fontanieu Commission cut down many of the Crown's debts.

Among the debts to merchants were wartime loans to the naval establishments at certain ports. For instance, in 1757 four merchants of Le Havre had lent 124,000 livres to the Marine Intendant, Ranché, at 6 per cent annual interest. Two years later, the Fontanieu Commission was examining the five credit notes with suspicion, inquiring whether the loans had been authorized by the Minister, and so on. When they decided that 6 per cent interest was 'against the general laws of the State', and that Ranché had no business borrowing on his own personal signature but should have arranged for the naval treasurer's agent to borrow, they were putting the merchant lenders in an awkward position.[12] Furthermore, they were ignoring the desperate circumstances that must have driven Ranché, even in 1757, to borrow as he did. We have no records concerning the treasurer's agent at Le Havre, but the agents at Lorient and Rochefort were already in difficulties.[13] At the end of the previous war, to take another example, the Intendant at Rochefort had borrowed 126,000 livres from various merchants of La Rochelle, the Treasurer General being some 176,000 livres behind in the payments authorized for that port, and had been begging for permission to borrow a great deal more.[14]

[10] AN, Colonies B 112, fol. 128.

[11] BN, ms. fr. 11336, fols. 14 ff.

[12] BN, ms. fr. 11337, Fontanieu to Berryer, 27 Apr. 1759.

[13] Arch. de la Marine, Lorient, 1E5 1, Laurent Bourgeois (Lorient) to de Selle (Paris), 14 June 1758.

[14] Arch. de la Marine, Rochefort, 1E 145, Maurepas to de Givry, 14 July 1748 and 17 Nov. 1748.

More damaging for the Canada merchants was the government's suspension and reduction of the Canadian bills; that is, the bills of exchange and promissory notes that had been common currency in Canada. These had long been issued in all French colonies by the governing authorities in payment for goods and services. According to the Bourbon financial system, an Intendant or other responsible official authorized payments in the form of signed *ordonnances* but did not make payments. To be cashed, an *ordonnance* had to be taken to the agent of a Treasurer General for Marine and Colonies who was one of those venal financiers or *comptables* entrusted with the management of all government funds from the collection of taxes to the payment for goods and services. The Treasurer General's agent at Québec might cash *ordonnances* with silver coin if he had it, as in 1755 and 1756 when coin had been shipped out from France, but he usually issued his own promissory notes (*billets de caisse*) or the famous playing-card money which he later took back in exchange for the bills of exchange he would draw once a year on his employer in Paris, the Treasurer General. These payments in paper need careful study because much nonsense has been written about them, chiefly in the antiquated belief that the only sound currency is gold or silver coin.

The Crown paid merchants at Québec in somewhat the same way that one merchant paid another. For most debts of more than a few livres, merchants everywhere used some form of paper payment because coin was awkward and costly to transport, scarce and consequently hoarded, and kept in reserve for a few special purposes: dowries for daughters marrying or entering convents; advances to the crews of departing ships; occasional household spending to maintain the family's local credit; and paying certain local debts, such as bills of exchange presented when due, also in order to maintain personal credit. The credit thus maintained was the basis for business transactions. Merchants usually opened current accounts with one another, as with their suppliers far and near, and their local tradesmen. Accounts were reckoned up and settled periodically. Otherwise, a payment might be made with a promisory note or a bill of exchange, and these were endorsed from one person to another until they fell due. Most notes and bills–millions of them–were thrown away when they had served their purposes, but in notarial minutes we find copies of those few that were rejected, protested, or not honoured for one reason or another, and these show that this type of payment was scarcely any different from bills drawn by the treasurer's Québec agent on the Treasurer General in Paris.[15] The only real difference was that the Treasurer General, like a dead, dishonest, or bankrupt merchant, failed to honour the bills drawn on him at Québec. He failed, first, because the Crown could not supply him with the funds he needed and, secondly, because on 15 October 1759 the Crown ordered him to accept no more of them, and publicly suspended all Canadian bills.

This was the first step in a general financial disaster that amounted to the bankruptcy of the French government. On 26 October, the Crown was obliged to suspend the *rescriptions* of the Receivers General of Finance and the notes of the General Farm of Taxes, and on 14 November the notes of the consortium of *Beaujon, Goossens et Compagnie* that had been financing the Marine and Colonies since the beginning of the year. But these were the principal paper currencies with which the Crown had been paying merchants and others in France, the metropolitan equivalent of the Canadian bills. Its paper notes discredited, the government was now bankrupt; that is, unable to pay its debts or to meet its commitments. Had it been a private firm, its creditors would now have assembled to press its debtors, sell its property, cash its other assets, and generally recover whatever they could from the wreckage. That is, in fact, what the revolutionary National Assembly began to do in 1789. In 1759, however, the Crown was still determined to defend itself with its own absolute authority. It dismissed the Controller General of Finances, Étienne Silhouette, on 21 November. By royal decree it defended *Beaujon, Goossens et Compagnie* and the other paying services from prosecution in the courts, took stock of its own debts, decided which to honour and which to repudiate, marshalled the funds accumulating meanwhile from tax revenues, slowly resumed payments with some of the suspended notes, and by such authoritarian means gradually restored its normal financial procedures and the public confidence that depended on normalcy. On 2 February 1760, Berryer told the naval Intendant at Bordeaux to be ready to send to Canada three boxes containing 30,000 printed bills of exchange and 18,000 *billets de caisse* that were to arrive shortly from the director of royal printing, Anisson Duperron.[16] Normal payments were never resumed, however, on the

[15] I have found copies of about forty such bills of exchange from Québec in the minutes of half a dozen Bordeaux notaries between 1716 and 1756: Bernard, Lagénie, Lamestrie, Parran, Rauzan, and Séjournée *l'ainé*.

[16] AN, Colonies B 112, fol. 35, Min. to Rostan, 2 Feb. 1760.

Canadian bills in which so much of the profit from the Canada trade was still held.

For at least three reasons, the Crown made a special case of the Canadian bills. First, Canada being now in British hands, the holders of bills that were still there were likely to become British subjects, and their payment was a contentious diplomatic issue. Secondly, the Crown, unfamiliar with the phenomenon or even the concept of inflation, was convinced that the enormous sums paid out at Québec during the war had been fraudulent, and acted on that conviction by arresting its officials in the *affaire du Canada.* The third reason was to cut down government debt. The Crown was able to use the *affaire* as a moral justification for deferring and reducing its payments on the Canadian bills. Of the original 90-odd million livres, only 37,607,000 livres were eventually recognized, and this sum was converted into *reconnaissances* bearing interest at 4 per cent per annum, a rate at which the French government could not borrow on the money markets at the time. This policy had a devastating effect on many of the Canada merchants, and its consequences were also felt throughout Europe. 'Nothing has been paid since 18 October 1759,' *Paillet et Meynardie* wrote to their Montréal agent on 1 February 1761, 'and so long as the war lasts nothing will be paid. At the peace, arrangements will be made but not sooner, from which you see how distressing this is for those who counted on being paid.'[17] From the merchants' point of view, this was the most discreditable of the crises that racked France in the years 1759-63, and it was remembered years later on the eve of the French Revolution.[18]

The bankruptcies that ensued among some of the biggest Canada merchants are attributable partly to the suspension of the Canada bills, partly to wartime losses of ships and cargoes, partly to the loss of Canada and Louisbourg, and partly to unpaid accounts of bankrupt debtors. *Bérard et Canonge* of Bordeaux, in whose firm Testas of Amsterdam held a one-third interest, collapsed on 22 November 1759, listing among their bad debts some 3,841 livres due from Bossinot, Denel, Giron and Quenel (*sic*), all of Québec.[19] When Jacques Garesché of La Rochelle went bankrupt on 28 July 1760 he claimed

[17] Bibl. mun. de La Rochelle, ms. 1954, *Paillet et Meynardie* (La Rochelle) to François Chevalier (Montréal), 1 Feb. 1761.

[18] Simon-Joseph-Louis Bonvallet des Brosses, *Moyens de simplifier la perception et la compatibilité des deniers royaux*, 1789 (BN Lb^{39} 7248), p. 89 note.

[19] ADG, 7 B 428; Butel, 'La Croissance commerciale', vol. i, pp. 176, 687-8.

among his assets 12,000 livres owing by the Crown for ships rented, 40,000 livres owing at St Domingue, and 23,000 livres owing by insurers on *Gracieuse*, seized on 7 February 1758 returning from Canada and St Domingue. He also claimed a staggering loss of 38,000 livres owing by the bankrupt Canada merchant Pierre Blavoust.[20] At Montauban, Étienne Mariette soon went bankrupt, pulling down other merchants with him, and turned over all his assets to his creditors on 18 April 1760.[21] At Bordeaux, Étienne Caussade failed on 2 August 1762.[22] Pierre Boudet was immediately in difficulties in the autumn of 1759, but managed to stave off bankruptcy until 31 December 1764 when his creditors forced him to retire on an allowance of 600 livres a year, and his sons went off to seek their fortunes, one to Louisiana, the other to Pondicherry.[23] Simon Lapointe's widow at La Rochelle failed on 9 March 1764, unable to recover from the loss of her well-established trade with friends and relatives in Canada.[24] When the Bordeaux firm of *Fesquet et Guiraut* failed in 1765, they claimed losses of 40,800 livres on three vessels sailing to Québec, *La Fortune, Le Rostan*, and the schooner *Les Bons Amis*.[25]

On 3 March 1766, *Paillet et Meynardie* of La Rochelle reported to their creditors that they were forced to stop making payments owing to 'the misfortunes that have affected their trade since the seizure of Canada by the English, either by losses suffered, by the delay of funds in royal paper, of funds in America, or by the scarcity of money which prevents the recovery of what is owing to them'.[26] Seven years later, Jean-Mathieu Mounier, who had returned from Canada with a fortune of 300,000 livres, intending to continue his trade at La Rochelle, ascribed his bankruptcy of 8 November 1773 to many causes, but prominent among them were the loss of Canada and the Crown's failure to honour the Canadian bills.[27]

The financial collapse of the French government had led directly to the collapse of many Canada merchants, but it had also led indirectly to that end. That is, the war was lost in 1759-60, and Canada was not relieved, partly because the Crown could no longer make payments.

[20] A. D. Ch. Mar., Fredureaux-Dumas (LR), 28 July 1760, *Traité du sieur Jacques Garesché . . ., [sic]*.

[21] A. D. Tarn-et-Garonne, David Delmas (Montauban), 22 Dec. 1762, *Accord*, 13 pp.

[22] ADG, 7 B 528.

[23] A. D. Char. Mar., 4 J 5, notes Garnault, and Tardy (LR), 31 Dec. 1764 to 16 June 1765, *abandon de biens*.

[24] A. D. Ch. Mar., Tardy (LR), 9 Mar. 1764, *abandon de biens*.

[25] ADG, 7 B 429.

[26] A. D. Ch. Mar., Tardy (LR), 3 and 10 Mar. 1766, *Réunion des créanciers*, 7 pp.

[27] A. D. Ch. Mar., B 1757, *État à peu près . . .*

By 1758, the war in all its theatres was being fought on credit, not only the organized credit of the Estates of Languedoc, Brittany, and other provinces, but the short-term, haphazard, private credit of the government's own financiers, including the Treasurers General for the Navy and Colonies. As early as 1750, indeed, they had raised a loan of four million livres that was still outstanding in 1758, by which time the accumulated interest totalled nearly two million livres.[28] In 1758, the Treasurers General and their agents in the ports were being pressed for more and more payments at a time when they could not recover their money by the usual method of negotiating rescriptions drawn by the Receivers General of Finance on their own agents in provincial towns. The correspondence of Laurent Bourgeois, naval treasurer's agent at the small ports of Lorient and Port Louis, shows him advancing more and more of his own and his friends' money to settle naval debts with such merchants as Robert Dugard of Rouen, whose sailors, he reported, 'have been in the most frightful misery for a long time'.[29] By October 1758 he was desperately begging for funds and quoting his own advances in thousands of livres.

His personal predicament reflected a general situation. A naval official wrote to the Intendant of finance charged with assigning tax revenues to the spending departments, 'Our poor navy is already in disorder by its inability to cope with an infinity of essential payments. . . .'[30] The ministers were particularly alarmed at the enormous sums the colonial Intendants were drawing in bills of exchange. If these bills were ever to be suspended, the Secretary of State for Marine and Colonies wrote to the Controller General of Finance as early as February 1758, the navy would be discredited and unable to carry on.[31] Some of the bigger Canada merchants in France were aware of the danger. 'Paper on the treasury is being scorned,' Admyrault *fils* wrote to a correspondent at Québec on 28 January 1759, 'No one wants to take it, though it is being paid punctually at maturity. People fear a

[28] AN, f[4] 1008, *Mémoire: situation du Sieur de Géorville*, 3 Feb. 1762; Armand Rébillon, *Les États de Bretagne de 1661`1789* (Paris, 1932), p. 730, shows six million livres lent to the Crown in 1758 and another six million in 1760, all at 5% interest.

[29] Arch. de la Marine (Lorient), 1 E[5] 1, Bourgeois to Mouffle de Géorville, 23 Jan. 1758 etc.

[30] AN, Colonies B 108, Le Normand de Mézy to Boullogne, Intendant of Finance.

[31] AN, Colonies B 108, fols. 64-7. By April 1758, the Treasurers General for the Colonies were unable to find a million livres to pay Simon Darragory, a French merchant in Spain, for shiploads of food sent to Canada on Spanish ships with false neutral passports.

distressing emergency (*un évènement fâcheux*); may this serve you as a warning.'[32]

It was in these difficult circumstances, and to avoid discredit, that the firm of *Beaujon, Goossens et Compagnie* were called in to assist in financing the navy and colonies. At the same time, a merchant banker of Bayonne, Jean-Joseph Laborde (1724-94), was called in to furnish a million livres a month to the army by a contract of 3 December 1757; then, by another contract of 13 October 1758, to take charge of military financing in general up to 50 millions or more a year; and finally, as Court Banker, to pay French diplomats abroad, subsidies to foreign allies, and other such obligations, this beginning on 4 February 1759 with the retirement of the previous Court Banker, Jean Paris de Montmartel.[33] When the crisis came the next autumn, *Beaujon, Goossens et Compagnie* went bankrupt, on 14 November 1759, and Laborde nearly did. The French government, now unable to pay for goods and services, called upon old friends and anyone it could think of in a desperate effort to send out ships and men.

Early in December, the Minister, Berryer, composed a letter proposing to that old friend of the ministry, Abraham Gradis at Bordeaux, that he send a military expedition to Canada disguised as a trading expedition because 'at the moment the navy has not enough vessels to detach a force sufficient for that expedition'.[34] He soon thought better of this idea, and decided on 10 December not to send the letter. But in January 1760, Berryer hatched another scheme for a privateering expedition to Canada to consist of three ships of the line, a frigate, and two fly-boats to be financed by selling 400 shares worth 4,000 livres each and so producing 1,600,000 livres. The Crown was to take 150 shares, Gradis 50, and the banking firm of *Banquet & Mallet* were to sell the remaining 200 shares in Paris.[35] This scheme, too, was dropped. The tiny merchant fleet that sailed for Canada from Bordeaux in April 1760 acompanied by *Le Machault*, a royal naval vessel, was a subject of hard bargaining between the minister and some merchants of Bordeaux, notably Lamalétie recently returned

[32] Université de Montréal, Collection Baby, U 21.

[33] On *Beaujon, Goossens et Cie* see Bosher, 'Financing the French navy'; Laborde's career is explained in his memoirs, edited by Yves-René Durand, in *Annuaire-Bulletin de la Société de l'Histoire de France, année 1968–1969* (Paris, 1971), pp. 75-162.

[34] AN, Colonies B 110, Berryer to Gradis, a letter dated only December 1759 with a note added, 'Le 10 Dec. 1759 monseigneur a suspendu l'expédition de cette lettre et de l'état dont il y est question.'

[35] Jean de Maupassant, 'Abraham Gradis et l'approvisionnement des colonies (1756-63)', *Revue historique de Bordeaux*, 2e année (1909), pp. 250 ff.

from Québec, to make them pay for as much as possible.[36] In this 'violent crisis in French finances', as Berryer afterwards called it, funds were so desperately scarce that he refused all unnecessary expenses, such as a subsidy the Abbé Reignière all unnecessary expenses, such as a subsidy the Abbé Reignière requested for his new invention of 'an inflammable and inextinguishable firework suitable for being thrown by arrows, cannon or mortars on to enemy vessels'.[37]

The crisis was compounded by the reluctance of investors to place money in French government funds. Foreign investors tended to avoid French loans. 'The last loan in England in December [1759]', Bertin, the new Controller General of Finance, wrote to Miromesnil on 23 June 1760, 'was subscribed by capitalists whose funds had been intended for our loans; this is established by details I have from Holland, from Switzerland and from Germany that would make you tremble . . .'.[38] In a humbler way, French loans were being abandoned in Canada also. When Guy *fils* stopped for a month in London on his way home to Montréal in May 1763, he decided to have Goguet send the family's funds from France so that he could invest them 'in the public funds or annuities on the company for which the State is responsible, and therefore nothing is more secure,' as he wrote to his mother. 'This money will yield at least 3 per cent in the worst circumstances. It would have yielded up to 5 per cent, 10 per cent or even 15 per cent if I had been here two months ago. I might have bought into some of those funds that would have yielded up to 15 per cent and better. There is another advantage. This is that the exchange rate is at thirty-two and one-eighth *deniers sterling* for a crown (*écue*) . . . etc.'[39]

Canada was lost in battle and in bankruptcy. But it was also abandoned, as historians have pointed out. Choiseul foresaw the possibility of a rupture between Great Britain and its North American colonies once the threat of attack from New France was removed.[40] However, a policy of abandoning Canada, for whatever reason, could only have been adopted by abandoning the religious policy that had sustained the colony since Cardinal Richelieu's time in the early

[36] AN, Colonies B 112, *passim* from Jan. to Apr.

[37] AN, Marine B^2 362, Berryer to Regnières, 23 Nov. 1759

[38] Marcel Marion, *Histoire financière de la France* (Paris, 1914), vol. i, p. 209.

[39] Université de Montréal, Collection Baby, U 5065, Guy (London) to Mme Guy (Mtl.), 20 May 1763.

[40] For example, Marcel Trudel, *Louis XVI, Le Congrès américain et le Canada, 1774–1789* (Québec, 1949).

The City of Quebec in 1759 by Captain Hervey Smith R.N.

seventeenth century. To Church and State, Canada was a Roman Catholic imperial outpost. The French Church supported the Canadian Church as a mission; most of the Canadian clergy came from France; and the Crown paid them.[41] Supporting Canada and persecuting Huguenots were parts of the same religious policy, much weakened in the eighteenth century, but still established. In the 1750s, however, the Crown gave up its old religious policy. This was a profound change.

The change was first visible when the enlightened Chancellor, Lamoignon, and other royal officials began to urge the bishops to adopt a more lenient policy towards Protestants.[42] The bishops remained firmly opposed to recognizing Protestant marriages and baptisms, but in the middle 1750s–in 1757, according to Dale Van Kley-the Crown washed its hands of the *dévôt* clergy's repressive cause and ceased to enforce the declaration of 1724 against Protestants and the edict of 1695 against Jansenists.[43] In the 1750s, Protestants at La Rochelle and Bordeaux were unofficially allowed to worship in private and to keep parish registers for the first time since the seventeenth century. The humiliating brass plaque that a royal Intendant had fixed on the door of the Minimes church at La Rochelle, to celebrate the King's defeat of the town in 1628, was ceremonially removed by royal orders on 1 November 1757.[44] At Versailles during the 1750s, Lamoignon de Malesherbes, the Chancellor's son, directed the government censorship service in a new liberal spirit.[45] In the 1760s, certain ministers and officials of the Crown responded sympathetically to Voltaire's appeal on behalf of the abused Huguenot merchant, poor Jean Calas, and his English Huguenot wife. Here and there during these years, some authorities began to remove the dangers and anxieties that had beset Protestants for more than a century. In the 1770s, the tolerant Turgot and the Protestant Swiss banker, Necker, were destined to become ministers of the Crown, and in 1787, a royal decree was at last to take the first step towards offering Protestants legal recognition as citizens.

[41] Guy Frégault, *Le XVIIIe siècle canadien* (Montréal, 1968), ch. 3, 'L'Église et la société canadienne'; Cornelius J. Jaenen, *The Role of the Church in New France* (Toronto, 1976), ch. 3.

[42] Grosclaude, *Malesherbes*, ch. 15, 'Les Affaires des Protestants'.

[43] Dale Van Kley, *The Damiens Affair and the Unravelling of the ancien régime, 1750–1770* (Princeton, 1984), pp. 269, 351 note 17; and see above, pp. 116-18.

[44] Père B. Coutant, *Les Minimes* (La Rochelle, 1968), ch. 4, 'L'Affaire des plaques'.

[45] Grosclaude, *Malesherbes*, ch. 3.

Already, thirty years earlier, Huguenot merchants from Canada found Bordeaux and La Rochelle less oppressive than before the War of the Austrian Succession (1743-8). A certain relaxing of the old anti-Protestant laws made life less insecure and less disagreeable. When Jean-Mathieu Mounier returned from Québec at the conquest, he lived for a few years like a minor *philosophe*, accumulating a library of some 1,500 works, many of them in several volumes, and a collection of scientific instruments with which he made experiments in the manner of the age. In 1760 and again in 1764-5, he visited several French towns, and he also spent two years in Paris. By 1774 and doubtless earlier, he had learned to use the deists' expression, 'l'être suprême'.[46] For him and other Huguenots, France was becoming less oppressive and less dangerous. In a famous study, Daniel Mornet saw a major change after 1748 when Montesquieu of Bordeaux published his influential *De l'esprit des lois* based on a comparative study of different civilizations.[47] One of Montesquieu's friends, Mathieu Risteau, was a Huguenot merchant at Bordeaux who sometimes sent ships and goods to Canada. Risteau and his wife, Marie Renac, were in close touch with other Huguenot merchants, such as the Goudal, Rauly, and Dumas families. These and their friends cannot have been ignorant of the changing climate of opinion which Montesquieu expressed and which this later phase of Mounier's life illustrates.

One of the forces that helped to create that climate was the famous movement of Jansenists and Richerists among the clergy and magistrates. This movement triumphed just as the Seven Years War was coming to an end, when the Society of Jesus, so powerful in France and Canada alike, was brought to trial and soon afterwards suppressed.[48] The triumphant followers of Edmond Richer (1560-1631) and Cornelius Jansen (1585-1638) had not forgotten how Louis XIV and the Jesuits had crushed them in obedience to papal orders expressed in bulls like *Unigenitus* (8 September 1713). *Unigenitus* had condemned 101 Jansenist propositions which read like the theology of a Protestant group in favour of simplicity of worship, Bible reading in

[46] A. D. Ch. Mar., B 1757, *État à peu près de mes malheureuses affaires*, 28 Jan. 1774.

[47] Daniel Mornet, *Les Origines intellectuelles de la Révolution française, 1715–1787* (1933), 4th ed. (Paris, 1947), part ii, ch. 1, p. 71; ADG, Rauzan (Bx.), 27 Oct. 1753; Bernard (Bx.), 7 Aug. 1718, marriage contract of Risteau and Renac.

[48] Jean Egret, 'Le Procès des Jésuites devant les Parlements de France 1761-1770', *Revue historique*, vol. cciv (1950), pp. 1-27; D. G. Thompson, 'The Fate of the French Jesuits' Creditors under the ancien régime', *English Historical Review*, vol. 91 (1976), pp. 255-77.

the vernacular, the voice of the laity, the power of divine grace, and much else.[49] When Louis XIV died in September 1715, many opponents of *Unigenitus* were recalled from exile or pardoned and began their teaching again, especially in the Faculty of Theology in Paris. In the 1720s and 1730s some tried to bring about a union with the Anglican and Russian Churches.[50] Meanwhile, radical Richerists still in exile, a sort of French presbyterian movement, secretly circulated Jansenist books printed in Holland, and a weekly journal, *Nouvelles ecclésiastiques*, and drew the support of many *parlementaires*.[51]

They eventually succeeded in discrediting their worst enemies, the Jesuits, in a celebrated affair that began in 1755 when British ships seized several French ones that happened to be carrying goods to France for the Jesuit West Indian mission on the island of Martinique. As a result of these losses at sea, the Jesuits' correspondents at Marseille, *Jean Lioncy et Gouffre*, went bankrupt in February 1756. Their assembled creditors tried to make their debtors pay, according to the usual procedures of the times, and soon discovered that the biggest debtor was Antoine de La Valette, the head of the Jesuit mission at St Pierre, Martinique, who managed large plantations and a considerable transatlantic trade. As the many legal cases arising from this bankruptcy proceeded, de La Valette's superiors and the entire Society of Jesus were dragged in. The Paris Parlement held them responsible for La Valette's unredeemed bills of exchange and so declared in a decision of 8 May 1761. By then the struggle had blossomed into a noisy political affair in which Jansenist magistrates succeeded in having the Paris Parlement condemn the Society, on 6 April 1761, as illegal and dangerous because of its 'vicious nature' and 'anarchical, murderous and parricidal doctrines'.[52] Other Parlements rallied to this view, and after much deliberation and negotiation, Louis XV and his council issued an Edict in November 1764 which finally suppressed the Society of Jesus throughout the kingdom. Their many houses, colleges, and estates were confiscated, and this once-great Catholic agency disappeared from France, and, after Clement XIV's encyclical, *Dominus ac Redemptor Noster* (21 July 1773), from the world. One of the greatest pillars of the Counter-Reformation, and of clerical power in New France, had been laid low.

[49] Anne Fremantle, *The Papal Encyclicals in their Historical Context* (NY, 1956), p. 99.

[50] Edmond Préclin, *Les Jansenistes du XVIIIe siècle et la Constitution Civile du Clergé* (Paris, 1929), p. 545.

[51] Ibid., p. 132.

[52] Van Kley, *The Jansenists and the Expulsion of the Jesuits from France*, pp. 92, 134.

This great revolution–for such it was–fascinated all observers at the time. A clerk in the offices of the Treasurer General of the Marine reported on it to the treasurer's agent at La Rochelle, while also reporting news of the *affaire du Canada.* 'Monsieur de Vaudreuil, Governor General of Canada, was put in the Bastille a few days ago', he wrote on 3 April 1762, 'and they say he was arrested with fifteen other people who are not named. That is all the news I can tell you except about the Jesuits who are at last *f[outus]*. They shut up shop on the first of this month and they are all in their house on the rue Saint Antoine.'[53] The suppression of the Jesuits was a step towards the destruction of the Church's power that was accomplished in Canada at this time by the British conquest, and in France thirty years later by the French Revolution.[54]

While the affair of the Jesuits was in full swing, another affair held the French administration of Canada up to public scrutiny in a general arrest and investigation of some fifty colonial officials. This, the famous *affaire du Canada*, exposed the greedy machinations of the Intendant, the naval controller, the purveyor, a long list of King's storekeepers and military and naval officers.[55] The Minister of Marine and Colonies, a former Lieutenant-General of Police, was already talking in 1759 of giving orders 'to stop the calamities that bad administration has brought upon that colony, or at least to have those who have taken part in them punished'.[56] For the observing public, this affair began on 17 November 1761 when the Purveyor General, Cadet, and the Intendant, Bigot, were arrested with many other officials from New France, high and low, about the same time. On 12 December, a commission or tribunal of the Châtelet criminal court was named to investigate and to judge the various crimes of which the arrested men were to be accused.

During the next two years, a very black picture of the colonial administration was gradually revealed and summed up at last in the final judgement of 10 December 1763, printed and published in many copies. Bigot was banished from the realm for ever, Bréard for nine years, and immense fines were imposed on most of the principal accused in order to extract their ill-gotten gains from them.

[53] A. D. Ch. Mar., B 4055, Couteau (Paris) to Brunet de Béranger (LR), 3 Apr. 1762.

[54] Hilda Neatby, *Québec, The Revolutionary Age, 1760–1791* (Toronto, 1961), 300 p. p. 19; Marcel Trudel, *L'Église canadienne sous le régime militaire, 1759–1764*, 2 vols. (Québec, 1956-7).

[55] Bosher, 'The French Government's Motives in the *affaire du Canada*, 1761-63'.

[56] AN, Colonies B 110, fol. 220, Berryer (Paris) to Péan (Que.), 22 July 1759.

Meanwhile, other colonial officials were under scrutiny, and several were arrested, denounced, and sentenced to various punishments. For instance, the treasurer's agent in Louisiana, Destrehan, was dismissed in 1759, and their former agent at Louisbourg, Jean Laborde (1710-81), for many years a busy transatlantic shipping merchant on the side, was imprisoned in the Bastille on 16 March 1763 and held until 25 August 1764 after he had signed over all his assets to the Crown in a detailed notarial document.[57] The Intendant at Martinique and such scriveners in his service as Lachenez were suspected of trading and cheating like their colleagues in Canada.[58]

The *affaire du Canada* was intended to persuade the French public that the defeat of the French forces in Canada was owing to corrupt, self-seeking officials. The *affaire* was timed, furthermore, to coincide with the negotiations that ended with the ignominious Peace of Paris signed on 10 February 1763. If much public opinion easily blamed the condemned officials, some observers saw them as mere scapegoats for the failures and misdeeds of higher officials and financiers in Paris. 'You know that the Sieur Cadet, Purveyor General in Canada, has been put in the Bastille,' wrote François Havy to Robert Dugard on 14 February 1761. 'There are at present a great many in Paris who would deserve it much more than he because they were the cause of the trouble.'[59] In the words of Mouffle d'Angerville, nephew of a Treasurer General for the Marine and Colonies, the government made scapegoats of the Canadian officials because it was 'too weak to attack the abuses at their source and to punish the big culprits'.[60] The biggest 'culprit' of all, as the revelations of these *affaires* suggested, was Bourbon society itself, anchored as it was to the absolute authority of Church and State.

When the trade and graft of royal officials and financiers was shown together with the official and financial connections of Catholic merchants, the fabric of Bourbon society appeared as tainted with corruption as Guy Frégault, Cameron Nish, and others have presented it.[61] But most Huguenot or New Convert merchants had only

[57] An, MC, Étude XXXIII 553, 12 July 1764, *Compte et transport de créance au Roy le Sieur La Borde.*

[58] AN, Colonies B 111, fol. 65, Minister to Le Mercier de la Rivière, 13 Oct. 1761 and 31 Oct. 1761.

[59] AN, 62 AQ 36, Havy to Dugard, 14 Feb. 1761.

[60] Moufle d'Angerville, *Vie privée de Louis XV*, vol. iv, p. 71.

[61] Frégault, *François Bigot, Administrateur francais*; Nish, *Les Bourgeois-gentilshommes de la Nouvelle-France, 1719–1748.*

the most superficial connection with it, and were scarcely part of it all, being social outcasts. The principal exceptions to this general statement were a few New Converts like François Maurin, Pierre Glemet, and Abraham Gradis. Maurin's name appears in connection with the depredations of the officer, Péan, the Purveyor General, Cadet, the Intendant, Bigot, and several King's storekeepers. A relative of the Mouniers, Maurin had served as Cadet's Montréal manager under Péan's direction from 1756 to 1760, married a Dagneau Douville de Quindre in 1758, generally blended with Bourbon society, and returned to France in 1760 with a fortune of nearly two million livres. He was sentenced with the rest, banished from Paris for nine years and heavily fined. So well did he mix with Bourbon society that his twentieth-century biographer apparently did not know he was a Huguenot.[62]

Glemet had a somewhat similar connection with the condemned officials, though he made less profit and accordingly suffered less. Abraham Gradis had been deeply involved with Bigot, Bréard, and the rest, and was saved from incrimination only by Choiseul's repeated intervention on his behalf. On 12 October 1762, for instance, Choiseul wrote to Sartine to stop any further investigation of Gradis' affairs: 'I desire that the last documents Sieur Gradis sent me, and which I gave you yesterday, should suffice for Messieurs the Commissioners.'[63] Gradis had served the Crown during the war, as well as the colonial officials, and was to go on being useful to Choiseul in the future. But such cases as these were exceptions. The few Jews and Huguenots who had been in business with the condemned officials from Canada had not been related to them in the way that Catholic merchants had. Merchants such as those whom Cadet had used as his correspondents at Bordeaux and La Rochelle had not intermarried with officials and financiers.

Choiseul and Sartine thought well enough of several New Converts during the *affaire* to consult them in establishing standard prices for the decade 1749-59. By an order of 6 September 1762, the Châtelet court in Paris and the *Présidial* court at La Rochelle ordered the police to consult *Meynardie frères*, Thouron the younger, François Havy, Admyrault, and Jean-Mathieu Mounier.[64] The Catholic, Soumbrun,

[62] *DCB* vol. iii, pp. 441-2.

[63] Bibl. de l'Arsenal (Paris), Bastille ms. 12, 145, fols. 83-4, 323, 374; Bibl. nat., ms. fr. 11338, Berryer to Fontanieu, 25 Jan. 1760.

[64] A. D. Ch. Mar., B 1796, *Procès-verbal destinés des négotiants faisant le commerce du Canada*, 14 Sept. 1762, 35 pp.

was mentioned, but not consulted. At Montauban, the Huguenot merchants Pierre de Lannes, Jean-Jacques Gauthier, and Joseph Rouffio were also trusted in establishing standard prices.[65] One Catholic merchant, but only one, Lamalétie of Bordeaux, was asked for his account books.[66] Thus, in seeking honest merchants seriously engaged in the Canada trade, but not too deeply involved with the criminal officials of the colony, the Crown eventually consulted seven Huguenots and only one Catholic. We can easily see why as we follow the French authorities in their investigation of the Canadian officials and their business partners, merchants such as Guillaume Estèbe, Jean-Patrice Dupuy, Denis Goguet, Louis Pennisseault, Lemoine Despins, and the many who had become King's storekeepers.

Much of their shady business is revealed in the biographies of Estèbe, Pennisseaut, Bréard, Cadet, Bigot,and others in the *Dictionary of Canadian Biography*, volume iv (Toronto, 1979). By way of example, let us here sketch the business dealings of one who does not appear therein, Jean-Patrice Dupuy (1732-86) of Bordeaux. He served his cousin, Lamalétie, and Lamalétie's partner, Admyrault, as a commission agent at Montréal from 1754 to 1756; and in 1757, back in Bordeaux, he sent consignments of merchandise out to Lamalétie and Estèbe, still in Québec.[67] Meanwhile, on 20 October 1756 he formed a company with Péan, the notorious adjutant at Québec, and Jean-Baptiste Martel, the royal storekeeper at Montréal. It was a transatlantic trading company founded for seven years beginning on 1 January 1757 under the name of *Dupuy fils et compagnie*, and Dupuy directed it and had a one-third interest in it representing 133,333 livres of the total capital fund of 400,000 livres, whereas Péan had a one-quarter interest, or 100,000 livres investment. It seems that Martel was to put up five-twelfths of the capital fund and hold the largest interest, but in any event the company dissolved on 14 May 1760 and re-formed without Martel on the basis of an equal sharing of profits and losses. This new partnership was to continue without term until either Péan or Dupuy decided to withdraw, and when at last they wound up their affairs on 30 May 1768, Dupuy in effect bought out Péan with

[65] Bibl. de l'Arsenal, Bastille ms. 12, 144, fol. 162, Choiseul to Sartine, 28 June 1762.

[66] ADG, 3 B 248, Sénéchaussée-présidial, *Procès-verbal transport*, 14 Sept. 1762, 5 pp.

[67] Dupuy's story is told in another context in J. F. Bosher, 'A Quebec merchant's Trading Circles in France and Canada: Jean-André Lamalétie before 1763', *Histoire sociale* (Ottawa), vol. ix (1977), pp. 24-44.

payments totalling just over 51,000 livres and a promise to take over all the company's debts as well as its assets.[68]

Long before this, in 1759, even before the Crown had begun to prosecute the Canadian officials and others of the *grande société*, Dupuy had begun to serve as a business agent for two of those officials who were later arrested, prosecuted, and sentenced to heavy fines. For one of them, the aforementioned Martel, Dupuy purchased for 100,000 livres a furnished house 'with six statues in the garden, each on its pedestal, a little mutilated and blackened by time', in the expensive Chartrons district of Bordeaux, this in his own name to conceal the identity of Martel for whom he acted as *prête-nom*.[69] And three years later, after Martel's arrest, Dupuy rented the house for him to another Bordeaux merchant for seven years at a rent every six months of '3,800 livres while the present war lasts and 4,500 livres in peacetime'. Meanwhile, by a formal agreement of 9 February 1760, Martel paid another 100,000 livres for a one-third interest in Dupuy's share in the *Régie ou ferme générale des droits réunis*, a tax-collecting agency founded in September 1759 by the Controller General of Finance to help in meeting the financial crisis of the time. Already, on 20 October 1759, Dupuy had sold another third interest, also for 100,000 livres, to Jean-Victor Varin de la Mare, the notorious former *commissaire de la Marine* at Montréal. A royal commission set up to deal with the property of Bigot, Varin, and the other major criminals of the *affaire du Canada* traced this transaction in 1764 and soon recovered from Dupuy what he still held of Varin's 100,000 livres, but I have no evidence that they knew of Martel's share.[70]

As if this were not enough, on 31 December 1760 Dupuy went to one of the business agents (*prête-nom*) of Péan and Bigot, and others from Canada, a certain Nicolas-Félix Vaudive, who was an *avocat au Parlement et greffier de l'audience du grand conseil du Roi*, and the son of a merchant jeweller and goldsmith of Paris, and borrowed 50,000 livres to invest in the tax farm of the *Devoirs de Bretagne.* The Crown confiscated this sum in 1764 as being part of Bigot's estate and Dupuy handed it over.[71] Another of Dupuy's unsavoury business arrangements showing how widely he cast his net in the field of maritime and

[68] ADG, Faugas (Bx.), 30 May 1768, *Cession et dissolution de Sossiété (sic) Péan et Dupuy*, 8 pp.

[69] ADG, Guy (Bx.), 16, 17 Feb. 1769, and 8 Oct. 1762.

[70] AN, MC, Étude XXX, 9 Feb. 1760, *société*, and 20 Oct. 1759, *société* with attached notes; V^7 353, entry for 3 Apr. 1764.

[71] AN MC, étude LVII, 8 May, 31 Dec. 1760, and 20 Feb. 1761.

colonial business was made in 1762 with a well-known financier, the *régisseur des économats*, Marchal de Sainscy, who managed the Crown's funds from vacant benefices and other ecclesiastical property. De Sainscy took a one-quarter interest in a project of Dupuy's for buying large quantities of the sort of merchandise that would sell in the colonies, and two ships, *Le Casque* and *Le Cheval Marin*, but by 1771 this project had proved to be a failure.[72]

Notwithstanding Dupuy's shady dealings with officials arrested in the *affaire du Canada*, he was not himself arrested. But he was denounced to the investigating commission, evidently by someone who knew much about his affairs. The denunciation illustrates the hostile public feelings the *affaire du Canada* aroused against what I have called, for convenience, Bourbon official society. It runs,

> The most important man to arrest in the *affaire du Canada* is a certain Dupuy, merchant, living at Bordeaux in the Chartron quarter, formerly a clerk in Canada. He is the secret confidential agent of Messieurs Bigot, Péan, Varin, and Martel. It is he who has cashed for them, in France and here, the Treasury bills of exchange they have entrusted to him.
>
> He used to return to France almost every year with these gentlemen's papers. He would collect the sums from the Treasurer General and with that money would buy a prodigious quantity of notes of the royal lottery. He has bought thirteen millions worth of thousand-livre shares in the general farms [of taxes] from the late Monsieur du Vergier, cashier to Monsieur de Montmartel. He has bought all the good bearer notes (*papier au porteur*). He has bought land for these gentlemen. He has bought Martel's house in Bordeaux which is rented in his name. In a word, that man is informed of all the money they have invested. The Commission would learn more from that man alone in a week than they could learn in six months by a lot of research.[73]

Dupuy was one of those Canada merchants from a family that was a part of Bourbon official society, related to the Lee, O'Quin, and Bennet families who had come to Bordeaux from Ireland in the seventeenth century, and related also to the Lamalétie family which had married into the Foucault family of officials in Canada. He was typical, then, of the merchants linked in business and marriage with officials and financiers.[74]

To sum up, France lost Canada in the course of financial, military, and religious crises that simultaneously undermined Bourbon official

[72] AN, MC, Cordier (Paris), 18 Mar. 1771, *procuration* of which a copy in ADG, Faugas (Bx.), 6 Apr. 1771.

[73] Bibl. de l'Arsenal, Bastille ms. 12, 145, fol. 6; 12, 143, fol. 313.

[74] Bosher, 'A Québec Merchant's Trading Circles', genealogical chart.

society by revealing its weaknesses. The Crown went bankrupt, owing to faults in the financial system from which the English and Dutch systems did not suffer. The ministry blamed the huge Canadian debts and the loss of the colony on the rapacity of its own officials, and tried them in a noisy affair that revealed widespread corruption in Bourbon official society. The odium this trial brought upon the colonial administration helped the Crown to abandon New France without losing face altogether. When the Crown gave up Canada it was turning its back on a Roman Catholic imperial mission, and it could do this in the 1750s because it had at last given up leading the Counter-Reformation. As another result of the same change, the Crown also abandoned the Society of Jesus to its enemies and eventually banished it. As the Age of the Enlightenment dawned, Bourbon official society, always founded on royal policy, began to crumble. The old differences between Catholic and Protestant merchants were ceasing to matter in old France as well as in what had been New France.

Conclusion

FRANCE gave up Newfoundland and Acadia in 1713 and the rest of New France half a century later. This was the same half-century in which the aggressive Roman Catholic empire of Louis XIV was transformed into the crumbling, tolerant monarchy of the pre-revolutionary Enlightenment. At the beginning of it, Catholic families with branches on both sides of the Atlantic had a monopoly of trade and shipping to New France; at the end, Huguenot families had a large share, perhaps most of it. At the beginning, the typical Canada merchant was a man with relatives in the magistracy, in the priesthood, in the ranks of the government financiers, and so was part of the society that had formed around the ruling families at court, part of the hierarchy of patronage created by the Bourbon kings. At the end, the typical Canada merchant was related to other merchants in Amsterdam, London, Hamburg, Geneva, even Boston, and so belonged to the cosmopolitan world of maritime business that had grown up in the Protestant seaports. In the early eighteenth century Church and State kept Protestant merchants out of the Canada trade unless they disguised themselves as Roman Catholics; in mid-century the State abandoned the Church's cause, even abandoned the Society of Jesus, and tolerated Protestants who conformed to Catholic practices.

A social study of merchants in that half-century, those in the Canada trade at any rate, shows basic religious differences. Most Huguenots and Catholics, like most Jews, married within their own religious communities. A marriage in that age was a family treaty based on a negotiated contract, just as a business partnership was. Contracts in marriage or in business were usually founded on the trust that grew out of a common religious tradition. For merchants, the two religious traditions were, moreover, profoundly different in that French Catholics were part of the approved, legal society of Bourbon France in which the clergy were extremely powerful. French Protestants, on the other hand, were outcasts and outlaws who survived by submitting themselves and their children to Catholic baptism, marriage, and other sacraments.

The two traditions were politically different also: a Catholic merchant belonged to the authoritarian hierarchy of Church and

State; whereas a Huguenot merchant was part of the Calvinist or reformed Church that had no priestly hierarchy and had not submitted to secular authority. In addition, the Huguenot merchant had strong ties with the communities of Huguenot refugees in Protestant cities. Merchants had a strong voice in the governments of those cities, and also in the central governments of Holland and Great Britain. The cosmopolitan business world of those countries, which for convenience we may call Atlantic trading society, was much freer than society in France, where Church and State censored the press, interfered in municipal government, and even controlled people's movements between France and the colonies. Religious differences were thus linked with different political traditions.

The Huguenot merchants who stayed in France did so for a variety of reasons. Some were from families too poor and numerous to emigrate. Lands and houses, kith and kin, kept others in those Huguenot communities which survived collectively at La Rochelle, Bordeaux, Rouen, Nîmes, Montauban, Paris, and other towns. The *abjuration* or 'conversion' that was rewarded with official posts or advantageous marriages kept some in France, apparently 'New Converts' but often merely trimming to the political winds and hoping for better times later. Historians have been too quick to think that any Huguenot who abjured had truly converted. Then, in the eighteenth century many Huguenots found profit in their position as French 'agents' of Atlantic trading society. With relatives in the ports of the Protestant Baltic and North Sea, and the Protestant Atlantic, they were well placed to export wine and brandy, woollens, furs, and colonial sugar, and to import American tobacco, Baltic naval stores, and Irish foodstuffs. These trading families found life easier in France as persecution died down gradually here and there after Louis XIV's death.

The Canada trade was opened to them, it is clear, in the 1730s. In the 1740s the Crown began to call on them, and on Jews also, to transport men, munitions, and foodstuffs to the colonies. Long wars at sea against heavy odds drove the French ministers to rely more and more on New Converts with their foreign trading networks and their ample resources. Religious scruples began to be set aside, and the Canada trade became increasingly cosmopolitan, less and less in the hands of the old Catholic trading families. German, Swiss, and Austrian fur buyers began trading with New France. The established Catholic families were hard-pressed. Those who could–Pascaud,

Goguet, Lamalétie, Trottier Désauniers–bought offices and married their children to noble or office-holding families, which had always been their inclination in any case. Others failed and went bankrupt: Bourgine, Blavoust, Soumbrun, Jung, Guillaume Pascaud, and more. Still others carried on in partnership with government officials in Canada, as indeed did a few New Converts, Jewish and Protestant.

Army officers, naval officers and storekeepers, and government financial agents had always traded in the colonies, adding to their meagre and uncertain emoluments by using their power for profit. They have to be counted as part-time merchants in any serious study of the Canada trade. After all, officials and financiers dominated the business life of Paris and the great monopoly companies, and had much authority in Bourbon official society. The mid-century wars offered them unprecedented opportunities in New France, where the Crown was spending more and more in the imperial cause. In old France, too, agents of the Treasurers General of Finance went into maritime trade. Government financiers invested in privateering ventures or speculated, like Prévost, in marine insurance.

The French government depended on its financiers for loans as well as for services, and in the Seven Years War strained their resources beyond the limit. Efforts to supplement the financiers' resources with the funds of merchant bankers could not save the rickety Bourbon credit system, and its collapse in autumn 1759 began on 15 October when it suspended the Canadian bills. As a result, the Crown could no longer send out ships and men, or command the services of merchants in the Canada trade. Nor could it pay its debts to them. Added to the cruel blow of the colony's loss to Great Britain, the government's bankruptcy set off a series of failures among the Canada merchants. To save money and to save face, the government blamed its own officials in Canada for the Canadian debts and defeats. The trial of these scapegoats revealed much corruption in Bourbon official society, and some of the big merchants were implicated.

The revelations of the notorious *affaire du Canada*, beginning in 1761, helped the government to turn its back on New France, an expensive white elephant it then seemed, and no efforts were made to recover the colony thereafter. The Huguenots who stayed in Canada suddenly found themselves free and respectable, eligible for offices from which Catholics were now excluded. But the trade between New France and old France was just as suddenly stopped. Many a cargo intended for Canada, in a warehouse at La Rochelle or Bordeaux, had to be disposed of elsewhere. 'There is still no news concerning the shipping of the merchandise in storage here belonging to Canadians,' Goguet wrote from La Rochelle to Madame Guy at Montréal on 1 May 1763, and went on to explain that the British government would allow no such shipments.[1]

Suddenly passengers between Canada and France had to go by way of British ships and British ports, like young Guy who spent some weeks in London in May 1763 on his way home to Montréal from La Rochelle, 'which will give me the time', he wrote to his mother, 'to make acquaintances here, which is very easy to do'.[2] Suddenly the ships in the Canada trade were British or British-American ships, such as the *Nettleton* which reached Dartmouth from Québec on 1 January 1760, the *Experiment* which landed on the same day in Virginia, having come from Québec, and the *Peter Beckford* which landed at New York on 11 January; and the sixteen vessels at the Downs, not far from London, announced by *Lloyd's List* on 11 April 1760 as 'remains for Québec'. The ports in the Canada trade were soon established as London, Bristol, Cowes, Falmouth, Plymouth, Cork, Greenock, and a dozen colonial ports. The Canada merchants now had names like William and Robert Hunter, William and John Grant, John Schoolbred, Robert Ellice, James Phyn & Co., Muir & Co., Buchanan, and John Cochrane.[3] But theirs is another story.

[1] Université de Montréal, Collection Baby, U 4663.

[2] Ibid. U 5065, Guy (London) to Mme Guy (Mtl.), 20 May 1763.

[3] R. H. Fleming, 'Phyn, Ellice and Company of Schenectady', *University of Toronto Studies in History and Economics*, vol. iv (1932), pp. 7-41; Jacob M. Price, 'Buchanan & Simson, 1759-1763: A Different Kind of Glasgow Firm Trading to the Chesapeake', *William and Mary Quarterly*, 3rd series, vol. xl (1983), pp. 3-41; David Geddes, 'How Habeas Corpus Came to Canada: the Bills on Credit Scandal in Quebec, 1783', *Three Banks Review* (London), no. 112 (Dec. 1976), pp. 50-65; and 'John Cochrane's Troubles', ibid., no.. 111 (Sept. 1976), pp. 56-60.

Note on Sources

THE principal sources for this study were the collections of notarial minutes, of official records and correspondence, and of random letters and accounts at archives in Bordeaux, La Rochelle, Paris, London, Québec, Ottawa, and Montréal. Another major source, the parish registers of births, marriages, and deaths–what are mistakenly called *l'état civil*–were even more widely scattered, being kept at the town halls or municipal libraries of the towns where they originated. Much supplementary information turned up in municipal, naval, and departmental (*départementale*) archives on the French Atlantic coast from Dunkirk to Bayonne, and inland at Rennes, Pau, Montauban, Agen, and Geneva.

Only two large collections of family papers are known to survive, those for the Dugard family kept in Paris, which I read, and those for the Gradis family, also in Paris, which an amiable descendant, Henri Gradis, was too busy to let me see, though much useful correspondence of Abraham and Moise Gradis is on microfilm at Bordeaux. As it happens, the Gradis papers could have added little to this study, devoted as it is to the Canada merchants in general rather than to any particular family, or to the trade itself.

The most useful papers may be summarized as follows:

BORDEAUX: 1. Archives départementales de la Gironde, minutes of the notaries Banchereau, Barbaret, Bedout, Bernard, Bolle, Faugas, François, Guy, Lagénie, Lamestrie, Lavau, Mansset, Pallotte, Parrans and Parrans *fils*, Perrens, Rauzan, Roberdeau, Séjournée, and Roussillon; the registers of the *Contrôle des actes des notaires* (B 12-170); Admiralty papers in the 6 B series, notably *Procédures* (6 B 1147-1195), and the several series concerning departures of ships and passengers; court records, especially the *juridiction consulaire* on bankruptcies (7 B 396-530); the collection of letterbooks and account books (7 B series); and papers of the *Chambre de Commerce de Guienne* and of the Intendancy at Bordeaux (both in the 'C' series).

2. Archives de la Ville de Bordeaux: alphabetical tables of the parish registers, the registers themselves; the *Fonds Delpit* and other collections.

LA ROCHELLE: 1. Archives départementales de la Charente-Maritime, minutes of the notaries Chameau, Delavergne, Desbarres, Fleury, Fredureaux-Dumas, Goizon, Guillemot, Rivière and Soullard, Solleau, and Tardy; registers of the *Contrôle des actes des notaires* (II C series); Catholic and Protestant parish registers (E supplément, 2 J 94 etc.); various Admiralty series (B); the *Présidial* (B 1796 etc.); the *Juridiction consulaire* (B 413, 4202 etc.).

2. Bibliothèque municipal: most of the parish registers and alphabetical tables for them; *Paillet and Meynardie* papers (mss. 1954 and 1960).

PARIS: 1. Archives nationales: minutes, mostly for the 1750s and 1760s, at the *Minutier central des notaires* for the notaries, Armet (Étude VII), Le Noir (XIII), Delage (XIV), Prévost (XX), (XXX), Poultier (XXXIII), Baron (XXXV), Bontemps (XLV), Patu (XLVIII), Le Pot d'Auteuil (LIII), Charlier (LVII), Arnoult (LXII), Patu (LXVIII), (LXXXIII), Regnault (LXXXIV), (XCI), de Ribes (XCIII), Hazon (XCIX), Godefroy (CVII), Vanin (CXV), and Leverrier (CXVIII); claims on the Crown (V^7 342-365); naval and colonial debts, and *Amirauté de France* (Z^1 series); colonial correspondence (Colonies B); naval correspondence with Bordeaux, Bayonne, etc. (Marine B^2); naval personnel (Marine C^7); colonial personnel and memoranda (Colonies C^{11A}); *Châtelet* death reports and inventories (*scellés*) (Y series); papers of the *régie* in charge of the property of fugitive Huguenots (TT series); files on *secrétaires du Roi* and other officers (V^1 and V^2); parish registers for Île Royale (Colonies Gî 406, 410, etc.).

2. Bibliothèque de l'Arsenal: Bastille papers, ms.

3. Bibliothèque nationale: papers of the Fontanieu Commission on debts to merchants etc. (mss. fr. 11334-11342).

QUÉBEC: Archives nationales du Québec, minutes of the notaries Barolet, Becquet, Chamballon, Dulaurent, Genaple, Hiché, Saillant, Lanouiller des Granges, and Panet; fugitive admiralty papers (NF series).

OTTAWA: Public Archives of Canada: transcriptions on paper and microfilm of many French series, such as papers on colonial funds (F^1 A), lists of Protestants in Canada (C^{11A} 75, and D2D carton I), and the parish registers of Louisbourg (Colonies G^1).

MONTRÉAL: Université de Montréal: Collection Baby (U series).

LONDON: Public Record Office: admiralty prize papers for the War of the Austrian Succession (HCA 32: 94-160), and for the Seven Years War (some 75 ships in the Canada trade) (HCA 32: 161-254); captured mail and 'intercepted papers' (HCA 30).

Books: A few scholarly books were particularly useful:

Brown, George W., *et al.*, *Dictionary of Canadian Biography*, vols. i-v (Toronto, 1966-83).

Butel, Paul, 'La Croissance commerciale bordelaise dans la seconde moitié du XVIIIe siècle', thesis, 2 vols., with continuous pagination. (University of Paris, Lille, 1973).

Clark, John G., *La Rochelle and the Atlantic Economy during the Eighteenth Century* (Baltimore and London, 1981), 286 pp.

Dardel, Pierre, *Navires et marchandises dans les ports de Rouen et du Havre au XVIII siècle* (Paris, 1963), 787 pp.

-, *Commerce, industrie et navigation à Rouen et au Havre au XVIIIe siècle: Rivalité croissante entre ces deux ports: La conjoncture* (Rouen, 1966), 454 pp.

Dechêne, Louise, *Habitants et marchands de Montréal au XVIIe siècle* (Paris, 1974), 581 pp.

Dickson, P. G. M., *The Financial Revolution in England: A Study of the Development of Public Credit, 1688–1756* (London, 1967), 580 pp.

Durand, Yves, *Les Fermiers généraux au XVIIIe siècle* (Paris, 1871), 664 pp.

Forster, Robert, *Merchants, Landlords, Magistrates: The Depont Family in Eighteenth-Century France* (Baltimore, 1980), 275 pp.

Frégault, Guy, *François Bigot, Administrateur français*, 2 vols. (Montréal, 1948).

Giraud, Marcel, *Histoire de la Louisiane française*, 4 Vols. (Paris, 1953-68).

Godbout, Archange, *Émigration rochelaise en Nouvelle-France* (Québec, 1970), 276 pp.

Lévy, Claude-Frédéric, *Capitalistes et pouvoir au siècle des lumières*, 3 vols. (The Hague, 1969-80).

Lüthy, Herbert, *La Banque protestante en France de la Révocation de l'Édit de Nantes à la Révolution*, 2 vols. (Paris, 1959-61).

Miquelon, Dale, *Dugard of Rouen: French Trade to Canada and the West Indies, 1729–1770* (Montréal, 1978), 282 pp.

Nish, Cameron, *Les Bourgeois-gentilshommes de la Nouvelle-France, 1729–1748* (Montréal, 1968), 202 pp.

Pariset, François-Georges *et al.*, *Bordeaux au XVIIIe siècle* (Bordeaux, 1968), 723 pp.
Price, Jacob M. *France and the Chesapeake: A History of the French Tobacco Monopoly, 1674–1791, and of its Relationship to the British and American Tobacco Trades*, 2 vols. in 4° (Ann Arbor, 1973).
Van Kley, Dale, *The Jansenists and the Expulsion of the Jesuits from France 1757–1765* (New Haven, 1975).
Wilson, Charles, *Anglo-Dutch Commerce and Finance in the Eighteenth Century* (Cambridge, 1941), 235 pp.

Index

The entries 'SHIPS' and 'SEACAPTAINS' list the names alphabetically.